# CHILD OF THE BLITZ
# MY STORY

By

NORMAN COTTEE

Grosvenor House
Publishing Limited

This book is published by
Grosvenor House Publishing Ltd
Link House
140 The Broadway, Tolworth, Surrey, KT6 7HT.
www.grosvenorhousepublishing.co.uk



A CIP record for this book
is available from the British Library

ISBN 978-1-80381-134-5

*Since no man has aught of what he leaves, what is't to leave betimes*

## INTRODUCTION

"Since no man has aught of what he leaves, what is't to leave betimes?" The quote is taken from Hamlet, Prince of Denmark, by William Shakespeare. Roughly translated into modern English, it means that you cannot take earthly possessions with you when you die, and consequently, it is no loss to hand them down to others in good order while you still have the chance. In this spirit, I want to pass on to my descendants and anyone else who might be interested, the memories and the knowledge I have accumulated during my lifetime; and this is why I am telling this story. I begin with my personal recollections, contained in this volume and will continue later in a separate volume with the fruits of my research about my wider family and ancestors.

# CONTENTS

# LIST OF ILLUSTRATIONS

# THE WAR YEARS

I was born during the 'Blitz' in my parents' modest, semi-detached, suburban home at around 2 o'clock in the morning on the 3rd May 1941 during a German bombing raid over London. As luck would have it, I endured the 'Blitz', witnessed the winning of the Second World War, the subsequent death throes of the British Empire and emerged unscathed from the underlying ever-present threat of nuclear annihilation in the Cold War. Thus, some good few years later, I find myself sitting here, still breathing, with pen poised and keyboard at the ready to begin my story

The 'Blitz' as Londoners affectionately called it, or Blitzkrieg as the Nazis termed it (Lightning War), launched as a prelude to what most people in 1941 believed would be the imminent invasion of our country, continued into the summer of the following year when the Germans turned their attention to the invasion of Russia. My mother used to say that, when I had learned to speak a little and heard the drone of enemy aircraft approaching, I would always call "Under the table Mummy" and, she and I would shelter under the dining room table, made of sturdy English oak, that she retained as a valued possession throughout her life. I entered the world backwards; that is to say bum first. I believe the medical term is 'breach born'. I claim no credit for the timing or the no doubt painful manner, for my mother, of my birth but was often told about it by her, my grandmother and my aunts as I grew up.

The heaviest bombing raid of the war occurred just seven days after I was born. This may well have been the night that my maternal Grandmother Arber, or 'Tootsie' as she was known, accompanied by my Aunt Dorothy and my godmother, Aunt Margaret, crossed London from Chingford Essex to see me for the first time. Because of the severity of the raid that night, they had to pick their way over ribbons of fire hoses and rubble as fireman struggled to extinguish blazing buildings. My aunt Dorothy still recalls walking across London Bridge and seeing the fire boats on the River Thames. With the indomitable spirit that characterised Londoners at that time and the Underground Railway out of action south of the Thames, they walked the remaining 10 miles or so to our house at 25 Wolsey Crescent, Morden Park to welcome me into the world.

Although I was born in Morden Park, Surrey, my earliest memories are of my Arber grandparents' house at 5 Forest View, Chingford, Essex, on the edge of North London, looking out over Epping Forest. This is because my mother and I went to live there in 1942 when my father, having been conscripted into the RAF, left these shores to help fight the Germans and Italians in North Africa. Also living in the house was my aunt Margaret, my grandparents' eldest daughter, whose husband, Bill, captured by the Germans in Northern France prior to the evacuation of the British army from Dunkirk in 1940, was being held in a prisoner of war (POW) camp in Poland. I suppose that after my father left for the African theatre, my mother moved to Chingford for the security and consolation of being with other members of her family, rather than remaining by herself with me at Morden Park. Meanwhile, my father had arrived in North Africa unscathed, after the troopship immediately before his had been torpedoed.

The first experience I can recall is of being in the Anderson shelter at night in the back garden of 5 Forest View. I imagine that an air raid must have been in progress. I see the black stove and the black metal chimney pipe leading upwards through the corrugated iron ceiling and two bench type beds running down each side: it was cosy and warm with the fire burning in the stove. Anderson shelters were air raid shelters named after Sir John Anderson, the government minister responsible for air raid precautions. Families were encouraged to build these shelters in their gardens to protect them from the damage caused by exploding bombs. The shelters were half submerged in the ground, topped with semi circular corrugated iron panels and padded with a thick layer of earth and grass turfs. You entered down three or four steps, through a door at one end and left the same way. There can't have been much room inside; only enough for half a dozen people at most. After the war was over, I remember 'helping' my grandfather Arber with a sledgehammer to demolish the concrete and brick foundation of the shelter. It was hard work. The concept and construction were perhaps sounder than might have been thought.

I also remember one afternoon at Chingford, slumbering in what seemed a huge bed in the ground floor living room overlooking the rear garden, when there was a sudden whoosh knocking me out of the bed and onto the floor. I lay there bemused and unhurt, watching flakes of ceiling plaster gently floating down. The next thing I knew was my grandmother and aunt rushing in and picking me up. A V2 rocket had fallen and exploded with considerable force about half a mile away in the forest, close to a pub on the main Epping to London Road, creating a large crater which I later, sometimes viewed during walks with my mother and brother Roger in the forest. Luckily for the majority of Londoners, many of the V2s were overshooting the city creating little damage to life or property. The government kept this secret, pretending that considerable damage was occurring in the city itself so the V2s would continue missing. Cunning or what! This happened between September 1944 when the V2 onslaught began and March 1945 when the launch sites in northern Germany were overrun by British troops in the last few weeks of hostilities.

I loved our walks in Epping Forest, and remember that my mother would 'discover' an orange, "left by the fairies as a treat", in a particular fallen tree trunk. As young as I was, I realised that she had hidden it there earlier. My mother loved oranges: and fish and chips which she regarded as the ultimate culinary delicacy. Subtlety was not her strongest suit. However I inherited from her an enjoyment of walking in the countryside, particularly in the flickering silence and mystery of woodland. I also remember lying one day in an open field towards Chingford Mount listening to the call of the cuckoo. The smell of bluebells was in the air. My mother wore a light blue dress with white spots, her naturally wavy, brown shoulder-length hair glistening in the clear blue sky. I had no concept of a war being fought. All was lovely and peaceful.

My brother Roger had been born in Chingford General Hospital in May 1943 and I vaguely remember going there with my mother, probably some considerable time later, wheeling a pram. I also have a vague memory of seeing a small number of young men dressed in light blue uniforms ambling towards Chingford Mount and being told that they were German prisoners of war. I believe they were based in a POW camp at Pole Hill up towards the Mount.

My last distinct memory of my earliest days was of going with my mother and grandmother one evening to Chingford Green, close to Chingford Church, and seeing an enormous bonfire onto which a life sized effigy of Tojo, the Japanese military dictator, was tossed and burnt to cheers from the crowd. This must have been VJ (Victory over Japan) night on 15 August 1945 when World War II was brought to a dramatic conclusion by the dropping of atomic bombs on Hiroshima and Nagasaki by the Americans. I knew nothing of that. But it was an enjoyable night with lots of people happily milling around. I was given a toffee apple in celebration.

There are two good British films and a BBC documentary which are redolent of the spirit, feelings, patterns of speech and preoccupations of these times and I have recoded them on DVDs as part of this history. First is the film 'This Happy Breed' dealing with the life of an ordinary family in London in the years leading up to the war and second 'Hope and Glory' which looks at the war years in a London suburb, through a child's eye. Lastly, the BBC documentary 'Hop Skip and Jump' perceptively reflects much of the freedom and innocent happiness I enjoyed growing up in the dozen or so years following the end of the war.

The other day when visiting Hughenden Manor, Disraeli's Buckinghamshire country house now owned by the National

Trust of which I am a member, I spied on sale in the gift shop, for £10, a CD entitled 'Music That Won The War' that included, according to the cover notes, the sound of the familiar air raid warning and all clear sirens. Being the last of the big spenders, I overcame my instinctive - 'to make do' - sentiment ingrained in me by the war, and bought it. I am pleased I did. Listening to it, I relive those enjoyable days.

# AFTERMATH

At some point, after the end of the war, we returned to Morden Park. The house at 25 Wolsey Crescent was semi-detached with a reasonably long garden at the back. It was built in 1936 in the mock-Tudor style common to most London outer suburbs of that era and was named 'Merioneth' by my mother after the town in West Wales where she and my father had spent their honeymoon. They owned the house outright, my grandfather Arber having purchased the property for my mother as a wedding present.

While settling back in, we still made frequent visits to Chingford. We would travel by red London Transport double-decker bus to Morden Underground Station, the southern terminus of the Northern Line and from there by Tube train to Liverpool Street Station where we would catch a steam train, operated by the London & North Eastern Railway Company (LNER), to Chingford. I used to find these journeys incredibly thrilling: I still find travelling exciting. Liverpool Street Station was a dark, cathedral-like, soot covered, Victorian warren of a place; dirty and noisy, bustling with taxis, luggage, passengers, porters, guards, engine drivers and firemen. Billowing clouds of smoke rose effortlessly toward the acrid vaulted roof. Even now, if I concentrate hard, I can almost hear and taste the wonderful surge and panting power of the engines as they waited, brooding to depart, the cacophony of shouting, doors slamming, whistles blowing and flags waving as first one then another locomotive would take up the strain, begin slowly increasing momentum, steam pulsing, pouring from the funnel, drive cylinders and valves, straining, slowly inching serpentine carriages forward until, with gathering freedom, the cascade of lung bursting steam and smoke ripples into a gentle clickety-clack and a bang as mindless carriages knock into one another trying to obey while trailing behind their mechanical master. Suddenly almost immediately after having left the station, plunging into a long, infernal tunnel, enveloping the whole train and pouring soot and smoke inside the carriages, the engine urges forward with gathering speed and energy. My mother and I would try and shut the carriage windows to keep the worst of the smoke out but usually this was not possible because the notched leather belts that were supposed to hold the sash type windows in place would not purchase on the heavily worn brass prongs at the bottom of the window frames. Personally, I didn't care; it was all too wonderful. The smell was fantastic and the fact that I often ran my fingers along the bottom edge of the window frames picking up a covering of pitch black soot did not worry me but did not please my mother, especially when I tried to wipe my fingers on my clean clothes. I knew the name of every station on the line; for instance Highams Park and Hackney Downs which the station master would shout out at least twice in an operatic voice as the train ground to a halt at each. Chingford was the last station on the line "All change". Here the locomotives, which on this branch line were tank engines, were detached, rotated on a turntable, refilled with water and coal from track side butts and yards and reconnected to what had been the rear carriage, becoming now the front carriage for the return trip to Liverpool Street – 'and the first shall be last and the last shall be first'. It was just a short walk from the station down Chingford High Street and round the corner into Forest View to get to my grandparents house. As you turned the corner into the unmade road which was Forest View, the view that greeted you, consisting of grassland serving as a golf course, framed by the thick hump of the low hills and the forest beyond, was always calming.

I retain a kaleidoscope of other memories of Chingford either relating to the period before returning to Morden Park after the war, or to the visits we made by train subsequently. My grandfather who wore striped shirts with a collar stud and a thick brown belt and braces to support his trousers had a shed at the end of the garden where he nurtured plants. It smelt wonderfully of seeds and garden implements. He grew his own shallots which he bottled in large glass airtight jars. In the scullery, the most lived in room in the house, adjacent to the kitchen, he would sit me on his knee and play games, including Peter and Paul with pieces of paper on his fingers which he would make disappear and reappear “fly away Peter, fly away Paul – come back Peter, come back Paul”. He would drink his tea by pouring it from the cup into the saucer from which he would sip and would eat multilayered sandwiches which he referred to as ‘Dagwood’ sandwiches. He was a kindly man, although he got cross with me once when I stepped on wet concrete he was laying to make a path down the side of the garden. However he quickly relented and carved my initial letter ‘N’ in the damaged section juxtaposed with my brother’s initial ‘R’. ‘NR’ may still be there if the path has not been dug up by now. His father, a pub landlord by trade, transferred his licence to the Duke of Sussex public house to my grandfather when the latter married my grandmother on 20 July 1908. His father who had been living in the private accommodation above the pub moved to a house at 57 Albion Road, Hackney, allowing my newly married grandparents to move into the rooms he had vacated. There they lived and raised their family until grandfather retired, at which point, he and my grandmother bought and transferred to the semi-detached house at 5 Forest View. None of their eight children raised above the pub, the girls in particular, became drinkers in either teenage or adult lives, no doubt having witnessed too many ugly and violent alcohol fuelled scenes in and around the pub over the years they lived there. By the 1930s my grandfather Arber was a man of financial consequence and a leading light in the Freemasons with the status of Worshipful Master. He was one of the few people to possess a motor car, a 'Standard', and owned a much used and much loved holiday house in Cliftonville. He retired in 1937-8 and when he died of Pleurisy on 13 June 1947, he left business interests and an estate worth over £1 million in today's money (2010) to his sons and in trust to his grandchildren, having purchased outright a house for each of his daughters as and when they got married. Under the terms of the will that my grandfather left, my mother and her sisters were allowed to draw interest from their share of the capital during their lifetime but the capital itself was held in trust to be disbursed, on their death, to their children. My grandfather was a great believer in fairness and treating everyone equally. However, my grandmother, mother and her sisters always resented the fact that my grandfather had treated them less favourably than his sons, not only in the way he settled his will, but in other ways, in terms of educational and occupational opportunities. No doubt he was only following the prevailing social norm at that time in giving pre-eminence to the male members of his family. Nevertheless it is surprising that he undervalued his daughters in this way, given that they were all without exception strong, assertive, competent personalities and he habitually deferred to my grandmother 'Tootsie' in the home.

The kitchen at Chingford was rudimentary. It featured a small stove where the household food was cooked, a coal fire, a china wash basin, a mangle for removing water from washed clothing and a clothes airing frame that could be hauled up and down for loading and unloading by means of a rope and pulley. There was a toilet upstairs in the house but also one outside in the back garden where the toilet paper consisted of torn squares of newspaper hanging from a metal hook – it was numbingly cold venturing out there in winter time having to expose your nether regions.

My grandmother always served meals that were scalding hot and I was encouraged to clear my plate "waste not – want not". My grandmother had a wicked sense of humour and a sonorous, bubbling laugh. She swore frequently in a good natured way, albeit usually in German. Her father, Friedrich Hecker was a nineteenth century German immigrant. As a teenager, she had stayed with his Volland step siblings and children in his home town, Tübingen in Schwabia, Baden Württemberg in South West Germany, acting as companion to one of the Volland girls who had an eye complaint and had gone to school with her in Kornthal, north of Stuttgart, for a while. As befitted a former publican's wife, she enjoyed a drink. She was to all intents and purposes the landlady of The Duke of Sussex, and ran it effectively for many years. Guinness was her favourite tipple, gravitating on medical advice in later life to Martini, acquired from what she termed the Doctor's Surgery which was, in fact, the local off-licence. She was the core of the household and the dominant personality. My aunt Margaret was a saintly drudge, who spent all her time slaving away in the kitchen and doing the housework. Even when invited, she would not sit down or stop working. Her husband Bill after capture by the Germans had been repatriated to this country on health grounds via neutral Spain before the war ended and they had married in June 1944. I never saw them together or speaking to one another. His appearance when we were there was rare but when he did appear it would be for Sunday lunch in the best (front) room overlooking the forest. He was invariably accompanied by a bottle of Burgundy for which he had acquired a taste whilst serving in Northern France. He had been born into a farming family in Sussex and became a professional soldier in the Life Guards, seeing service in the First World War (1914-1918). Although over age when the Second World War started in 1939, he volunteered and was posted to Calais with the Military Police where he was captured in the run up to the famous evacuation from the Dunkirk beaches. He was then marched on foot by his captors 800 miles to a prisoner of war camp in Poland. Many of the younger soldiers died on the way. Bill was the senior Non-Commissioned officer in the camp and fought for better conditions for his men as per the Geneva Convention but the camp's Commandant had to abide by Nazi rules. Bill established some rapport with the Commandant based on their mutual service in the 1914-1918 war but many of the prisoners died of disease and starvation nevertheless. By 1944, Bill aged 53 was a sick man. Mercifully, the Red Cross were able to arrange for his re-patriation on the hospital ship 'Grisphom'. A photograph taken of him at that time shows a man like a skeleton, with a cardboard label hanging round his neck inscribed with his prison identity number, and eyes staring from deep sockets that looked as though they had seen hell on earth. My mother and grandparents rather frowned on his unwillingness to fully participate in family life but in view of all he had been through, it is not surprising that he was self-contained and wanted to keep his own space around him. I sensed this but actually found him quite engaging and sympathetic towards my brother and me. In his slow rural Sussex drawl, he would tell us stories of his time in the POW camp, smuggling messages to the Red Cross and the outside world, hidden in broom heads and of his fellow villagers throwing an American soldier in the duck pond who had become over familiar with a local girl. He also took us for walks with him on the golf course across the road where he played a little.

As a young boy growing up after the war, the nemesis whine of air raid sirens was a natural part of my world; similarly with bomb sites barrage balloons and prefabs. The latter were cheap pre-fabricated bungalow style buildings erected to house people whose homes had been destroyed in the bombing. This was the way things were. I didn't question it. I didn't realise that this audiovisual landscape had been created by the life and death struggle with Nazi Germany that my parents' generation had been engaged in, directly and indirectly, over the preceding five years. I suppose I made the connection later. But by then, events had moved on; the Malaysian Emergency, the Korean War with the Glorious Gloucesters and jet aircraft in combat and the ignomy of the Suez debacle which finally put the skids under the old guard and the days of Empire - not before time I thought. Speaking of deprivation, I remember when we were living again at Morden how pleased my mother was when she received a food parcel from her brother, my uncle Wallie (Walter) from New York, USA. I particularly remember that it contained egg powder, among other things, so obviously we had not been getting fresh eggs as part of our ration. Most foodstuffs were strictly rationed during the war and for several years afterwards. Wallie had been a conscientious objector who, at the beginning of the war, had spent time in prison for his sincerely held beliefs before being freed to enlist with the United Nations. He went to Greece with that organisation where he met a Greek American co-worker who he returned to marry and live with in New York, working in her father's ice-cream parlour.

My father had been serving with the RAF in a radar tracking and guidance unit attached to the American 1st Army advancing eastwards from Casablanca in Morocco to link up with the British 8th Army (The Desert Rats) advancing westwards from El Alamein in Egypt. He passed through Mersa Matruh, Benghazi, Bizerte (Binzert) along the North African Mediterranean coast before taking part in the Anglo-American invasion of Sicily and Italy, finishing up at Caserta near Naples. He was an intelligent man and had been allocated to the radar unit because he was able to read and assimilate numeric co-ordinates from an upside down viewing position and translate them quickly into meaningful information for the pilots to act on. He was invited to become an officer but declined, much to my mother's chagrin, because he didn't want the responsibility and was unwilling to leave his comrades of the same rank. I think his tour of duty was pretty leisurely. While in North Africa, he swam in "The Med" an experience, in later family holidays on the South Coast of England, he often recalled as relaxed and pleasurable. "Swimming in the Med is like being in a warm bath; it spoils you for anything else". This was the mantra to which he regularly resorted as an excuse for not joining the rest of us in taking a dip in the rather more bracing waters of the English Channel.

For his part in Hitler's downfall, my father was awarded five medals. The accompanying citation reads 'The Under-Secretary of State for Air presents his compliments and by command of the Air Council has the honour to transmit the enclosed Awards granted for service during the war of 1939-45.' These were the '1939-45 Star', the 'Africa Star - North Africa 1942-43', the 'Italy Star', the 'Defence Medal, and the 'War Medal 1939-45'. No doubt he was among hundreds of thousands of other servicemen who received similar recognition for their humble yet valuable contribution to the successful prosecution of the war. To me, the medals represent a tangible reminder of his self-deprecating approach to life: I never knew he had received them or the circumstances in which he had received them until my sister and I discovered them in my parent's bedroom dressing-table drawer when we were clearing the contents from their second and final home in Bradpole near Bridport in Dorset following my mother's death during the British Lions tour to New Zealand in 1992. Among them we also found another medal, the 'LCC (London County Council) Kings Medal 1919-20' bearing the head of the reigning monarch King George V. I have no idea whether this was given to my father or mother or a member of their respective families or the nature of the achievement that the medal commemorated. It is an interesting object in itself, as are the war medals. I have had them all mounted and framed together with the accompanying citation certificate and have presented them to my eldest son Simon for safekeeping, who, like me, is interested in history.

I remember visiting at some point my grandfather's bottle factory, C T Rouse Ltd of Whiston Street, Haggerston, and East London, in which he had invested and was a majority shareholder. The factory was dark and warm. I saw gin and medicine bottles of all sizes and descriptions being hand blown from molten material drawn from the furnaces and laid in moulds to solidify into the appropriate bottle shapes, some of which were ribbed denoting dangerous medicines. It was a thriving business only to be frittered away, after my grandfather's death, by his eldest and most untrustworthy son, my uncle John. My mother used to keep the books for John but resigned and ceremoniously handed them back when she discovered that he and his colleague in the business were embezzling the company and defrauding its customers.

I also remember being taken one summer's day by my godmother, Aunt Margaret, to London Zoo in Regents Park and being fascinated by a cascade of concrete steps which I ran up and down again and again. According to my aunt, I found the steps far more exhilarating than watching the penguins in the adjacent penguin pool. Animals are all right but I much prefer plants. Neither overrides my love of physical and sporting activity.

My father returned from the forces overseas sometime in 1946. In the parlance of the times, he was being 'de-mobbed' or de-mobilised from active service. One day my mother told my brother and me that he would be coming home that evening. My brother, Roger, and I slept in the front bedroom of the house overlooking Wolsey Crescent and I remember that evening, getting out of bed, alerted by the noise of a vehicle drawing up outside the house, a rare occurrence in those days when almost nobody owned a car of their own. I pulled back the bedroom curtain in time to see in the darkness, illuminated by a lamppost, half a dozen or so uniformed men crouching forward, in the open back of bull-nosed Bedford truck. They sat there silently, a metal frame, over which tarpaulins could be dragged in inclement weather, arching over them. Almost immediately one of the men wearing a back and front style RAF cap got to his feet and clambered over the back of the truck with a kit bag over his shoulder and walked up our garden path. The lorry chunked into gear and sped off up the road before my father, for I presumed it must be he, reached our front door. There was no wild greeting. I went back to bed where Roger and I remained until, after a while, this same uniformed figure stole into our room and without turning on the light, placed two or three presents for us each beside our beds and retreated quietly. I can't remember anything being said. He was a stranger. He had left home before I had developed any conscious memory of him. Roger had been born while he was away. I was pleased with the presents and played with them for a bit before going to sleep. That was it. Whenever I call to mind that moment or am reminded of it in television documentaries, I chide myself for failing to suppress convulsions of deep welled tears and sob "why didn't he come to me and hug me to show me that he loved me! - and I would have loved him." As it is, he remained a comparative stranger to me throughout my life.

Although nothing was ever said, I got the feeling in later life, that it was not easy for my mother and father to resume their married life together having lived separate lives for so long. My mother had firm views about the way in which the house should be run and the family brought up. She had been brought up herself in a household with strong feminist leanings where she and her sisters were encouraged – not that they needed much encouragement - to stand up for themselves and to take responsibility. My father's scope for influencing our young lives was somewhat circumscribed therefore. He was passive and unambitious by nature which enabled the partnership with my mother to work most of the time with the occasional clash of mutual frustration. Having said that I don't think my father was altogether untypical of many of the men of his generation who tended to value routine, stability and family values more than self-fulfilment and achievement. Both socially and economically the country was still constrained by the class system and the 'stiff upper lip' approach to adversity and the war had left an indelible mark on all those who had seen active service. As a boy my father won a scholarship to Charterhouse Public School but his family lacked the financial resources and determination to maintain him there so he never took advantage of this opportunity. Throughout his life, winning the 'Pools' so that he might retire and do nothing more taxing than looking after his family remained his chief ambition.

# RECONSTRUCTION

My first day at school must have been in early September 1946. I remember it well – and it wasn't a pleasant experience. I was taken by my mother to Morden Farm Infant School in Grand Drive, Morden about ten minutes walk away from where we lived, and left on my own with a swirl of other kids. I felt lonely and uncertain in the playground and couldn't wait until the school bell rang at the end of the day and it was time to go home. But by the end of the week I had made friends and loved it.

My best friend at school was David Brown. Though he was more nurdish than me, we got on well. He used to enjoy swapping cigarette cards and playing charabancs which was the early name for bus-type coaches whereas I preferred more physical activity such as British Bulldog, Jump Jimmy Knacker, and football and cricket played in the school playground during the breaks with a moth eaten tennis ball. In British Bulldog you had to run from one chalk line to another evading capture by the catcher who stood in the middle. Anyone caught joined the catchers until the catchers so outnumbered the runners that no runners were left. I was quite good at dodging and getting across successfully – good training for playing rugby later on. I also adored Jump Jimmy Knacker. This was a game for two teams. The first team would choose a team member to act as the 'pole'. The pole would stand with his back to a wall and the rest of the team would bend down facing him and form a human bridge by sticking their heads through the boy in front's legs. The other team would form a line and take it in turns to run and jump on the backs of the other team with the aim of collapsing the bridge. The most effective approach was to land as many jumpers as possible one on top of the other on the weakest member of the bridge. We also played games of marbles, which began with the invitation "Lardie on yer", conkers in the autumn season, kiss chase and generally rushed around the playground at break time, sometimes watching the girls swinging from the railings displaying their woollen school knickers dyed bottle green or navy blue. Outside school we played cowboys and Indians using the shed at the bottom of our garden as a base come-hideaway and gang games in the orchard at the back of the house where we built camps and sometimes lit fires. I remember smoking hollow plant stalks lit from such fires in imitation of our parent smoking habits and playing doctors and nurses with other girls and boys on a building site halfway between home and school. For cowboys and Indians We would construct our own bows and arrows, swords and guns from pieces of wood and string. If we were lucky for Christmas or birthday we might get a toy cap-firing revolver and a cowboy or Indian hat and costume to add to the fun. Similarly, we would build our own self propelled vehicles from planks of wood, string and old pram wheels. We did get a metal pedal powered toy jeep one year for Christmas with a US style star on the bonnet. To the chant of "Eee Vaa Voo" we often played the hand gesture game representing scissors, paper, or stone concealed from your opponent behind your back till the final call of "Voo". Scissors cuts paper; paper covers stone; stone blunts scissors.

David often came to my house and we played in Morden Park usually accompanied by my brother. I can't remember ever going to David's house. Somehow I think my mother slightly disapproved of our friendship because David's father worked in a factory (Fosters Electrical Transformers in Merton) and they lived in a terrace house on the main road in Wimbledon Chase. Such were the niceties of class distinction in those days. We lived in a similar house but semi-detached and in a better, quieter location adjacent to Morden Park. They had a London postcode; we were in Surrey – just, and my father was an office or so called white collar worker in London. After leaving school around the age of fourteen to fifteen, my father had joined J H Bance & Company, named after the founder, situated in Victoria, central London. Starting as a boy clerk, he later became a travelling representative for the company which acted as export agent for Sheffield steel manufacturers who produced railway lines and other items much of which was exported. My mother considered that we were middle class. This was probably true at the time but although she never admitted it openly, I think she looked down on the Browns as working class.

On the naughtier side, we would play 'Knock Down Ginger' a 'dare' game involving knocking on people's front doors and then running away and hiding before the occupants opened their doors and looked around in some confusion for the source of the knocking. In the lead up to Guy Fawkes Night we would throw fairly lethal lighted bangers at other gang members and fire roman candles at them while trying to evade incoming missiles ourselves. Every year, as a result of such antics, perhaps not surprisingly, children would be injured suffering serious burns, including the loss of eyesight. There was no age limit when it came to buying fireworks and little restriction on the size of the bang you were able to buy for your few penny's worth of pocket money. One year during our fireworks party in our back garden to which a couple of neighbouring families had been invited, my father ignited a so called Jumping Jack firework on the strip of concrete, a sort of primitive patio where we were standing, that separated our house from the lawn. The Jumping Jack was a standard firework contained in most packs available for purchase in local shops at that time. It was coiled a number of times like a rearing serpent and bound tightly with string. The idea was that once lit and laid on a hard dry surface the little monster would explode repeatedly, jumping in the air a foot or two as it did so. Because of the way it was put together, it was difficult to predict the intervals between each bang and jump. It was fun. We dodged successfully until it landed in a boy's Wellington boot and continued exploding. He cried in pain and hopped about with each successive explosion before the adults present could catch him and remove his boot. Unfortunately he had suffered quite a nasty burn on his calf where the exploding firework had lodged. Later when I was at grammar school my best friend Terry French and I, used the little knowledge we had gleaned from our chemistry lessons to concoct an explosive mixture which we stuffed in a metal bicycle pump and detonated to loud effect in the back alley that ran behind our house.

David Brown, my brother and I often played cricket or just messed about together in Morden Park along the brook that flowed in a six foot deep gulley through it. We built makeshift bridges from tree roots and branches and would try to catch small fish that we referred to as 'tiddlers' and remove them to a jam jar where we could observe them more closely. If you were unlucky enough to fall or be pushed in you would get what was known as a 'bootie'; a shoe full of water. Once when we were mucking about by the brook we were asked by a local newspaper photographer to pose for a picture. Although he later provided my mother with a free copy of the photograph he had taken, it never appeared in the local paper. Local excitement and drama must have crowded out our frolicking in the park as a newsworthy item. Occasionally we would notice other less straightforward men lurking in the woods surrounding the park. They usually wore macks (raincoats) and I assumed that these were the men that my mother had cautioned me against from time to time when we went over the park ..."don't talk to any strange men". We didn't know why we should not get involved with them but we avoided them nevertheless. In our teens we ridiculed them as DOMs (Dirty Old Men). Little did we know!

At Morden Farm, in addition to David Brown, I was friendly with the Waite twins, Rosemary and Diane and like most other boys in my class, fancied a plumptious, curly haired girl named Maureen James. I also recall Mrs Leadbetter, a grey-haired, metronomic, music teacher, appropriately nicknamed Mrs Leadbasher.

I did well in end of term examinations regularly coming third in class in most subjects. I also remember one year, in the school sports, winning three prizes, including a seaside bucket and a plastic ball. I was, with David Mathieson, the fastest runner in the school over 100 yards and represented the school in the District sports. I came third. My theatrical career began at Morden Farm where, in the annual nativity play, I took the non-speaking part of one of the three shepherds abiding in the fields and later, the Angel Gabriel, representing a distinct step up on the ladder to thespian stardom.

I collected quite a few toy vehicles which I used to buy with my pocket money saved religiously for the purpose. These were miniature metal, rubber-wheeled cars, vans, buses and lorries made to a high standard of detail and sold under the brand name Dinky Toys. In good condition they would probably be worth quite a lot of money now. I played with them endlessly at home. I used the lino (plastic 'linoleum' floor covering popular in the 1950s) in our living room, patterned as it was, as roads for my various dinkys. My pride and joy was a yellow articulated lorry marked with the Weetabix logo, with doors that opened and closed at the back. I also enjoyed building different things with pieces from my Meccano set also made of metal, a sort of precursor to Lego. I remember building a crane, complete with winding gear, the metal struts of which were held together with tiny nuts and bolts which were inevitably the first things to get lost.

I hated rainy days and would sometimes have to resort to playing games of cards to while away the interminable drizzly hours. I have never been particularly fond of playing cards, partly because, along with horse racing, I find it a highly boring way to spend my time and partly, I suppose, because it reminds me of those dull rainy days. I much preferred reading or drawing, colouring or painting and was proud when one of my pictures depicting cowboys and Indians was displayed in an exhibition in the local library in Lower Morden Road. When we went to view my masterpiece, the lady in charge told my mother that the picture was praiseworthy and interesting because I had imagined and depicted some of the figures outside the frame. I remember I had drawn an Indian showing his head and trunk at the bottom of the picture, leaving the lower half of his body to the imagination of the viewer below the frame as it were. She said it was unusual for an artist of my age to have an awareness of space outside the formal frame of reference – or words to that effect. I was quite pleased. My reading consisted of weekly comics like 'The Eagle' and 'The Beano' and the series of 'Biggles' and 'Just William' books. I also loved the 'Robin Hood' story – he was very much the hero of my dreams - and 'Alice in Wonderland' that together with the 'Tinderbox Man' sometimes prompted nightmares.

My sister Susan was born on Cup Final day in the local maternity unit on a bright, sunny afternoon on 24 April 1948. When I was told about my new sister's arrival in the world, I was in the garden, so perhaps it was half-time or the match had finished. At any rate, I thought her birth on such an important day was most auspicious. In those days the FA Cup final was a truly national event alongside the Oxford and Cambridge Boat Race, the Grand National, the Epsom Derby, the Wimbledon Tennis Championship and the summer Test Match Cricket series. There weren't all the distractions and attractions there are nowadays. Partly because there was no alternative, but partly also because these events brought the whole country together in the difficult years following the war they provided something to enjoy and celebrate against the prevailing mood of gloom and decline. People were captivated by these events and would discuss them enthusiastically at work, at school, in the streets, shops and pubs. When the relevant day came, virtually everything stopped so that people could listen on the radio to the event unfolding or, if you were lucky enough, watch grainy pictures on early black and white television. I don't think we had a television then, although we were the first in our street to get one. It was a Phillips, combining in a tall wooden cabinet a radio and a television incorporating glowing, bulbous glass valves. The picture was black and white or more various shades of grey. The screen was nine inches in size. It was rare to get to the end of a programme without a break in transmission, announced with the statement 'Normal service will be resumed as possible' and accompanied with instantly forgettable background music. This was frustrating but at the same time the message was faintly reassuring while we waited and waited. Transmission of programmes which were all live started in the afternoon and finished with the national anthem in the late evening. When no programmes were being transmitted a test card appeared enabling engineers to carry out repairs and the picture to be tuned. There were also 'interludes' between programmes that lasted for ten minutes or so, the most well known of which was the 'Potter's Wheel' featuring a potter making a pot – gripping stuff!

Speaking of the Derby, in the days leading up to the race, which was held on the Downs outside Epsom some five miles or so from where we lived, we would be visited by a string of fortune tellers, tinkers, tramps and gypsies travelling on foot to the meeting. I remember one flamboyant individual who called himself Prince Monolulu, knocking on every door in the street including ours every year without fail, offering for a small monetary consideration to give us the name of the certain winner of the race. He was of Caribbean or Pacific Island descent. A big tall man with curly hair and a jolly face, whose chant was "I've got a horse!", he sported a multi-coloured cut skirt over his trousers and a red Indian style headdress with foot long coloured feathers sprouting from a band round his head. Some of the tramps who called would come every year and were indulged as 'regulars'. They arrived, not necessarily at Derby time, but according to their own calendar and familiar haunts as they plodded their way round the country.

More frequent visitors to our street and a step up from the vagrants and itinerant beggars were the horse and cart fraternity immortalised later by the BBC in their popular comedy Steptoe and Son in the 1960s. There was the rag and bone man, the scrap metal man who cried stentorously, "Any old iron?" and of course the daily horse drawn milk cart, later replaced by an electrically powered milk float. In spring and summer there was often a race among housewives and family members to collect any horse manure deposited as the horse and cart passed along the street. People, me included on some occasions, would rush out armed with a shovel and bucket and scoop up as much as you could to use as a fertilizer on the garden. Horse manure was particularly good for roses which grew well in the local clay soil but came on a treat with a helping of said nourishment.

In winter the coal dusted face of the coalman appeared. Sporting grimy leather caps and dust-encrusted flaps over their coats they would hoist heavy sacks of coal onto their backs from the wagon and, bent almost double, stagger down our sideway to the coal bunker my parents had built at the back of the house below the kitchen window. There were two sections to this bunker with a wooden lid to each on top through which the coalman emptied his sack and a sliding hatch at ground level through which we later extracted the stored coal. One section provided storage for normal coal for the main fire and the other section was reserved for anthracite which was burnt in the kitchen boiler to provide our hot water. Later my father had an electric immersion heater fitted to the hot water tank upstairs that meant that with the flick of a switch, after a short while, you could have hot water for a bath, winter and summer alike, without the chore of first having to light the downstairs boiler. The immersion was supposed to be expensive to run but we used it regularly, regarding it as a fortunate luxury. In one skilful well practised movement employing hand, arm and shoulder, the coalman would tip the content of the sack into the bunker producing a thundering roar accompanied by thick black clouds of coal dust billowing upwards. We had to stand sentinel during this operation to make sure that, first of all, they delivered all the bags we had paid for - it was not unknown for them to cheat on this score - and secondly, to see that coal was not tipped in the anthracite section of the bunker and vice versa. In winter as soon as we got out of bed, no matter how cold it was outside, it was my brother's job and mine in weekly rotation - my mother termed it being 'Duty Wallah' - to shovel this fuel from the bunker – no easy task - and to bring it into the house in a metal hod called the coal scuttle. There, having first removed the ashes of the previous night's fires, disposed of them in the dustbin and swept the grate and surrounding hearths clean, we laid and lit the dining room fire and kitchen boiler using rolled up pieces of newspaper as tinder. Often we would hold an open sheet of newspaper over the gap between the hearth and chimney breast to create a draft up the chimney to encourage the flames to take hold. This was quite tricky because the newspaper sheet tended to billow inwards getting ever closer to the fire as you created the vacuum effect accelerating the flow of air up the chimney. If you weren't careful, the sheet you were holding could easily catch fire, disintegrating spontaneously in a flurry of lurid flames. Then you had to clear up that mess and start again. That was nothing to the mess created when, intermittently, the chimney sweep came to call armed with long scrapers and brushes which he poked up the chimney pulling down clods of black sludge and showers of soot. With luck, most of the debris landed on the cloth he laid round the base of the fire place and could be easily removed. Roger and I also had to help our mother in the day to day running of the house by doing the wiping or washing up for a week each; we could choose which. I always chose wiping up; my brother washing up.

Sundays were deadly. Everything was closed apart from the churches and Sunday Schools. As a child, I had to attend Sunday School. I think this was excused on the grounds of accepted custom, religious duty and to give Mum and Dad a 'well earned rest on Sunday afternoon' after the strains of the preceding week and the effort put into delivering Sunday lunch consisting of the obligatory roast beef and two vegetables followed inevitably by the sweet course such as rhubarb, which my mother loved, a taste I never shared despite her admonition "It's good for you". Sunday School was held at 3 o'clock in the afternoon in the library down in Lower Morden Lane. I hated it and tried to get out of going but to no avail. Mum and Dad had to have their Sunday afternoon rest. Were they resting, I wonder now?...know what I mean ...nudge...nudge... wink...wink!? I'm afraid I thought Sunday School was trite, patronising and boringly unbelievable from a doctrinal point of view. I did eventually persuade my mother not to send me. Although I have always accepted Christian moral philosophy as a basic tenant in my life, I have never had a religious experience. I believe Jesus of Nazareth was a powerful moral teacher and philosopher but not that he was unique or that he was divine. I don't subscribe to the virgin birth and resurrection myth. Indeed, I regard a lot of religious dogma as positively harmful with its tendency to promote exclusivity and to constrict rational human thought to the detriment of more natural altruistic human emotions and impulses. The only tolerable part of Sundays was listening to the radio in the mornings. Family Favourites was a music request programme uniting men and woman in the services in BAOR (British Army Over The Rhine) in Germany with their loved ones back home. It was listening to this programme that I fell in love with classical music. Tchaikovsky's first Piano Concerto featured regularly along with more mainstream popular pieces of the time. Jean Metcalf hosted in London with her welcoming svelte voice combining seamlessly with her avuncular husband, Cliff Michlemore in Germany. This was followed by The Billy Cotton Band Show, a mixture of humour and light jazz style music, also featuring Archie Andrews a dummy dressed as a schoolboy. Then came Life With The Lyons, a half hour family comedy show starring Bernard and Barbara Braben, two Canadians; again a husband and wife team. The BBC was very strong in promoting family values in those days. There were no other broadcasters then. Apart from the cinema, it was the

BBC or nothing. Still there were some BBC programmes that proved popular with the young. I remember Dick Barton Special Agent with fondness and later as a teenager, I was captivated, along with many of my contemporaries by the Goon Show.

Sunday was also the day when, in winter, a fire would be lit in the lounge and we would have tea there. The room was used only for Sunday tea and occasionally for entertaining. It was the posh room. The room was decorated in 1930s art deco style with a light green tiled fireplace with narrow contrasting black lines and, hanging from the ceiling a matching light green segmented glass lampshade. There were small alcoves either side of the fire place and a bay window, overlooking the front garden. In the bay stood a circular wooden coffee table on which tea cups and saucers and the teapot were placed over patterned paper doyleys. My mother also possessed a metal-framed, two tier wooden-trayed trolley on which cakes, bread and butter, jam and honey would be ceremoniously transported from the kitchen to the lounge. Sometimes for tea we had winkles with our bread and butter which we had to extract from the shells with a pin before popping them in our mouths. We would count the empty shells on our plates repeating out loud the old rhyme 'tinker-tailor-soldier-sailor-rich man-poor man-beggar man- thief' to discover our destiny in life; jokingly of course. Sometimes, somewhat gingerly, we would make toast by impaling slices of bread on a three pronged metal toasting fork which was held over the fire. Occasionally, through inattention or poking the fork too close to the flames, the slice of bread would catch fire and have to be extinguished leaving a wholly or partly blackened piece of bread that could be quite tasty topped with a knob of butter. The finishing touch for my mother and for us was the tarts she bought from the tennis club in Raynes Park to which she and my father belonged. These delicacies were referred to by my mother with startling originality as 'Tennis Club Tarts'. They had round light pastry bases that were topped with red jam and a dab of cream. They would sometimes be accompanied by fruit cake and my mother's homemade bread pudding that looked to me like congealed grease dotted with dead flies, which I didn't altogether care for, either in appearance or taste and rock cakes, aptly named, although to be fair to her, these weren't bad. Whenever my parents entertained it was only ever with family. I can't remember them having friends round although they were by no means anti-social and enjoyed the company of fellow members of the tennis club who my mother used to gossip about. The club also organised social events from time to time which they used to attend. Mum and Dad often went to dances in the evening or so it seemed. My mother always looked wonderful in her evening gown and she would let us smell the perfume she had dabbed behind her ears before they left for the evening. I think her favourite perfume was called Soir De Paris which smelt wonderfully sophisticated and rapturous. My father usually bought her a bottle of Soir De Paris for Christmas and her birthday. In the early years before we acquired a television, they would take it in turn to go to the cinema once a week while the other baby-sat and I remember my mother enthusing over Gone With The Wind. We didn't know what it was but joked after repeated mentions about 'Gone with the wind up' as an indeterminate expression for someone retiring in high dudgeon.

I remember with embarrassment the dreadful silences that sometimes occurred when we were sitting in the lounge for Sunday tea entertaining guests. The conversation always seemed stilted and would either peter out or would be brought to a juddering halt by my father making an inappropriate or incontrovertible remark. One Sunday my adult cousin Brian and his fiancée came to tea. We sat in the habitual serried and opposing ranks either side of the art deco fireplace while Cousin Brian, a jolly, straightforward character, told my parents how he had been getting on with his driving lessons. When it came to describing the procedure for executing the emergency stop, my father took issue with him, claiming that you should "slam your foot on the footbrake" not push simultaneously on the clutch pedal to disengage the engine as Brian was saying he had been told by the driving instructor. When Brian persisted that this was what the driving instructor had told him to do, my father became more loud and hostile, accompanying his mantra "just slam your foot down on the footbrake!" with ever more exaggerated and violent jabbing of his right foot against an imaginary brake pedal. The ensuing silence was cavernous. Brian and his fiancée politely made their apologies and left.

Entertaining was more about observing the necessary etiquette rather than having an enjoyable time. I carried with me into later life an aversion to mannered behaviour and snobbery. But these were very much the driving forces behind personal relationships, both formal and informal, in those days. It was while my parents and I were being entertained by the Ridgwells who lived a couple of doors up the street from us at one such Sunday afternoon session that I innocently got drawn into my first sexual experience by their elder daughter Barbara as we played together in the broom cupboard in their hallway. She was older than me and more sexually aware, I suppose, and invited me to rub my private parts against hers. Somewhat surprised, I complied, sensing that I was being quite daring but any pleasurable physical feelings excited by the encounter were minimal as far as I was concerned.

One night, I unintentionally shattered a small part of that posh, Sunday-room ethos. For some reason my brother and I were given our bedding and told we would be sleeping that night on the floor in the lounge. Had we got guests in the house staying overnight? If so, it was a most unusual departure from the normal tea-time visitation when guest were expected to arrive around 3 pm and leave shortly after 5 pm. Anyway, having been put to bed in the lounge, warned to behave and to go to sleep, there we were. Voices from the adjoining dining room where my parents were presumably entertaining percolated through intermittently. It was all frankly rather exciting. Not being in the mood to go to sleep and finding our unfamiliar night time surroundings full of intriguing possibilities, I suggested to Roger that we pretend to be flying angels by scrambling onto the arm of one of the armchairs, and then jumping off flinging our arms into the air to represent the angels flapping their wings, our fall being broken by the soft bedding material on the floor. This worked well and we each had a couple of goes. However on my next attempt, as I flung my arms up into the air, my left hand inadvertently hit the art nouveau glass lampshade, my parents pride and joy, bringing the whole thing crashing down in a tinkle of breaking glass. Next thing my father was storming into the room and beating me repeatedly with a stick which left deep oblong shaped bruises on my back, bottom and legs for several weeks afterwards. At the time I felt I deserved the punishment and never held it against him but looking back I think that, though generally docile and passive, my father was prone to occasional ill-judged, uncontrollable outbursts of rage which demeaned him in my eyes.

That is not to say that in some ways I admired him. He was tall and handsome and unlike my mother with her laboured attempts at humour, he had a quick wit. However, I was always wary of his unpredictable outbursts of temper. For all her faults and her considerable strengths, I loved my mother throughout her life but never grew close to my father. No doubt the fault is partly mine: I should have tried harder. But somehow I don't think the outcome would have been much different. One piece of advice he gave me when I was being bullied shortly after starting school was something I valued at the time and stayed with me. My mother gave me two or three sweets each day to take to school. One of the boys at the school, not in my class, obviously found out and began to demand in a threatening manner that I hand them over to him, which I began to do. When my parents found out - I must have told them - my father told me that the next day when the boy demanded his ransom of sweets, I should refuse and if necessary fight him. He said that even if I lost the fight, the boy would not bully me again – bullies don't like opposition. The next day I followed my father's advice and sure enough I was never troubled by this boy again. My mother would also repeat, whenever I was facing a new challenge, the old adage, that a coward dies a thousand times a brave man but once.

My school diet supplemented by my precious sweets consisted of a free bottle of milk at break time each morning and school dinners. There was no choice of menu. You had to have what they gave you whether you liked it or not. I remember on one occasion they served fish cake. The smell put me off and made me feel sick. I couldn't bring myself to eat it. I sat at the table throughout the lunch period unable to take a bite and was obliged to take the offending cake back to the classroom for the start of the afternoon's lessons. There in the presence of my classmates I was forced to swallow a few bites before honour was satisfied and the plate with the remains of the cake was finally removed from my unwilling gaze. I have never eaten fishcake since although I love fish and seafood. One afternoon after school dinner, I can't remember what I had eaten and much to my considerable embarrassment, I shit my pants in the classroom. Too frightened to say anything, I sat at my desk in this smelly and uncomfortable state until the blessed relief of the school bell rang signalling home time. I rushed home and confided in my mother who cleaned me up and re-asserted my self esteem in an unfussy and understanding way. At school I also developed a chronic dislike of macaroni served from time to time in a sweet milky cream as a dessert. Much to my chagrin, it was also given to me when I was confined for six weeks in the isolation hospital with scarlet fever. I think I was probably around five or six years old at the time. I was denied all visitors. Even my parents could not come to see me. I took with me into the hospital, my beloved cuddly, a brown soft toy duck, whose neck I had twisted in love and I dare say childish anxiety so that it had become a mere thread holding the duck's head on to the rest of its body. Unfortunately because of the highly infectious nature of the disease I had to leave my toy duck behind when I eventually recovered and returned home. It was hard but I accepted it as part of the process of growing up and having to learn to live with loss and disappointment like being told that there was no Father Christmas. When I got back home, I was given a Daimler ambulancc Dinkey toy with a red cross on the side. I enjoyed playing with it unaware of any accidental or deliberate symbolism my parents intended to impart. If it was a deliberate choice - a palliative memento for my incarceration in the hospital, I remain unclear to this day what the intended subliminal message might have been.

As we grew up, my classmates, brother, sister and I spent periods away from school with illness. The average illness lasted three weeks. We went through the card; tonsillitis, influenza, chicken pox, measles, mumps, to which, in my case, was added the aforementioned scarlet fever. I also suffered quite badly from earache at night. Hearing my groaning, my mother would console me and would tie a woolly sock round my head covering my ear, keeping it warm and would then give me a sip of brandy to help dull the pain. This seemed to work. These enforced absences from school and normal life were not only painful, irritating and debilitating at the time but left you in a weakened state afterwards when you had to catch up with the schoolwork you had missed. I suppose, in a general sense, this unavoidable suffering taught me the value of endurance and perseverance in the face of hardship and difficulty and that in the end things would get better.

Enforced absences from school of a different kind were the school holidays, the longest and most pleasurable of which was the summer holiday. It lasted a mere six weeks but to me, at the time, it seemed almost endless. Two of these six weeks were devoted to the annual seaside family holiday. In the early days we went to Bognor Regis. I counted the days leading up to our annual summer holiday with mounting excitement, spending part of my time designing miniature gardens on a tea tray using flowers, moss and earth from our own real garden and a mirror to represent a pond. On the appointed Saturday we would at last depart from home, travelling by taxi to Sutton, Southern Region RailwayStation and from there by electric train to Bognor. We stayed within walking distance of the pier and the beach in a Fawlty Towers type Guest House in the town on a half board basis. We ate our meals in silence with a few other guests in the front room of what was really a terraced house. I remember junket and blancmange appearing regularly on the menu for dessert neither of which appealed to me. We were promised that if we behaved ourselves, Roger, Susan and I would be treated to a Knickerbocker Glory ice cream on the last day. We always got one and were taken ceremoniously to an ice cream parlour cum café near the main bus station to receive our due reward although I am not sure that we always entirely deserved it. I never wanted to go home at the end of the family seaside holiday and would feel sad for days afterwards. This was always the time when I felt most alive. Whenever I go away on holiday, I still feel the same emotions of excitement and anticipation beforehand, freedom, stimulation and enjoyment during and sadness afterwards.

Also as a special treat my mother always asked me what I would like to do on the last day of the school summer holiday. My answer was always the same – to go on a boat trip on the River Thames at Kingston. We travelled there by red, single-decker, London bus which was unusual because most were, as now, double-deckers, including the electric, overhead cable powered trolley buses that operated between Raynes Park and Kingston and trams that ran between South Wimbledon and Elephant and Castle in London. Thc trolley buses were virtually silent but had a fierce acceleration. It was wise to find a seat as quickly as possible after boarding or you could be thrown back violently. The trams were more sedate and although similarly powered by electricity made a clanking and grating sound as they ran along steel rails embedded in the middle of the road and best avoided on a bicycle or car in wet weather. We had no car and nor did anybody else that I knew. We relied totally on public transport and 'Shanks Pony', that is to say, our own two feet, for getting around. This didn't inhibit my mother. She loved walking and the outdoor life and it was a question of using public transport or staying at home which she was not keen to do. I remember waiting at a bus stop in teeming rain for a bus outside the catholic Convent at Hindhead where my father's sister Noll spent the larger part of her life and who we visited periodically. This moment sticks in my mind because of the force of the rain and the sudden appearance of a tank rather than the hoped for bus to take us home. The rain was coming straight down in stair rods when an olive green tank came roaring towards us ejecting spray from either side of its tracks. It swished past, driver and occupants invisible, seemingly unconcerned about the fact that my mother and I were already soaked and feeling abandoned in the middle of nowhere miles from home.

My father travelled around the country in his job and sometime around 1952 was given a company car. As I have said, car ownership then was negligible, so we were lucky. It was a grey, four door, leather seated, 'Flying' Austin Standard 11. 'Flying', I suppose, because of the body design, the most notable feature of which was a one-piece, sloping rear end. My mother loved the sea and on summer weekends we would often drive in the car to Bognor and later to West Wittering near Chichester. We broke down so many times just short of our destination that the local AA man on his motorbike, whose duties included amongst other things, saluting every passing motorist sporting the Automobile Association badge, always managed to get us going again and came to know us quite well. We took a picnic lunch with us which we ate on the beach or in the car if it was raining and bought fish and chips along the Epsom Road on the way home to save my mother cooking, which she never liked doing. Sometimes, while sunbathing, playing on the beach or swimming, RAF Gloucester Meteor jet fighters would swoop across on practice runs, firing on a target ship moored out to sea. This area of rolling sand dunes and gently sloping, fine-sand beach is still largely unspoilt. We also regularly went, rather proudly, across London in this sleek vehicle to visit my grandparents in Chingford. We accomplished this trip without breaking down although I can remember gently colliding with a bus on one occasion at the Elephant and Castle crossroads. Traffic at this five road junction was controlled by a policeman standing in the middle on a circular podium. He sported broad white arm bands and directed the approaching vehicles with a series of well practised and exaggerated arm movements. These consisted of the flat hand denoting stop: the windmill rotation of the arm and hand to denote come on: and variations to indicate turn right and left. Many junctions in London and throughout the country were controlled in this way rather than by traffic lights.

In 1952 the returning Conservative party under Winston Churchill as prime minister abolished the last vestiges of wartime food rationing. Certain commodities such as confectionary and sweets inessential to the war effort or the subsequent recovery of the national economy could only be purchased by surrendering government issued coupons contained in coupon books. Imagine our joy when the appointed day arrived. We kids all went round to our local sweet shop knowing that for the first time ever we could buy as many sweets as we liked within the limit of our weekly pocket money. Sweets were displayed behind the counter contained in enormous glass jars with screw topped lids. We would spot what we wanted, point to the appropriate jar and licking our lips in anticipation, wait for the shopkeeper to take down the jar from the shelf, slowly unscrew the lid and pour the contents into the scale before transferring them to a crisp white paper bag. I bought a whole bag of liquorice sticks and other delicacies but I only remember the liquorice sticks.

There were no supermarkets then to compete with local shops and very few chain stores although Sainsburys who maintained a fascinating long narrow shop in Morden across the London Road from Morden Tube and Bus Station was popular and gave good value for money. Butter, cheese, bacon and ham was cut to individual order using wire cutters fixed to stone boards for the cheese and backward and forward motion scything machines for the meat. In Morden there was also an 'Are You Being Served' style department store called Hawes and a Co-op where you earned dividends from your spending. The Co-op always bore the taint of a socialist experiment in common ownership and resembled inside, both in décor and products alike, its Soviet retail exemplars: we didn't shop there. My mother as I recall had to go round the shops locally at Stonecot Hill each day to provide us with our staple food and beverages with perhaps a weekly trip to Morden. We had a cool larder in which my mother kept perishables. We had no fridge then or washing machine. Washing was performed in a metal tub or in the sink filled with hot water and soap suds. Clothes, sheets and so on were laboriously rinsed dry by feeding them through the mangle screwed temporarily, for the purpose, to the draining board and consisting of a metal frame supporting wooden rollers turned by a metal handle. With the larger thicker items of clothing and sheets for example, this required a lot of sweated effort to turn the handle and push the items through the rollers.

Around this time, I sat the 11 Plus examination in Rutlish Grammar School and much to everyone's surprise, I failed. My mother and my teachers, including the Headmistress, Miss Baker, could not understand it. I had always been in the top three or four in my class and although the percentage of grammar school places available in Surrey was low at around 10% making the competition more intense, I should have secured a place based on my school work. The school and my parents took up my case as a result of which my parents were invited to an interview with an official in the County Education Department in Kingston, the County Town, which I also attended. The gentleman we saw admitted that errors had been made and that there were irregularities in the marking in my examination paper, although some weaknesses in spelling were evident: I had consistently misspelled the words 'their' and 'receive' transposing the 'e' and 'I' letters. It was agreed that I should be allowed to re-sit the examination at the earliest opportunity. This meant that I wasted a couple of terms in the Morden Farm Secondary Modern School where I came top in everything by a mile before eventually re sitting the examination successfully.

# ELEVEN PLUS

While waiting to start at the grammar school, I was walking home one day from the secondary modern school at Morden Farm when I saw for the first time in the sky above me, a jet propelled aircraft. It looked clean but odd, having no visible means of propulsion. It seemed smoother and quieter than the increasing number of propeller driven passenger aircraft I had become accustomed to seeing gently descending from the navigation beacon near Epsom Downs to land at the recently designated London Airport at Heathrow. This strange metallic beast in the sky was the world's first jet airliner, the British designed and built De Havilland Comet which first flew on 2 may 1952 and was taken out of service after suffering several fatal crashes brought about, as it was subsequently discovered by metal fatigue inherent in the design. The field was then left clear for American aircraft companies, notably Boeing, to learn the technical and production lessons from this classic example of late British imperial folie de grandeur and to virtually monopolise the subsequent commercial airline business.

The much heralded Festival of Britain in 1952 celebrated the centenary of the Great Exhibition of 1852, when Britain was the undisputed workshop of the world and through its official and unofficial empire effectively ruled over half the world. It was a rather half- baked attempt to recreate the country's former prestige, albeit in a forward looking way. The exhibition took place on the South Bank where the Festival Hall now stands. We went with my mother, brother and sister, known to me as 'Dood', stemming from her difficulty in aspirating the letters 'S' in her name when learning to speak. She would say 'Doodan' not 'Susan'. The exhibition was popular and colourful and we lost Dood for several minutes in the melee of people. Wc found her again at the eccentric moving sculpture created by a man called Emmett. A new monarch Elizabeth II came to the throne in June 1953 after the old king, her father, the reluctant but still comparatively young King George VI, had died on a dull day in November the previous year. At school every child throughout the land received a gaudily decorated china Coronation Tea Cup and Saucer to celebrate her accession which some, more in hope than anticipation, were hailing as the start of a new Elizabethan age. I found the gift puzzling and un-necessary. I knew why it had been given but not what to do with it. I disposed of it to my mother without a moments further thought. I don't think that anybody in their heart of hearts really believed that we were entering a new Elizabethan age. Nevertheless the 1950s showed a gradual improvement in living standards, mirrored by a steady decline in our international influence which sank to humiliating depths during the Suez crisis in 1956.

I started at Raynes Park Grammar School in the autumn term of 1953 carrying a brown leather satchel, proudly if awkwardly dressed in my brand new school uniform, shirt, tie, short trousers, blazer and cap sporting the school badge. The school badge was and remains unconventional which in many ways sums up the school. Also, the cap badge was made of silver chrome and, uniquely, was pinned to the cap. It represented the road system and electric railway that bounded the school – our place in the modern world.

I loved the school and its ethos – 'From each his own to each his need'. I subscribe to that philosophy. Although traditions were respected, you were taught to think for yourself, not to be hidebound by prevailing views and norms and to draw your own conclusions defending them when necessary. This was not an overt policy but a deeply ingrained part of the culture of the school imparted by the founding headmaster John Garrett, an intimate in more ways than one of the famous poet W H Auden. This founding ethos was continued and nurtured by all succeeding headmasters. The school was built in conformity with the 1930s standard rectangular two storey government funded model, with a central quadrangle, wood panelled assembly hall, playground on one side, orchard and playing field. It stood on a roughly triangular piece of land sandwiched between a commercial building owned by Bradbury Wilkinson, printers of bank notes, on one side of the triangle, from which it was separated by a brook, iron railings and footpath. On the second side it was bordered by two other schools, Bushey Primary and Bushey Secondary Modern from which it was separated by a twelve foot fence, high enough to preclude fortunate boys like myself who had succeeded in getting to grammar school from mixing with the common herd. The base of the triangle was formed by the Kingston Road where it joined the Kingston By-pass. On the other side of the by-pass stood

Shiphams canned meat factory. There were two school entrances, one on the Kingston Road and the back one that I used that led from the road adjacent to the railway level crossing at Motspur Park running along the Bradbury Wilkinson brook and one side of Bushey Secondary before opening out into the grammar school playing field known as Little Side. Big Side, or Oberon to give its formal title, had been acquired from a bank or insurance company shortly after the school was founded and was situated a mile or so away from the school on a remote sight surrounded by big detached houses and an extensive allotment area. It had space for several pitches and a huge stylish pavilion in which you changed. It had enough room for dining and functions although this facility was never used except on the annual school sports day to which parents were invited.

For the first couple of years, I walked to school; a distance of about three and a half miles each way; summer and winter, in all weathers. Then, when I was in the third or fourth form, I was allocated a space in the school bike shed and cycled instead. I had been given a pre-war iron frame Raleigh bicycle by my uncle Bob, one of my father's two older brothers, which I had customised by fitting drop handle bars, flash red plastic racing mudguards, chrome, streamlined, dynamo powered front and rear lights and a narrow leather racing saddle. It still weighed a ton and the Sturmey Archer gear system was unreliable. Under heavy tension when I was pumping the pedals to climb a steep hill, it tended to slip sending the pedals suddenly in to free spin and landing my crotch on the cross bar with a painful and embarrassing bump. All the pupils walked, cycled or used buses and trains to get to school. Nobody came in a car; not even the teachers. One Saturday, with a school friend, I cycled all the way to Brighton and back, a feat of which, though saddle-sore, we were proud.

I enjoyed and was inspired by French, Latin and later Greek and Russian language lessons but most of all by History. Mathematics and Physics were interesting. Biology and Chemistry lessons were fun. We were taught Biology by our form master, Mr Trinder. He was a knowledgeable man as were all the masters. He had a jovial character which we exploited. In reply to his question to the class as to which age came after the Pleistocene Age, my friend Terry French answered amid general laughter with a query in his voice "The Sausage Sir?". We learnt the wonders of Osmosis, a word which the whole class would repeat with heavy emphasis followed by gales of furtive laughter every time Mr Trinder uttered the word. We found out about Spirogyra and asexual biological reproduction by which time we had a pretty good idea where this particular line of study was leading, especially when we started considering the lifecycles of tadpoles and frogs. Sure enough when we reached human reproduction, it became an absolute riot. Mr Trinder after persevering for a while, abandoned the project after our amusement and mockery became too much. He did so in a way that surrendered nothing of his authority and strengthened the teacher-pupil bond. Everybody in the class had known for some time how human babies were conceived. I first learnt about sex when somebody at the secondary school told me in the playground one day. To begin with I didn't believe what I was being told. It seemed weird and a bit disgusting – putting your willy in a girl's hole. But I was persuaded that this was so and that it was apparently very enjoyable. Long after Mr Trinder's lessons on the subject, my mother said to me one evening that my father had something to tell me about how babies came about. The atmosphere became suddenly formal and my father was clearly embarrassed. I could tell that he was being prompted by my mother to do his fatherly duty. Fortunately he said "Well, you have biology lessons at school don't you?" With great relief, I quickly assured him that this was the case and that consequently, I knew all there was to know on the subject. That was that. I don't blame my mother for making sure that I knew. When she was growing up she was told that babies were either brought by storks or were found under gooseberry bushes. The subject was taboo in Victorian and post Victorian Britain and neither family members nor friends had told her 'the facts of life'. I am sure she was not alone in this. Incredibly, my father had to explain 'the facts' to her after they got married – presumably on their honeymoon. The final confirmation came for me one summer evening when, engaged on a so-called wide game with a few fellow scouts, I strayed over the London Road into a rectangular strip of land dotted with scrub, bushes and small trees bordering the Beverley Brook that ran across the lower part of Morden Park past our scout hut. It was dusk. Moving forward stealthily, we suddenly spied, in a small clearing on the other side of the brook, a man with his trousers down on top of a woman, white legs akimbo, reinforced hooped skirt in the air, in the act of copulating. At that moment I realised that what we had joked about and at times only half believed was actually true. Here was living proof. Much to the couple's embarrassment we began lobbing grass and lumps of mud in their direction until reluctantly and with a show of annoyance they gave up and hurried away adjusting their dress to regain a modicum of dignity as they did so.

Sexual encounters of a different kind were amusing and innocent. A boy called Davidson, for the general amazement and approbation of his fellow classmates would take pride in displaying his abnormally long todger through a hole in his trouser pocket. Whether the hole had been created especially for the purpose or was purely coincidental I never discovered. To add to the entertainment, conducted behind a raised desk lid, he sometimes drew a smiling head on the tip until one day somebody at the crowning moment hit the said todger with a wooden pencil box and the performance was never repeated. Roy Saunders, a fellow scout, who was also fairly well endowed, was fond of inviting and receiving fondling as a part of his growing sexual awareness and evolving puberty. As a rite of passage in transcending puberty, I remember being given my first pair of long trousers to wear. My parents bought me a grey pair to go with my school uniform. I first wore them when we drove to London Airport to greet my uncle Wallie on his return to the UK from his failed marriage in the United States. I felt very proud and grown up although the tailoring left something to be desired. At Heathrow there were a couple of large two story Nissan huts serving as arrival and departure halls inside a low wire fence running parallel with the adjacent A4 Bath Road. These makeshift buildings were connected to each other and to a rectangular tarmac area the size of a small football pitch by duck boarding. A twin engine De Havilland Rapide aircraft parked on the grass offered half hour pleasure flights for £5. No other buildings or aircraft were visible across the vast grassy expanse that was Heathrow. After a while a four engine propeller driven converted wartime Avro York pulled up on the tarmac, the corrugated metal panels of the fuselage and the rivets holding them together shaking with the vibrations created by the engines before they eventually slowed and stopped. The plane looked primitive and I was surprised it had come all the way from New York without mishap. My uncle emerged from the aircraft and we took him home but not before he told me how much I had grown which seemed to be the stock observation I received as a child from all my aunts and uncle when we met.

Chemistry lessons were enjoyable although I learnt very little and dropped the subject halfway through my A level studies. Peter Smith was the chemistry master. He was a lovely man of medium height with grey, combed-back hair and a thick goatee beard. However, he was not much good at explaining the mysteries of chemistry. On one occasion he pointed to a spot on the blackboard which he had completely covered in lines, whorls, words, numbers and symbols by exclaiming with great emphasis “This is the crux of the matter”. Everybody tittered. I had not got the faintest idea what he was talking about. To add a bit of spice to these lessons, I remember balancing as dangerously as I could on the back legs of the four legged tall stools we sat on behind a long wooden bench equipped with Bunsen burners, running water and sinks. Occasionally, I and others following a similar practice crashed to the ground when we leaned back too far and were greeted by jeers and laughter from the rest of the class. Pete, as the master was known, didn’t seem to mind too much. However he was a little put out one day when Terry French and I were conducting an experiment and we blocked the sink. In order to free the blockage, Terry inserted some metal callipers down the plughole and poked vigorously, triumphantly announcing after a few seconds that the liquid was draining away. Unfortunately, I had to tell him that he had dislodged the U bend in the drain pipe and the liquid was rapidly spreading over the Chemistry Laboratory floor. It may have been on the occasion of this mishap or some other that Pete asked Terry and me why we had to conduct all our experiments on an industrial scale. We thought this was quite amusing and probably true. Not that this mild admonishment changed our approach at all. Some pupils in our form had a gift for chemistry. One of them, a small, thin, pasty faced lad, called Mottershead with bulging tortoise like eyes, was an intense and successful chemistry student. I remember one of the other boys called Radford observing, aptly, that if Mottershead wanted to find out what was inside a caterpillar he would climb up its arse to find out. Radford looked and sounded perfectly unremarkable most of the time but he could come up with hilarious jibes and daring exploits. One such involved climbing into the loft above the Chemmie Lab to make strange ghost like noises during the lesson. Unfortunately while he was thus occupied he stepped on part of the ceiling unsupported by a joist and his foot and the lower part of one of his legs went through. All we could see was his leg dangling. Ordinary looking and sounding boys like Radford are the ones to watch.

Outside the formal curriculum, Pete Smith produced the school plays. He was brilliant. He had a great eye for casting, and a lively ability to draw subtlety, humour and drama from the script. Through his infectious and enthusiastic staging of these productions, he opened my ears and eyes to Shakespeare and other dramatists. I took part in both school and house plays appearing as Sir Andrew Aguecheek in Twelfth Night, as Trinculo in the Tempest, both comedy roles and in another comedy role in Ben Johnson's play the Alchemist. In the House Play competition in which Pete Smith was not directly involved, we took on the then revolutionary tragic-comedy by Samuel Beckett, Waiting For Godot where I had one of the leading roles as the aimless tramp Vladimir. Adjudicated by the popular radio-TV quizmaster and Raynes Park Old Boy, Robert Robinson, wc came a close second in the competition to the rather more worthy Duchess of Malfi, despite the fact that our offering had gone over a storm with the audience. I loved acting and developed good comic timing and the art of holding an audience. I loved getting into costume and trying to make my character come to life. My last two appearances were leading roles in The Frogs by Aristophones performed in the school quadrangle and as the young lieutenant in Once Aboard The Lugger a musical comedy where I had to sing as well as act. I remember after leaving school, meeting at the Oberon, the soft voiced, and terrifyingly parsimonious Jack Stratton my former Physics Master when to my astonishment he told me without a hint of his usual deprecating sarcasm how perfectly he thought I had suited the part and how impressed he had been with my performance in that role. I may not have won his approbation as a Physics student but his compliment was welcome and a boost to my morale. Perhaps I should have joined the Navy or the acting profession.

Before treading the boards at Raynes Park, I remember, as a member of the audience in the oak panelled school hall, watching Androcles And The Lion performed in the annual competition by my own House. Halfway through, the leading actors climbed on to a platform, constructed to represent the Coliseum in Rome and faced away from the audience to simulate watching Androcles fight with the said

Lion. Unfortunately the weight was too great. The Pillars holding the platform began to collapse, at which point characters who had been killed off in previous scenes rushed on stage to help support the platform enabling 'Nellie' Partridge, the best actor in the school, playing the part of the Roman Emperor, to deliver his lines, before he and the whole edifice came crashing down and the curtains were drawn. On another occasion, I can't remember whether it was a House or school production of A Midsummer Night's Dream, in the scene where Titania the fairy queen falls in love with the weaver, Bottom transformed by magic into appearing with an asses head, John Spencer, playing the part of Bottom, forgot his next line. There was an audible prompt to which Spencer responded by carefully removing his asses head, turning slowly to the prompter in the wings, saying loudly with mild irritation in his voice "I've said that before" and promptly put his asses head back on again. It did shatter the tenuous illusion a little bit, but it got a good laugh.

The school was an all boy's school and operated a House system to which every boy belonged. The houses were named after the original house masters appointed when the school opened in the 1930s. There were five houses – Newsom's, to which I belonged and whose house colour was mauve, Cobb's - green, Milton's - silver, Halliwell's – yellow and Gibbs – red. House ties instead of the school tie could be worn, one of the two light blue diagonal bands on the navy blue background in the school tie being replaced by the appropriate colour. Competition between the respective houses, in whatever field, from, debating and drama to rugby, cricket, athletics, swimming, or chess was intense but good natured. Without warning one day I was told I was representing the house in a boxing match after school that afternoon and would be facing Dave Wearn, a square shouldered giant from Gibbs house. To my eternal shame I failed to appear, my excuse being that I had never boxed before in my life and had no experience or training in the sport; which was true. However a large part of my motivation was that I was frightened of getting hurt and pummelled unmercifully by Wearn.

I had no such fear of taking part in my first rugby game. Before going to Raynes Park, I had read a story in a boys' own book in which a robber had been chased by the hero and brought crashing to earth with a flying 'rugby tackle'. The text was accompanied by an evocative line drawing showing the event. From that moment on I desperately wanted to learn how to perform this feat for myself so that I could apprehend any robbers or nefarious villains in the same heroic and admirable way. When we all turned out in our rugby kit including heavy ankle length leather boots with nailed studs, baggy shorts and hooped shirts for our first game, I asked Norman Bellis, the sports master, after he had explained the rules of the game to show me how to execute a flying tackle. He obliged. The game then began and very quickly the other team secured the ball. Terry French, my best friend and classmate, was hurtling towards the try line with the ball neatly tucked under his arm. Keen to find out if the instructions and demonstration given by Norm Bellis actually worked in practice, I lined Terry up and executed the perfect tackle on him. Steaming untouched towards our try line I brought him crashing to the ground and he never quite recovered. Emboldened by my initial success, I tackled everything in sight for the rest of the game and showed that I could run with the ball myself and elude tacklers with the speed and agility developed running and dodging other kids in crowded school playgrounds. I loved the game from the first and have never stopped loving it. I quickly found myself selected for the school team playing at fullback because of my tackling and running. I couldn't kick but gradually improved this part of my game by practicing. Gradually, I mastered drop and touch kicks and conversion kicks which I took for my house team. I was house rugby captain and we won the house cup every year. I adored the rough and tumble and the naked aggression in the game but also the rugby ethos requiring respect for opponents and referees. As the saying goes – on the pitch you try and knock seven bags of shit out of the opposition but after the game is over you shake hands cheer the opposing players off the pitch and enjoy a drink and friendly banter with them afterwards. When I got to the sixth form, I gained my school colours playing for the school first fifteen. I was very proud and was allowed to wear a special badge on my blazer showing the school insignia on a light blue background to denote my achievement. Throughout my life I have always tried to get into the first fifteen in a manner of speaking in whatever I have attempted. Or to put it another way, I have striven to get into the top ten percent. I think I have broadly achieved this aim both in my working and social life. By a combination of hard work, determination, enthusiasm and skill, I have managed to creep in at the bottom end of this segment and am comfortable with the knowledge that whilst I would ideally like to be at the very top, I'm just not good enough or lucky enough to scale the highest heights.

I have photographs of me proudly wearing my school blazer complete with my rugby colours badge on the top pocket and light blue edging denoting my status in the sixth form as a school prefect. At Raynes Park discipline was based on a culture of self-discipline, reinforced by the prefects. At the end of morning assembly which the whole school attended and which took the form of a semi-Church of England church service with a hymn to sing and a reading of the bible as well as notices from the Deputy Headmaster, the Head Prefect would read out the names of boys guilty of misdemeanours who as a consequence were required to attend the prefects' room during the morning break as punishment. On one occasion shortly after two top Cold war Russian spies Burgess and McClean, tipped off by the so called Third Man, had caused a media sensation after escaping from the country when they were about to be arrested, the Head Prefect announced "Would Burgess and McClean please report to the prefects' room at break." These were two boys in my form as it happened who coincidentally shared the same surnames as the infamous Cambridge spies aforementioned. Such was the routine of these announcements that I am sure that the head Prefect did not realise the implication of what he was saying. However the whole assembly burst out in spontaneous laughter which the head Prefect acknowledged with a smile once it dawned on him what he had just said.

For serious indiscipline there was the cane and permanent expulsion for repeated serious infractions. This would follow a report from the prefect or from a master and involve a hearing in front of the Headmaster, a mild mannered intellectual named Henry Porter and referred to by the pupils as just Henry. Henry had his own place in the local pub, The Duke of Cambridge, where he would sit quietly on his own with a pint of bitter, ruminating on the inner spirituality of some abstruse Greek text. The pub was also the school watering hole for older pupils. They never bothered Henry and he never bothered them, inside or outside school hours if they came across one another in this establishment. One day I was summonsed as a witness to attend a disciplinary hearing in Henry's study after reporting a boy for smoking on school premises. I cannot remember the boy's name but he looked like Mick Jagger of the Rolling Stones. The boy alleged that I had mistaken his breath congealing in the cold air for cigarette smoke. My evidence was accepted. The boy who had made it plain to me that he did not want to be at the school anyway and had several previous disciplinary offences against his name was expelled.

At the end of each term we all gathered in the school hall for the final assembly presided over as all school assemblies were by the formidable and intimidating 'Tiger' Raynham the Deputy Headmaster. A tall, straight backed, well built man, he sported bushy eyebrows and a lush military, mustard coloured moustache. He would walk with great presence onto the stage and turning towards the assembled throng, would look down, place his two large leather shoed feet with great deliberation in exactly the same two spots, look up, cross his arms and glower at us. Pushing and shoving and chatter would cease immediately and deathly silence and stillness descend under his penetrating gaze. This was such an awe inspiring ritual that before the final assembly one year some brave sixth formers drew two foot marks in chalk where he habitually placed his feet. The whole school waited with bated breath to see what his reaction would be. Nothing – he didn't bat an eyelid. We all felt he must have seen them but he never wavered a jot from his normal routine. We were all left feeling slightly cheated. The Tiger's tale was not for tweaking! At final assembly 'Tig' and all the masters wore their graduation robes over their normal cloaks and carried their mortar boards. We always sang the school song composed by the poet W H Auden, a close friend of the founding Headmaster William Garrett. This was a touching and stirring piece, both words and music, and we still sing it every year with much affection at the Old Boys Reunion Dinner which I normally attend. The final tear jerker and morale booster was the customary reading from the lectern by 'Tig' of Saint Paul's letter to the Corinthians (1 Corinthians 13). This was the magnificent King James Authorised Bible version "When I was a child I spake as a child, I understood as a child, I thought as a child: but when I became a man, I put away childish things. For now we see through a glass darkly; but then face to face: now I know in part; but then shall I know even as also I am known….etc" not the vacuous, modern Enid Blyton style, travesty.

The House system had also operated at Morden Farm School where the houses were named after the Tudor national naval heroes Raleigh, Nelson, Drake and Grenville. I was in Raleigh whose colour was red. Nelson was blue, Drake yellow and Grenville green. These gentlemen were very much my own personal heroes too: action men; brave and exuberant. One of my favourite pictures then and now is 'The Boyhood of Raleigh' depicting an old seaman pointing across the sea to an eager and wide eyed young Raleigh, telling him about the excitement and mystery that lies beyond the horizon in foreign seas and lands. The theme of adventure and exploration echoed the hunger I have always felt for travel away from home. A similar picture titled 'When Did You Last See Your Father' depicting two children, a boy and a girl, being quizzed by a parliamentary office in the English Civil War was influential in my childhood and has remained a favourite. For me, it offered a key to a door that revealed a distant but important time in our development as a nation; a door that was opened wide for me on a visit to Aunt Dorothy and Uncle Graham in my early teens. He was a grammar school teacher in Birmingham and had a gift for bringing history to life. His knowledge and memory was incredible. He knew the history of practically every field, castle and pub in England. My brother and I were despatched by my mother to stay with them for a week. We travelled up by coach – Midland Red – a journey which took several hours in those pre-motor way days. Graham took us around Warwick and Kenilworth Castles and various Civil War sights. He talked inspiringly about the Roundheads and Cavaliers and the important issues being disputed and of course about Oliver Cromwell who I mistakenly assumed he admired. The fact is that the more I found out about Cromwell, and I have since read several books about him, the more he has become my ultimate hero. Flawed though he was as he himself openly admitted, he stayed a modest and sincere man, un-phased by deserved celebrity. A man of reflection and decisive action when needed, I carried with me from that time his guiding mantra that fame and fortune should be the reward of those who earn it based on individual ability not on family inheritance. I remain persuaded that on balance, we would be more successful as a nation without the encumbrance of our constitutional monarchy and its sub-structure of snobbish drone-like hangers on.

# EXTRA CURRICULUM

In the Raynes Park years, not everything of most value to me then or in later life was learned as part of the set curriculum. Certainly I enjoyed and profited by the subjects I studied. I particularly liked History taught by Mr Rudgeley who had a distinctive burred accent. It was a school joke that he would pronounce words like forty-four with heavily rolled and emphasised 'r's; so much so that we sniggered and laughed whenever the number 44 was mentioned in any context. It became a secret laughter code that permeated the whole school from first years to sixth formers and bound us together in an absurd but very real way. As you passed through the school the difference in ages seemed enormous with sixth formers especially physically big and able ones like John Bray, the first team and later Old Boys Rugby Club captain, appearing like gods to more junior boys like me. My brother also attended the school two years below me and we were known as 'Big Bot' and 'Little Bot' respectively. The nickname derived from my habit of wandering around in the changing room and on overseas school trips in my underpants and the fine size and shape of my nether regions. 'Bottom' shortened to 'Bot' rhymed with the first syllable of my Surname 'Cot'.

I also enjoyed languages and was good at French, Latin and Greek all of which I passed at the age of sixteen at 'O' (Ordinary Level). I passed eight subjects in all with good grades, the others being Science, Geography, History, English and Mathematics. We also had practical classes in

Woodworking and Metalworking but I treated these lessons as a joke and had no desire or ability to become proficient in them. Encouraged by Harold Wilson the then Prime Minister to join the 'white hot heat of Britain's technological revolution', I unwisely from an academic point of view chose the Science Sixth rather than the Arts Sixth Form to pursue my 'A' Level studies. I got four modest passes in Physics Pure and Applied and Mathematics Pure and Applied for my pains. Nevertheless, although my natural talents lay more on the Arts side, I am grateful for the intellectual window that the study of these subjects opened up to me and I have retained an abiding interest in them ever since. I was accepted by London University to study Physics and my exam results were good enough to get me in but my heart was not in it and my mother was anxious about the expense involved; not just for me but for Roger and Susan if they followed suit. In those days very few university places were available and most parents could not afford to send their offspring to them. These were the days long before the advent of biros and calculators let alone computers when the most we had were logarithm tables and all work was done with pen and ink and coloured pencils. Each desk was furnished with an ink well and blotter and a wooden handled pen with a replaceable metal nib. Fountain pens were a luxury item along with propelling pencils and were awarded for passing exams not taking them. Fountain pen or not, unforced and deliberate ink-blobs represented an ever present hazard in producing neat, well ordered work.

We looked forward to morning break when each pupil received a free one third of a pint bottle of milk. For a small amount of money you could also purchase cream buns and doughnuts from the tuck shop provided you got in the queue early enough and resisted attempts to push you out of the way. School dinners were bulky hunger stoppers not fine cuisine. My favourite was 'Toad in the Hole' for main course and Jam Rolly Polly for pudding. Each table had a table leader who ordered one of the boys to collect the food cooked in brown ceramic bowls from the serving table erected close to the kitchen. The table leader then distributed the portions. If you finished quickly you could go for second helpings, when available. As a consequence and having a healthy appetite I learned to eat more quickly than anybody else I know until I was trumped much later in life by my daughter-in-law's father Howard. The staple concoction consisted of mashed potato with meat and veg for first course and what we called stog for sweet. Stog was a suet style pudding and came in every conceivable colour and consistency and was always accompanied by custard in consuming which, I tried to avoid the skin and the lumps. The kitchen was presided over by a podgy, abrasive woman, Mrs Austen, whose husband Stan, the school caretaker, was only ever observed leaning on his broom with a vacant expression on his face. His name became a byword for indolence and lethargy. The only other female in the school was a part-time teacher named Mrs Herdman married to Bill Herdman the Geography teacher. She was an innocuous grey-haired pigeon of a woman who insisted that we boys call her 'Sir'.

I enjoyed school trips. Once a week we went to the swimming baths in South Wimbledon. I was a member of the school team and the school breast stroke champion and record holder. Afterwards we were given a cup of Bovril to warm us – the pools in those days were unheated - and a packet of old style greasy potato crisps. My mother who loved swimming, especially in the sea, had taught me to swim at an early age. I joined Epsom Swimming Club for a short period but got bored with the tedium of training involving swimming endless lengths of the pool. I drank my first glass of beer in a dive bar off Leicester Square on a school trip led by the English master who had taken a small party of us to see an 'Angry Young Men' type play in London's West End. It was a half pint of Flowers Bitter. I forget the play but remember that first glass of bitter. School trips also led further afield. L R King our French teacher and form master took a party of us to Paris. He was known to everyone as Larkie following his initials and the in joke was that he was a Communist. It is true that he wore a Lenin style beard but there was no other evidence that in reality he was a party member or sympathiser. He was a tall, gaunt man and a good swimmer with a well developed torso. A bit of a soft touch from a disciplinary point of view, we played him up mercilessly at times, but he never lost his kindly manner and we liked him well enough. After I left school, I discovered that the innuendo directed at him about being a Communist probably stemmed from the fact that his mother was Russian. This no doubt also accounts for the most memorable moment of our Paris trip when, without a comment or warning, he ushered us into a Russian Orthodox Church as we were walking down a Paris street on a Sunday morning on the left bank of the Seine. The atmosphere inside the Church was spellbinding, the wafting of the incense and the sonorous chiming of the unaccompanied Gregorian chant created an unforgettable moment of serenity and beauty in the midst of the bustling, hurly burly of the city. Although confirmed in the Church of England, I've never had a religious experience: but that came close. In fact I only got confirmed in order to please my parents and to continue going to the church youth club. I suppose my lack of religious conviction was noticed because at the end of the series of weekly preparation classes that applicants for confirmation like myself were obliged to attend, I was summoned for an interview with Canon Livermore the head of the parish. We talked generally and after discussing the subjects I was studying at school, which included the classic languages of Latin and Greek, I read an extract of the bible in the original Greek to him and gave him a passable translation. This seemed to do the trick and he gave his approval for my confirmation to go ahead. Some months after my confirmation, I was challenged by Pop Dawson, our local curate, a rather pompous, bigoted Yorkshireman with a booming voice, about my failure to attend church regularly. I told him that, as far as I was concerned, I followed Christian moral doctrine and that going to church was an important and inspiring cultural experience equivalent to going to an art gallery or concert but nothing more. Over the years this has remained my view.

The school trip to Paris was the first time I had ever been abroad and I loved it. It was in the days before car ferries and channel tunnels. The boat that ferried us across the English Channel was a steam ship. She had a single tall, black funnel painted with a broad red horizontal stripe and two wooden masts. Moored along the quayside we boarded down a narrow gangplank. A single vehicle, a Mercedes saloon car, was hoisted by crane onto the main deck and secured by ropes and pulleys. Our voyage from England to France proved stomach churning to say the least. The weather was foul and the sea extremely rough. As we headed for France, the ship was rolling, pitching, yawing and performing every known nautical manoeuvre in order to stay abreast of the waves. Down below the fumes and stench of sea sickness were overpowering and we stayed on the exposed upper deck unable to stand, thrown backwards and forwards across the deck clutching the handrail on one side before lurching to clutch the handrail opposite in order to save ourselves from going over the side. We thought it was great fun. Mottershead appeared from below, his face a greeny-blue, the same colour as the sea. Observing our antics he groaned hopelessly and descended again into the murky and putrid depths of the vessel. When we reached Dieppe I was struck by the houses round the harbour which all had grey slate roofs and shutters on the windows. This really was a different country. I was excited and throughout my life have never lost that feeling of excitement when travelling to different places and parts of the world. The steam train that was waiting on the quayside was also different. The engine and carriages were all painted a dark olive green colour. There was no platform. The engine was covered in a mass of pipes. On the journey to Gard Du Nord in Paris we started singing. Schoolgirls in the corridor from neighbouring compartments evidently from the north of England, judging by their accents, mocked us light heartedly "What's all that warbling and singing", which they pronounced warboolin**g** and zin**g**in**g** with heavy emphasis on the '**g**'s. Frankly, they seemed to us to be more foreign than the French people whose country we had come to visit.

The following year, Larkie accompanied by his fellow teacher Pete Smith and the caretaker at Oberon, Peter Hillbury, took a party of us by boat and train to Lugano in

Switzerland to an area known as the Italian lakes. I was appointed a monitor, responsible for half a dozen of my fellow pupils and on the train from London as we neared the channel port of Newhaven, Larkie called the monitors together and asked them to check that the boys in their respective groups had their passports ready. I suddenly felt stupid. I had forgotten my passport. I told Larkie and he and Pete Smith between them managed to persuade the ship's purser, who was French, to allow me on board; but only after they had drafted and signed a handwritten statement asserting my nationality, identity and membership of the school group. Amazingly, I managed to enter France when we reached the other side of the channel and to cross the French and Swiss border without my passport. Nobody asked for it. Arrived in Lugano, I had to write to my mother who sent my passport in the post to me in time for my return trip. What an idiot!

Lake Lugano, enclosed by the Alps and the two other lakes we visited, Como and Maggiore, were stunning. The place where we stayed in woodland on the outskirts of Lugano town was less so. It was run by a German couple and consisted of wooden huts sleeping ten boys per room in bunks. It was surrounded by a ten foot wire fence with main gates of similar height which were locked at seven each evening. We reckoned they were ex Nazis and the accommodation had been a prison camp of some sort. Being teenagers we resented the discipline the couple were trying to impose upon us and in the early evening a few of us would slip out before the gates closed. At the end of an evening spent in the town in various bars we would congregate in the bar nearest the camp where we would meet up with Mr Hillbury who also enjoyed going out for a couple of drinks. We would then leave in a group and climb over the camp gates in the darkness trying to make as little noise as possible before returning to our huts. This scheme worked well for several nights until towards the end of our stay we were rumbled and caught by Larkie in the act of climbing over the gates. He read the riot act and we were confined to barracks for the remaining evenings of the holiday. On a visit to Lake Como, I remember Derek Furminger, lying out all day on a stone terrace in the full glare of the sun; his unprotected body save for a pair of skimpy white swimming trunks turning to lobster pink. Not surprisingly he suffered from sunstroke afterwards and was hors de combat for three days. We thought it was amusing – just the sort of thing that always happened to Furminger. At school we bullied him mercilessly at times but he was a member of our gang and in a curious way we loved him and he loved us. One day, four of us hired a small boat and rowed out into the middle of Lake Lugano. The lake was very deep and the water cold. Tim Biddiscombe and I persuaded Pete Williams, who was gullible and always eager to please, to swim in the nude. He duly jumped over the side of the boat and yelped as he met the cold water and yelped again when he claimed a fish had brushed against his bollocks. We were convulsed with laughter and rowed away leaving him in the middle of the lake. "Oi...you bastards...come back!" he shouted but we kept on rowing. In my mind we abandoned him in the lake but in truth we must have relented and took him back because many years later in 1995 we met up with him, quite by chance, in a bar in Cape Town, South Africa where we were celebrating England's win over Australia in the quarterfinal of the Rugby World Cup. Pete had become a successful mover and shaker in the international oil business, operating around the world, but sadly died of a heart attack back in England shortly before he was due to retire to the South of France. A stalwart supporter of Harlequins rugby club over the years, his death was commemorated by a plaque erected in the main stand, now demolished. Needless to say, in our innocence, we saw none of this unfolding as he flailed around in the lake.

I also remember my first trip to Twickenham the home of international rugby, arranged by the school to see the traditional varsity match between Oxford and Cambridge. I was amazed by the speed and flat trajectory with which the ball was passed between the players. John Spencer who forgot his lines playing Bottom in our House Play had gained a place at Oxford largely because of his rugby prowess and was playing when calamity struck again in the opening minutes when he conspicuously dropped a high ball punted in his direction.

This was the first of many visits to 'Twickers' over the years. I was in the old North Stand on a gloomy November day with my brother in the 1950s when we witnessed Peter Jackson the England wing three-quarter scoring a brilliant solo try directly opposite us at the other end of the ground against Australia, to win the match. His side step and swerve seemed miraculous and we and the huge crowd went wild. Since that match took place, the game has changed immeasurably and mainly for the better. Nevertheless, I enjoyed the camaraderie and excitement then just as much as I do now. Another famous try from that era was the one by the England left wing Andy Hancock against Scotland which I watched at home with my family on our black and white television. The weather for the game had been dour and was mirrored by the play on both sides. Nobody had scored a try and the match was heading for a tedious draw. Suddenly, from a scrum deep in their own territory, the England forwards won the ball. For once, instead of being kicked, it was passed to Hancock who ran the length of the field, head back, arms and legs pumping up and down and lungs bursting to elude the Scottish defenders for the winning try. When he made the line, my mother, in her enthusiasm, leapt up spilling the cup of tea on her lap all over the fireplace.

My mother loved sport of all kinds. She had played netball at school, was a good athlete and played tennis regularly at a club in Raynes Park to which my father also belonged and I joined in my teens. Nevertheless swimming remained her favourite form of exercise. When she moved to Bradpole in Dorset when my father retired, she swam in the sea practically every day throughout the summer and two or three times a week in an indoor pool in the winter. She continued swimming in the sea until she was eighty years of age and only stopped then because of health problems which culminated with her death a couple of years later.

Terry French and I, wary of the fact that on leaving school we would have to undergo our National Service for two years in the armed forces, decided to join the school ATS unit. I think the initials stood for Air Training Service. We attended on Tuesdays after school and were taught marching and other drills in the school hall. We were equipped with uncomfortable and ill-fitting light blue serge uniforms and leather boots and taught to identify enemy aircraft from silhouettes printed on sheets of dog-eared paper. We were given a rifle each– unloaded of course - for the evening. The idea was that by joining and completing our basic training in the ATS we would be more likely to qualify as non-commissioned officers during our National Service. We reckoned this would enable us to enjoy a cushier existence for these compulsory two years than serving merely as 'squaddies' like most people. Fortunately for us, we didn't have to put this theory to the test because in the late 1950s National Service was abolished. I believe we were the first year to benefit from this concession. We immediately withdrew from the ATS.

With Terry, I recall on one occasion going to Saturday morning pictures at the Morden Odeon. Many children throughout the country went regularly to their local cinema each week for this Saturday morning programme designed specifically for children. He suggested we go because the cinema was advertising the showing of the very first 3D (three dimensional) film for children. On arrival we were each given a pair of cardboard framed spectacles containing a pair of different coloured translucent plastic lenses, red and green I think, which applied to the eyes while viewing the specially engineered film, created the 3D effect. As was usual with all cinema audiences in those days, settling in to our seats, we were entertained to a short popular music recital played on an electric organ which disappeared below stage level when the film was about to begin. Having seated ourselves, the recital ended after a little while; organ and organist duly disappeared and the lights dimmed. A hush descended as everyone raised their 3D glasses to their eyes and waited for this new technological wonder to appear before us. Unfortunately nothing happened and after a while we kids started getting restless and noisy. The cinema manager appeared on stage and apologised for the fact that due to a technical hitch they were unable to show the 3D film after all. We booed. He said they would show us a film – not in 3D – instead. We were disappointed but lo and behold - the film, admittedly in black and white, was about the adventures of a young couple marooned on a desert island. The amazing thing was that they had no clothes on! You couldn't see this amount of nudity in an X rated adult cinema in those days let alone at children's' Saturday morning pictures. I don't know where they got the film from or whether they realised what the content was before they showed it. At the end everyone was cheering and shouting "Roll it back!" Nobody cared a jot about missing the 3D experience.

Terry's parents were mildly eccentric. His father was a very tall, well built man with large feet. He was a policeman and lived with Mrs French in a flat above Halfhides the jewellers in Wimbledon Broadway at the foot of Wimbledon Hill. He played the harmonium and saved money by taking his newspaper from a nearby waste paper bin each day. The marriage had become one of convenience. Mrs French would cook for him and he would pay her for each meal, calculating individually how much the carrots and other ingredients cost. She would wave romantically at passing bus conductors whose buses came to a halt at the bus stop outside the jewellers. Terry was envious of my family which he saw as the ideal.

One of the reasons I didn't go regularly like a lot of other kids to Saturday morning pictures was because I had a Saturday morning job. I worked in the local grocer's shop on the Epsom Road, tidying up the back room and trimming the cauliflowers and other vegetables for display in the shop. I didn't particularly like the work. In winter, trimming vegetables made my fingers go numb with the cold but I took pride in creating order out of the preceding week's chaos leaving everything in neat accessible piles by the end of my morning's exertions. I also shared a paper round with my brother which I hated. I have never been very good at getting up in the mornings and in the winter, particularly for the Sunday round, it took a great deal of will power to stick with it. Other jobs I took in the school holidays in order to supplement my pocket money were much more enjoyable.

For three successive years, I worked as a stagehand at the Wimbledon Theatre during the pantomime season. Topping the bill were music hall, radio and television stars Sandy Powell the ventriloquist, the cheeky cockney, Tommy Trinder, and the king of the 'odd ode', Cyril Fletcher. Cyril played the Dame and was perfect in this role, his deep voice contrasting wonderfully with his female character. In the main comedy scene, set in the castle kitchen, he was supposed to be making a cake but needless to say the pastry mix went everywhere but in the mixing bowl. In the slapstick antics with his incompetent assistant, the scene reached a crescendo when rolling his large, dark, mischievous eyes and poking his tongue into his cheek he mellifluously enunciated the line "...it went all up the wall...!" which always drew a huge laugh from the audience and everyone backstage. At the end of the scene, covered in pastry-mix, he exited stage right, where I was stationed, announcing that he was going to have a bath. His assistant left on stage shouted a warning after him about the precarious state of the hot water boiler. Cyril had to make a lightning change of costume, donning a bath cap and grabbing a large lufer while seating himself in a specially constructed wooden contraption running on casters at each corner, and made to look like a bath. The idea was that the boiler would explode and Cyril seated in the bath would appear on stage, bursting through the smoke wearing nothing but a bath cap and an amazed look on his face. For this to happen the special effects people had to simulate an explosion and it was my job with a another stage hand, simultaneously, to undo the catches on a hinged, concealed flap in the scenery, push the flap down so that it fell flat on the stage floor, grab either side of the bath and propel it with Cyril inside onto the fallen flap. The flap had to take the combined weight of Cyril and the bath. It was built of solid wood with a six inch ramp at the near end and guide rails to take the casters on the bath. Cyril was a big heavy man and had about five seconds to change costume and seat himself in the bath before the imaginary boiler exploded. We had rehearsed successfully with the empty bath but for some reason had not rehearsed with Cyril himself sitting in the bath. On the first night, Cyril made a lightning change, jumped in the bath, boiler exploded; flap crashed down, but despite our best efforts, the bath would not budge. We pushed with all our might but the front casters had jammed on the leading edge of the wooden ramp and as the smoke cleared we could see the audience and they could see us haplessly trying to get Cyril and bath on stage. Fortunately, the audience saw the funny side and much to our relief, so did Cyril. He suggested that for the next performance we take the bath further back and give it a run before engaging the ramp. And this is what we did and it worked perfectly thereafter. Cyril was a delight to work with. He was an intelligent and naturally funny man; a very polite and considerate professional, unlike some of his fellow stars.

For the most part, I spent my time erecting and striking sets, placing, removing and storing stage furniture and props. Periods of intense activity changing scenery were intermingled with periods of inactivity in the wings while we watched the performance, both matinee and evening, to the point where I and my fellow stagehands new the script and stage 'business' off by heart. The scenery was made from painted canvases stretched over wooden frames which were lashed together by deftly looping ropes round metal hooks at top and bottom and braced in some cases by extendable poles. These canvases known as 'flats' in the theatre were about six foot wide and up to thirty feet tall. It was quite an art to slide them single handedly into position, flick ropes over the top hooks and pull them together tightly enough to prevent them sagging or collapsing altogether and crashing down during a scene change or performance. During my final season, among other props, I looked after a double bed that was stored on my station in the wings when not required on stage. One of the chorus girls, pretty in figure and face, took to sitting on the bed with me when not dancing and we became friendly in a semi-romantic way. I was looking forward to spending time with her at the end of season party only to find that unknown to me she had become involved in a serious relationship with the stage manager who was a lot older than her and probably married. I was deeply disappointed: I knew she was older than me but hadn't realised that she was more worldly wise and experienced and the attention she had paid to me had been but a passing, inconsequential dalliance.

My romantic education progressed during the 1957-1958 summer holidays spent working as a waiter at the Sussex Club at Elmer Sands to the east of Bognor Regis on the south coast of England. This was a small holiday camp with a fresh supply of holidaymakers, including girls of my own age, each week. We waiters mostly came from a similar middle class, grammar school background and shared a chalet. We served breakfast, lunch and dinner each day to our designated holiday makers and tried our best to serve them efficiently and in a friendly manner, hoping and usually securing a good tip at the end of their allotted week or fortnight.

The rest of the time was our own which we devoted to sunbathing, swimming and playing rugby games on the sands. Every evening there was a live band that played dance music in the ballroom which gave us a good opportunity to meet and get to know the available female talent. These dances were open to the public which is how I met Suzanne Villiere whose father was French and mother English. Suzanne spent her summers with friends in a holiday home about a mile away in Feltham village owned by her parents and she and her friends attended the dances. She also held a lot of all night house parties. These drew in young people not only from the Sussex Club such as me, but local teenagers from around the Elmer, Feltham, and Bognor area. I remember midnight bathing in the sea from the beach near where she lived and starry nights walking home from her house to our chalet. I was also able to practice my schoolboy French with Suzanne with whom I went out briefly and with her French friend Dorothy Dauvissat with whom I had a more serious romantic relationship. This gave me the inspiration and confidence to improve my fluency in French and other foreign languages which I have never lost.

Following one of Suzanne's parties we learnt that the local Sussex police were investigating the theft of a portable radio. Portable radios were quite a prized novelty then. Those of us from the Sussex Club who had been to the party were interviewed individually by the police in the Sussex Club kitchen. I was asked to give my name and address, to confirm that I was at the party, and then the trick questions, asked in a heavy, slow, Sussex drawl - "Did you steal the radio?" followed by "Do you know who stole the radio?" to both of which I replied "No" trying hard not to appear smug and superior. I doubted whether they would ever find the culprit on the basis of this plodding approach. However some days later after we had all come to suspect the shifty looking, stubble sporting, Assistant Chef at the Sussex Club who was considerably older than most of us, we learnt that a young fair-headed, fresh-faced naval rating who had been at the party in his uniform had been arrested and had pleaded guilty. And the radio had been recovered. Quite how this came about we never found out. Perhaps the police hadn't been so bumbling after all – or naval officers or persons unknown, Miss Marple perhaps, had cracked the case. It taught me to be wary of judging character and probity by appearance. Nobody for one moment ever suspected the innocent looking naval rating.

I still laugh about the time at the Sussex Club when returning one afternoon from the beach, we noticed one of the bar staff gathering mint from a patch of the herb growing in the shade at the side of our chalet. The mint appeared that evening garnishing glasses of gin-based cocktails known as Pym's No 4 which was a popular drink among the ladies. We didn't like to tell them that in order to save a long walk at the end of the evening to the main toilet block, we waiters would urinate on the mint at the side of our chalet before going to bed each night.

Babes in arms, Norman and Cousin Richard with Aunt Hilda, surrounded by my Mother, Father, Nana and Grandad Arber and seated, Great Grandfather Hecker

1

Norman at one year old, at Chingford, during the war

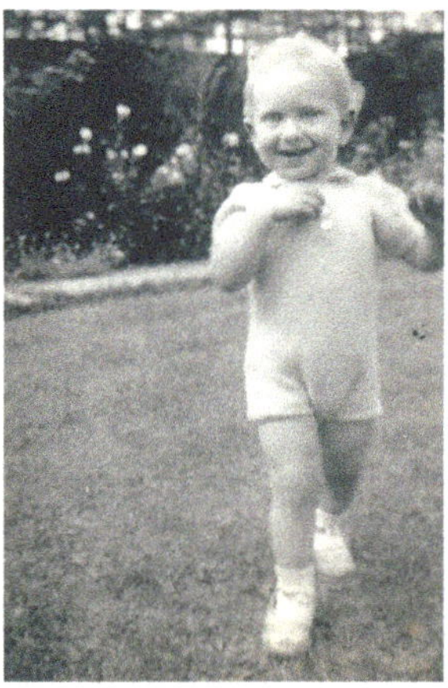

2

Formal photograph with mother, Mary Ann, in 1944

3

Family holiday at Bognor in 1946

4

At Morden Farm Primary School 1951

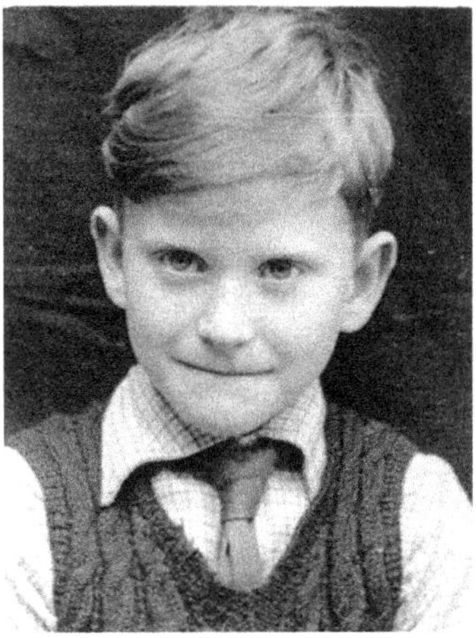

5

Holidaying in 1956 at Canford Cliffs

6

At Raynes Park Grammar School in 1957

7

Rehearsing Aristophanes 'The Frogs' in school quadrangle, 1959

8

Custom House London, Training Group, February1960

9

Looking cool with Martyn and Chris in 1961 in Tossa De Mar, Spain

10

Celebrating coming of age with Mum and Dad, May 1962

11

With Ros outside 'Casilla' 1962

12

# TOWARDS MATURITY

It was at the Sussex Club that I was encouraged by a fellow waiter to wear cut away shirt collars, to tie my tie in a 'Windsor' knot and to be bolder with the opposite sex and people in general. He was a local lad and a good mentor. These style adjustments went well with my 'drain-pipe' trousers which I had been one of the first to wear at my school. These were aptly named, narrowly tapered to the ankle and were happily unlike the baggy, largely shapeless trouser legs of the normally available garments. On the recommendation of Martyn Bond, with whom I played rugby at school and of whom more anon, I bought my first pair of 'drain-pipes' in a grey-green cloth at a small tailor's shop in Carnaby Street, long before this area of London became the fashion mecca of the beat generation in the sixties. The barber at the local Beverly shopping parade who, at my request, first cut my hair fashionably short in the 'Tony Curtis' style told me that I had a strong head of hair and would never go bald. I was pleased with the result and generally pleased with my appearance as a young blade. I took it for granted that he was right about keeping my hair. Sadly I did begin to thin in my fifties and by my mid-sixties had lost all the hair on the top of my head. Still, I fared a lot better than my father in this respect who was bald from his late twenties and my sons who thinned on top at about the same age. My father used to say that 'grass doesn't grow on a busy highway'.

Changing from my modern tailored drainpipe gear into scout uniform which included baggy short trousers was a bit of a wrench. I had joined the cubs originally and progressed to the scouts where I became patrol leader of the Beaver and then the Kingfisher patrols. I wasn't wildly enthusiastic about the cubs or scouts but it gave me another interest and outlook on life. I didn't care much for the rituals, instituted by Baden Powell, the 'hero' of Mafeking in the Boer War and founder of the cub-scout movement but went willingly along to the weekly meetings and to summer scout camps.

At one summer camp it rained for the whole fortnight. This was in the otherwise beautiful Wye Valley in Monmouthshire. The tent we pitched blew down in the middle of our first night under canvas and we had to cook everything in the open with damp firewood, foraged from a local forest a quarter of a mile away. From a railway bridge near Tintern Abbey, following the example of a fellow scout and egged on by him, I dropped a stone in the path of an oncoming steam train; an action I regretted at the time and afterwards. It was patently a stupid and dangerous thing to do and I should have refused to go along with him. Fortunately, no damage was done. Another year we camped in the New Forest in Hampshire. The weather by contrast was blisteringly hot. I developed painful blisters on my feet caused by going on rather pointless long hikes in ill-fitting heavy boots. I remember at this camp being astonished and appalled by the swearwords being used by some of the boys and the frequency with which they employed them in everyday speech. On reflection, I suppose I learnt some survival skills and to endure discomfort and deprivation. I enjoyed the camaraderie, the singing of songs and telling of ghost stories round the campfire in the evening and the songs and jokes that we shared travelling in the back of the lorry with our kit and equipment to and from our designated campsites.

Back home one evening, dressed in my scout uniform walking down Lower Morden Lane to our scout hut in Morden Park for our weekly meeting and carrying my regulation stave, a stout stick an inch thick and a meter long, I came upon a group of Teddy Boys surrounding my brother who had left home in his uniform a couple of minutes before me. They were ridiculing his dress which was certainly different from theirs and threatening him. They were known as Teddy Boys because they attired themselves in black Edwardian style jackets, the collars of which were edged in velvet, worn over white shirts with bootlace ties, extremely thin drain pipe trousers, white socks and black leather boots. They were generally feared and had a reputation for using flick-knives, knuckle dusters and bicycle chains and beating people up. I waded into them whirling my stave round and round to keep them at bay and managed to ward them off long enough for Roger and I to make our escape in the direction of the scout hut. This was a half built concrete and breeze block structure designed to replace a wooden building that had stood on the same site. The hut was being built by parents and volunteers and was still unfinished when I left the scouts. Gangs of youths were often to be found loitering in and around the hut situated as it was on the edge of the park and reached only by a dark, albeit wide, gravel path. There was always in those days the ominous presence of danger, or so we felt. When we went out, we had to walk or cycle on our own. We were not transported in cars or accompanied by parents. Fights between gangs of youths or individuals occurred both at school and outside. It would be wrong to exaggerate the prevalence of such violence but it did occur from time to time. One Saturday evening for instance at the Morden Assembly rooms in Grand Drive where, with friends, I had been dancing to a traditional jazz band, the half-time interval was shattered when lumps of rock and pavement stones came crashing through the windows causing the evening's entertainment to be abandoned. To this day I don't know why the Assembly rooms were targeted that night and who was responsible. This sort of incident was unusual but not isolated. We accepted and lived with the underlying threat of violence that existed and learnt to defend ourselves in physical encounters. From time to time, in junior and grammar schools, for reasons I cannot now recall, I got involved in fights with other boys and could give a pretty good account of myself especially when I could turn the encounter into a wrestling match – the half nelson and the head lock being my preferred techniques.

Towards the end of my scouting days, I led the Kingfisher patrol to second place in a weekend camping competition at Broadstone Warren in Sussex covering scout groups drawn from all over the South of England so I had at least gained some proficiency in the outdoor life and had the opportunity of taking responsibility for and leading other members of a team. I also gained leadership experience as school prefect and more particularly as captain of my house rugby team where, despite being saddled with a distinctly average, motley group of players, we won every match and carried off the house cup. For one match a boy who had been picked turned up with only soft-soled trainers to wear on his feet. I asked him why he had not brought proper rugby boots. His answer was unsatisfactory and his attitude so offhand, I told him he would not be playing and took the field with fourteen men. We still won.

I have a feeling I was wearing my old scout shorts when, with a couple of friends, I embarked one summer morning on an ill fated bike tour. We were supposed to be heading for the West Country for a couple of weeks. I had bought and fitted special panniers to my bike to carry my gear and we had a tent of sorts to take along with us. The plan was to cycle to the Stonehenge area for our first night and to pitch our tent in a farmer's field overnight. Unfortunately we hadn't allowed for the wind and rain and the weight of our equipment. We got as far as Thruxton, pitching the tent in a soaking wet field. The tent proved wholly inadequate for the purpose and by morning we were dejected and wet. We unanimously decided to abandon the trip and to return home. My mother was most surprised when we re-appeared so soon after leaving and I felt uneasy that we had not shown enough fortitude in braving the elements. Then again, I couldn't see the point of suffering extreme discomfort just for the sake of it.

By comparison with camping in the great outdoors, I much preferred the family holidays I had spent in the early 50s, knobbly knees competitions included, in various holiday camps in Southern England. In 1950 and again in 1951, we stayed at the Riviera Lido near Bognor Regis, then in 1952 at The Dolphin near Brixham, at Gunton Hall on the Suffolk coast in 1953 and in Sand Bay south of Weston Super Mare in 1954. There was always plenty to do come rain or shine and it was all great fun. Except one year at the Dolphin, when I was required to spend the day with the lovey-dovey couple whose table I was obliged to share in the dining hall each night. As the eldest son it had fallen to me to sit with them at their neighbouring table because the dining hall only accommodated a maximum of four people per table and with my parents, brother and sister we numbered five. So that left me as the odd one out. This soppy, stuffy couple were constantly calling one another 'darling' and I never achieved the slightest rapport with them: I felt like a surplus piece of crockery at their table. The day excursion with them I went on towards the end of the holiday in their diminutive Austin 7 car, complete with string door handles, was excruciatingly embarrassing and sheer torture as far as I was concerned. It seemed to me at the time that perhaps it was their way of showing their gratitude to me for nightly suffering their self-absorbed company. On the lighter side I remember, while staying at The Dolphin, my brother Roger and I, with another slightly older boy we had befriended, went fishing in Brixham harbour one afternoon. We hadn't got a rod or any bait; just a line with a hook on the end. We sat on the harbour wall and lowered the line into the water. In a matter of minutes we felt a tug on the line. We drew it up to find an enormous lobster on the end with its claw impaled on the hook. The lobster had obviously been minding its own business perambulating on the sea floor and had accidentally and absent-mindedly trodden on our hook. Our catch drew admiring glances from people in the vicinity. However, we were so frightened of this fearsome and unexpected apparition which was still very much alive and flailing around on the hook that we promptly dropped the line and the lobster back in the water and beat a hasty retreat to the holiday camp.

After the holiday camp era, we were privileged to be able stay in a large, wonderful, art-deco designed, detached house, appropriately named 'Waterfront', in Poole Harbour, belonging to the firm owned by Mr Bance for whom my father worked. It had a splendid, panoramic window in the living room and a small waterside garden both providing spectacular views over the wide expanse of Poole Harbour and of Brownsea Island and the Purbeck Hills beyond. There was a swing in the garden which my sister loved and a rowing boat that we were able to use. Roger, Susan and I went out in the boat one afternoon and were late returning because the wind and tide had turned against us. My parents were scouring the bay from a local beauty spot overlooking the harbour called Evening Hill and famed for its spectacular sunsets but in the failing light had not been able to spot us. They were somewhat relieved when we eventually returned and dragged our little craft back on the front lawn. With one exception, the weather was always hot and sunny when we stayed there – or so it seems looking back. Certainly I remember being in bed plastered with calming potion to take the worst of the sting from the sunburn from which Roger, Sue and I were suffering. Most days we went to the beach at Canford cliffs near Sandbanks: one of the best stretches of sandy beach in Southern England. The exception to the run of sunny holidays was during Whitsun week in 1957 when I was studying for my school O level examinations. A huge storm blew up that lasted for three days. It was fascinating watching the boats tossing and turning in the wind, rain and swell. At least I could get on with my studies instead of going out. My other consolation, while I revised, was a pre-war gramophone record player made of expensive wood that smelt of refined oil and spice. There were only two vinyl records that went with it; the first Bach's Air on a G String and the second, Noel Coward singing 'Mad Dogs and Englishmen, both of which I thought, and still think, are terrific pieces of music and remind me of those magical days at 'Waterfront'.

We were nominally self-catering but the house came with a live in maid, a dumpy, lovable lady named Gladys who cooked and cleaned for us. Gladys could be a bit domineering as far as the domestic arrangements were concerned. Not surprisingly she and my mother were wary of one another but my mother, who normally wanted to be in control but who never liked cooking and domestic duties, was content for once to bite her tongue. On several occasions, at low tide, we fished on the exposed mud flats for cockles using a rake and a bucket. The cockles were plump and plentiful and we became proficient in finding and digging them up. We took them by the bucket-load to Gladys who showed us how she cooked them and served them the same day with our evening meal. You can't get much fresher or tastier seafood than that!

It was still raining that Whitsun when we left. Much to my mother's annoyance, my father had been asked by the owner of the business, Mr Bance to collect some gulls eggs from Poole dockyard on our way home and to deliver them to him at his mansion in Bagshot, Surrey. In the shambles of the dockyard, my father eventually found the place he was looking for, collected the eggs, and drove us to Bisley where he was obliged to park outside the main wrought iron gates and to deliver the eggs on foot to Mr Bance at his front door. My mother was absolutely furious that we had to wait outside the front gate in the car in the pouring rain and had not been invited in or thanked. She was also annoyed that while he was dining on ducks eggs we were driving around the country in a company car, a Flying Standard 11, that by this time was so old and rusty, the water leaked through the sun roof, dripping on my father's right wrist as he held the steering wheel. Sometime later, Mr Bance committed suicide by shooting himself through the mouth with a shotgun. His body was found at the bottom of Beachy Head. My parents never disclosed the cause, even if they knew. It was an odd thing. I sensed something of a cover up by the Bance clan. His passing was not greatly mourned by my mother.

After leaving the scouts I attended the St James Church Youth Club. It was a great place to meet other young people from outside my school circle although my lifelong friendship with Robbie Stevenson who also went to Raynes Park Grammar really cemented itself here. We danced to the pop music of the time played on an electric turntable record player. The dance in vogue was the jive. We also played table tennis and sometimes went on rambles in the countryside. On one occasion I remember we hiked overnight in the Dorking area; a prickly and tiring endeavour which turned out to be harder and less fun than we had expected. Club evenings were presided over by the long suffering Dora and Bernard both of indeterminate age who just managed to maintain a semblance of order despite our teasing and fooling around.

On Friday evenings, I went regularly to a jazz club at a pub in Morden opposite the tube station called the Crown Inn which had a function room at the back. It was always packed and there would be the occasional fight outside but on the whole the atmosphere was peaceable enough. All the top British bands were featured. Chris Barber was my favourite with his smooth voiced vocalist Ottalie

Patterson. Lonnie Donnegan performed with his skiffle band and Kenny Ball, and Ken Kolyer with their traditional jazz bands. I also went a few times to a club in a similar but smaller function room round the side of the Alexandra pub in Wimbledon where I particularly enjoyed listening to the Temperance Seven.

I liked modern jazz too. My school friend Martyn Bond who was a bit of a self professed Bohemian and Beatnik, Chris Eggleton his friend from his Merton Park primary school days and I sometimes went up to London to Ronnie Scott's and the Flamingo nightclubs in Soho to listen to various modern groups of whom The Modern Jazz Quartet or MJQ were the most exciting and well......modern. I also loved Picasso and poets such as Ezra Pound and T S Eliot. Inspired by them, I started writing my own poetry and have continued, albeit with a long interlude between getting married and retirement from full time work and have published my poems. In the same modernist vein, I remember being impressed by the opening of the new Coventry Cathedral with its modern architecture, sculpture and Graham Sutherland tapestry over the main alter. I later visited the cathedral with my brother when we were staying on the outskirts of Birmingham with my Aunt Dorothy and Uncle Graham and was not disappointed. I confess that I also admired the clean lines of the new buildings including tower blocks that were springing up from bomb sites and replacing the old Victorian back to back slum housing. By and large, the office buildings have stood the test of time but the residential tower blocks became a mixed blessing and in some place a byword for grime, crime and desolation. They looked wonderful on the drawing board and in model form but the reality turned out to be altogether different.

As befitted his image, Martyn smoked French Gitanes cigarettes and Chris smoked Senior Service. I didn't smoke cigarettes. I had tried them behind the bike sheds at school - where else - and didn't like the smoke going up my nose or the idea of inhaling. However, I used to enjoy sucking the mouthpiece of a discarded pipe my father must have once smoked. It was kept in the main drawer of the bureau, a semi-sacred alter-piece occupying pride of place opposite the fireplace in the lounge. When I left school, with my first month's salary, I decided to buy a pipe for myself. I enjoyed pipe smoking for forty years never inhaling but contentedly puffing the smoke in and out. I liked the taste and the smell but didn't need or want a nicotine ingestion. I only smoked in the evenings and at weekends – never at work. I suppose I smoked about 2 ounces or 500 grammes per week. I tried a brand called Erinmore to begin with but soon gravitated to St Bruno a rich and mellow dark tobacco which I continued to smoke until I gave up when I retired from full time employment in 2000. I don't regret giving up: I felt better physically and more full of energy. But nor do I regret the years I spent enjoyably puffing away in my leisure time. I still enjoy a good cigar on special occasions with the same no haling-in proviso. Shortly after taking up pipe smoking I remember attending a party in High Wycombe one Saturday night. I smoked my pipe constantly that evening partly because I didn't know many people there. I think I was overdoing it because at one point I began to feel sick and had to go outside in the fresh air to recover. Although this wasn't the usual all night party held in someone's house while their parents were away that were so much in vogue, it was held in a hall somewhere in the town and finished too late for me to get the train back home. I was persuaded by some American servicemen who were at the party to go back with them to their barracks. I spent the night smuggled into the United States Airforce base situated on the hillside outside the town. The base was restricted to authorised US personnel and as a British civilian, I was worried that I might be arrested for trespass or as a spy. They told me not to worry and to just walk out past the guardhouse and security barrier when I left. I thanked them for putting me up and for their advice. The following morning, with my courage screwed to the mast, I strode out of the base with as confident an air as I could muster. Thankfully nobody challenged me and I regained national territory without causing an international incident.

When visiting pubs or jazz clubs, I would drink bitter, now called real ale. It was always served in pint sized dimpled glasses with a handle, not in the straight glasses that became almost universally adopted when the lager revolution occurred. Lager drinking was unheard of in those days. I am not naturally conservative in outlook – I prefer change and progress to the status quo but I still insist on a traditional glass with a handle whenever I go to a pub even though the bar staff usually have to scratch around before they find one. I am fighting a one man campaign to preserve this part of my country's heritage. Apart from bitter the only other alcoholic drink we had in those days was at Christmas when my father was given a case of wine. These were white wines such as German Hock and Moselle or French Sauternes and Barsac. As a special treat after Christmas dinner we were allowed a liqueur, usually Benedictine. I drank my first memorable glass of red wine when my brother Roger was training as a teacher at a college outside Bognor and we met in a local restaurant. We chose a Cotes Du Rhone from Chateaux Neuf Du Pape which went down exceedingly well with the steak we had ordered. The only red wine generally available at that time was Chianti from Italy which tasted like brick dust. It was sold in a bulbous shaped bottle protruding from a stout straw container. Many people made the empty bottle-baskets into lampshades that were regarded as quite fashionable.

# WIDER WORLD

My heart lifts and lightens whenever I recall the long hot summer of 1959. I was a carefree youth of eighteen years of age with hormones coursing through my veins. I stood relatively tall at just over six feet in height, lean in build with broad shoulders and a thick head of hair. I had passed my maths and physics A Levels and could have gone to university. However, despite Harold Wilson's boast about the white hot technological revolution that would be sweeping the country under his Labour government, the prospects for graduate scientists seemed poor. My mother wasn't particularly keen on the university option either, fearing the strain it would place on the family finances, the more so, because my brother and sister were following behind and would be expecting the same opportunity. At school I had wanted to be a doctor but my decision not to go to university scuppered that idea. So, armed with my A Levels, I returned to school in the autumn term to play rugby, act in the school play and learn Russian while I looked for a job.

Actually, I left my mother to do much of the job hunting for me. I told her that I didn't want a 9 to 5 office job, as they were known, and was looking for something more varied, preferably involving travel and foreign languages. She got hold of some recruitment literature for the Outdoor Service of HM Customs & Excise and for a trainee pilot scheme with the national airline, British Overseas Airways Corporation (BOAC), both of which seemed interesting careers and for which I had the necessary academic entry qualifications. Customs were first to reply. They offered me an interview and I passed narrowly and was offered a start date in February 1960. BOAC then invited me to an interview but, encouraged by my mother, I accepted the Customs job. She felt that Customs offered the greater job security – which was all important to her, remembering, as she did, the great stock market crash and depression of the thirties. Over the years, my family made a valuable contribution to the public service. My brother became a schoolteacher, married a schoolteacher and retired as Headmaster of a middle school in Mansfield. My sister joined the Department of Social Services as an Executive Officer and later worked at Heathrow for British Airways while the company was still in the public sector, finishing in Customs & Excise at Shepperton. She married Ken, a police constable, who finished his service with the Met Police having risen to the senior rank of Detective Superintendent. Compared with most occupations in both the private and public sectors the salary offered for the Customs position with a maximum annual salary of over £1000 was favourable. The press frequently headlined 'the £1000 a year man' as the ultimate goal for aspiring professionals. I assumed that in addition to working mainly outdoors, the Customs job was about travel, ships, docks, planes and airports and that my foreign language skills would be employed daily. I thought back to the time at junior school when we had been taken on a coach trip round the London Docks. Even though I was suffering from flu that day I was excited and inspired by the sights and sounds of enormous ships from all over the world with funnels and masts looming over the warehouses and bustling wharves.

I loved my school and was sorry to be leaving but fresh adventure awaited. When I told Henry Porter my Headmaster that I was joining Customs and would be leaving finally at the end of the autumn term, he expressed surprise at my choice and, disconcertingly, advised me not to do it. I think he was wary of me joining the public service and felt I was better suited to some other occupation which he did not specify. Perhaps he was right – who knows? With hindsight I would have liked to be an airline pilot or chef or worked in the private sector somewhere. However, the die was cast. In many ways the job lived up to my expectations. In some ways it didn't. I never travelled very far and spent most of my working life in and around London. The furthest I got was Hull for four days during my initial training, although some years later, when I was Assistant Collector at Heathrow Airport, I spent two enjoyable weeks in Lille in Northern France with a member of the French Collectorate on a Mattheaus exchange. I used my language skills then but this was the only occasion. Even allowing for the promotions I gained, the early pay advantage I enjoyed declined markedly over the years in comparison with the police and similar managerial positions in the private sector. Margaret Thatcher in particular made it clear as Prime Minister where her priorities lay in relation to civil service pay. I never became a great fan of hers.

I joined Customs as an Unattached Officer or 'UO' as we were called on the 8 February 1960 and went to the Collector's Office in Queen Anne's Chambers near Victoria to sign on. This was the head office of London South Collection, one of five London Collections at that time, each of which was presided over by a Collector appointed individually by the Commissioners of Customs & Excise who were in turn appointed by the Crown. Sobering to reflect that by the time I retired, under various modernising government changes, the London Collections had been reduced to one with similar reductions having been made in the rest of the country. On arrival, I was taken to a man who opened one of his desk drawers. It was empty apart from a tea pot, tea-cups, sugar bowl and two small piles of forms – Trade Union Membership and the Official Secrets Act. "Sign here and here" he said "one lump or two?" He then asked me where I lived. From the other drawer he took out another pad of forms, gave me the top copy and told me he was sending me to Wimbledon Excise Station in South London, about five miles from where I lived in Morden Park. I knew I had joined a section of the service that was a cut above the uniformed officers who checked passengers' baggage at the ports for contraband goods but was expecting to be posted to Dover or to London Airport as a Customs plain clothes equivalent to the police Special Branch. So being sent to Wimbledon, which did not seem to be the den of iniquity in smuggling terms, was a mild surprise. Confusingly, I was told that I would be spending the next four weeks in waiting room. This was not, so I learned, Wimbledon railway station waiting room at the bottom of Wimbledon Hill but the Excise Station, or office in normal parlance, at the top of the hill, where I was expected to report and wait for my six months basic training call up to the Custom House, London.

I left Queen Anne's Chambers, without meeting Queen Anne, and headed for Wimbledon. I walked up the hill and along a parade of shops at the top, eventually finding the address I was looking for. A heavy wooden door bearing the appropriate street number appeared between two shop fronts, concealing, or so I surmised, a flight of stairs leading to the Excise office above – many of the excise offices in those days were above shops. By this time it was about 10.30 in the morning; I rang the bell – no answer. Not a quill pen quivered, not a bird tittered: total silence. Somewhat non-plussed, I spotted a brass plate inscribed 'HM Customs & Excise – Wimbledon Excise Station – Office Hours – Tuesdays & Thursdays, 10 am – 12 noon'. Obviously I concluded, today being Monday, the officers are on their rounds trying to catch illicit gin and whisky distillers and won't be back in the office until 10 o'clock tomorrow. I went home somewhat to my mother's surprise and returned the next morning just after 10 am to find the door open. I climbed the stairs and was greeted with incredulity, feigned or real I'm not quite sure, by two middle aged gentlemen by the name of Mr William Bailey, with a pencil thin moustache and black crinkly Brylcreemed hair, known to his colleagues as Bill, and Mr Norman Mahoney, a bluff and sturdily built yeoman farmer type. I gingerly handed my appointment form over to them. They conferred and demanded to know why they had not been told to expect me and why I had not shown up the previous day as instructed on the form. Mr Mahoney immediately rang the Collector's Office and complained. I was summoned to the phone and told in a very formal voice that THE COLLECTOR in person wanted to speak to me. This was not the start I had expected. Not without trepidation but with the freshness and naivety of a new recruit, I explained what had happened. There was silence and I was asked to put Mr Mahoney back on the line. I was most disconcerted at having been shopped so readily by people I was expecting to look after my interests. However, their manner towards me changed immediately from indignation to warmth and friendliness and I realised that I had passed my first test as an Officer of Customs & Excise. I had shown that I could think on my feet and argue my way out of a tight corner with impeccable confidence and logic.

In waiting room I addressed and licked envelopes, kept the station register, a large, heavy, green covered, loose leaf tome known affectionately as the Green Dragon, accompanied Bill Bailey on visits and made the tea. Excise officers were autonomous, independent satraps in those days, unsupported by clerical staff, in complete charge legally and practically speaking for revenue raising and audit functions in their own individual geographical areas. They were not managed in the normal sense. Officials in the grade above, known as Surveyor from the French 'surveilleur' (supervisor or overseer) checked secretly and overtly from time to time on their activities. That was all. One afternoon, Horace Pett, the local Surveyor, whose office was in Richmond, was spotted parking his car and walking towards our office. Because he had not telephoned beforehand to say he was coming, Messrs Mahoney and Bailey told me to sprint downstairs to lock the front door. I complied and dashed back upstairs where we all three remained motionless and silent, heads bent below window sill level so that we could not be heard or seen from outside. Finally, Horace, having rung the bell increasingly insistently several times, gave up and drove back to Richmond. Officers of Customs & Excise had a reputation for being intelligent, resourceful, and idiosyncratic. I was now one of this rather unusual and elite band of brothers, having received my Commission as an Officer of Customs & Excise, that now, suitably framed and marked 'Cancelled' hangs in a prominent position on my study wall. I say brothers because the Outdoor Service I joined was composed of men only. Women were excluded on the well-intentioned, if patronising, grounds that men were better suited to working outdoors in physically demanding conditions and in dealing with physical confrontation that could and sometimes did arise with taxpayers, passengers and the like. There was no equal opportunities legislation in place then. Not until 1972 when the Department assumed responsibility for Value Added Tax (VAT) were women admitted.

In March 1960 I started my basic training in Custom House, London. The building designed by Sir Christopher Wren, stood next to Billingsgate fish market in Lower Thames Street and I carry in my nostrils to this day, the pungent smell of fish which permeated the place. As winter turned to spring and spring to summer, overlooking the bustling Pool of London, the smell in our wide, high ceilinged top-floor classroom, became stronger and stronger. We started with six weeks Excise theory covering the ways in which the Department controlled the collection of revenue in the country by indirect taxation and were then sent to various Excise Stations either singly or in pairs to learn from local Excise Officers how the theory and supporting legislation was implemented in practice. We visited breweries, distilleries, bonded warehouses, businesses registered for Purchase Tax (the forerunner to VAT) and to depots distributing road fuel all of which generated revenue. In total the Department collected over forty percent of total government revenue which rose to just under fifty percent with the advent of VAT. Excise practical lasted about six weeks and at the end we had to report back to Custom

House and were tested on the knowledge and experience we had acquired. The Principal of the Training Division, an austere, elderly, white-haired Scotsman named McCail, took great delight in quizzing us personally. A lifelong bachelor, wedded to the job he was reputed to retire each night at home with the Departmental Books of Instruction as his bedtime reading. I was unfortunate enough to get picked out by him for grilling. He started by asking me where I had done my distillery practical training knowing full well that I and a fellow ex-Waterguard, Preventive Officer from the uniformed section, named Don Holmans, an incurable practical joker, who sadly died in harness as Assistant Collector Dover some years later had been sent to Saltend Industrial Distillery standing on the windswept estuary of the Humber outside Hull. We had both hoped to have been sent to a small malt whisky distillery in the romantic Highlands of Scotland as most of the rest of the class had been but we had drawn the short straw. Saltend Distillery was a vast, ghastly place with rail yards, storage tanks and a sprawling chemical works that used the majority of the spirit produced in the distillery as raw material for the manufacture of various chemical products. Outside the distillery main gate in the middle of this industrial inferno stood two 'provided houses' owned by the Department and let at a nominal rent to two of the officers and their families stationed at the distillery. The notional rent was a huge financial bonus for officers with families who occupied these provided houses with the result that in the Highlands of Scotland where the location was desirable such appointments were sought after but I couldn't conceive of any officer in the service volunteering for appointment to Saltend for the sake of a provided house. It remained at the back of my mind to do whatever I could in future to avoid compulsory appointment to a place like that. McCail then proceeded to ask me what I had seen and to describe the distillation process which I did. He then asked me what happened to the spirits after they had been distilled which I did but he then started going in to even greater detail. I wasn't clear where all this was leading and why he was becoming so pernickety. Finally when I told him that the spirits were fed from the still house through a pipe that ran over the yard outside into receiving vats in a warehouse opposite, he asked me how I had followed the pipe; at which point, somewhat nonplussed, I replied "with my eye" – bearing in mind that the pipe was some thirty feet in the air where it traversed the yard and we had only been given four days on site instead of the usual five owing to the intervention of the Easter holiday. He then asked whether I had felt along it with my hand, whereupon, Don, to my relief, began to titter with laughter, as did some of his fellow ex Waterguard colleagues, despite McCail's glowering demeanour. "Well..." concluded McCail, half triumphantly and half defensively, taken aback by this unforeseen outburst "when I was there... (as an experienced inspector he might have added but didn't )... I climbed up a ladder and found a spiral in the pipe." We all felt like saying 'well... bully for you'. For the record, a spiral was a technical term for a hole drilled in a pipe that could be plugged and un-plugged, through which spirit could be illicitly extracted. I gained plenty of sympathy from my classmates for having been the victim of McCail's narrow-minded and humiliating interrogation.

It was while I was engaged on my Excise practical that I passed my driving test at the second attempt. I had been taught by my father and my first lesson with him had been a disaster. I got in the driver's seat of the family car, by then a Morris Traveller, parked facing uphill outside our house and when he said "put your left foot on the clutch pedal, engage first gear, put your right foot on the accelerator then take your left foot off the clutch pedal" this is literally what I did. The car leapt forward in huge, alarming, kangaroo jumps and I only managed to bring it to a halt before we reached the top of the road. After that I was very nervous about the mechanics of getting the car moving from a stationary position. I gradually got the hang of the process however and by the time I took my first test I was supremely confident. At one point I overtook a car parked at the curb on my nearside while another car was travelling towards me. I should have waited for the oncoming vehicle to pass but I thought the gap was wide enough. Unfortunately I clipped the parked car with my wing mirror. It was the slightest of contacts and fortunately no damage was caused to our car or the parked one. I recognised immediately that the game was up and I would fail as indeed I did - for lack of care while overtaking - despite executing every other manoeuvre perfectly. I was annoyed with myself and booked a re-test straight away and on this second test, some weeks later, I passed but not before nearly knocking the local vicar off his bike. Mind you it was his fault. He rode straight out across me from left to right as I was approaching a crossroads in a quiet residential area. In fact he came off the pavement into the road in front of me. I managed to slam on my brakes and just avoided hitting him. He wobbled a bit and proceeded on his godly way. The examiner congratulated me on my reactions and confirmed that the vicar was to blame, adding that I didn't need to do the emergency stop which was part of the test as I had already performed it in a real life situation rather than in the normal simulated way. The feeling of freedom I had when I subsequently borrowed the Morris Traveller and drove it unaccompanied by anyone else was a joy.

I also passed my induction as an established Unattached Officer of Customs & Excise after concluding three months Customs theory and practical during which, among other things, we learnt the ancient art of gauging wine and spirits casks using a variety of weird and wonderful measuring instruments such as dip rods, endometers and bung rods. At the end, each of us was invited to declare our preferences for the Collections where we wished to work and just to show who was boss, we were promptly assigned to places diametrically opposite. One family man from Glasgow was posted to Dover and vice versa. Don Holmans and I were appointed to Harwich Collection. Before taking up this appointment however, I took a holiday. Some weeks earlier, travelling up to Custom House by tube from home, I had met by chance one morning, Derek Furminger who we had all teased and bullied at grammar school. To my surprise he seemed to have matured and become more likeable and we agreed to stay in contact and to go to Paris on summer holiday together. Off we set therefore, at the beginning of August 1960 for two to three weeks in France together. Unfortunately after three days in Paris he was beginning to get on my nerves. The weather was hot and sunny and on the fourth day, we decided to go to the Piscine Deligny, an open air swimming pool by the side of the River Seine. There by chance, and much to my relief, we bumped into Martyn Bond and his friend Chris Eggleton. Martyn was an old school friend who like me had joined Raynes Park Old Boys Society and had been playing first team rugby with them in the 1959/60 season.

Martyn and Chris said that evening they were meeting four female English friends transiting Paris on their way by train for a holiday in Northern Italy. They suggested that Derek and I come along. In continental Europe, travelling by train was the only realistic option in those days apart from hitchhiking. It was unheard of to travel by air. Short haul journeys were accomplished by ferry and train and long haul by ocean liner. That evening we all met up and waved the girls goodbye as their train left the Gare De Lyon bound for the Mediterranean. The four of us spent the next couple of days mooching about Paris surviving on a diet of tartines and coffee for breakfast followed for the rest of the day by hard boiled eggs and Rose d'Anjou wine. Somehow we conceived the notion of following the girls and surprising them by meeting up with them again in Italy (no mobile phones then). We were young, footloose and fancy-free and agreed to set off from Paris the following morning on foot and once in the suburbs to hitchhike the rest of the way. We also decided that we would stand a better chance of getting a lift if we split into pairs and drew lots as to who should go with whom. Luckily, Martyn and I were paired and Chris was lumbered with Furminger. Martyn and I spent most of the day walking out of the Paris area and it wasn't until we reached Fontainebleau that we picked up our first lift in a rather smart British manufactured Sunbeam Alpine car. A little further down the road we spotted Chris and Derek and the driver kindly stopped for them. He turned out to be the British Vice Consul in Naples returning to his post after a dirty weekend in Paris. He was upper class, but an absolute hoot and we got on famously. He was very pro-British and hated the French. He was intending to drive through the night which suited us. Travelling for hours southward on Route National 7, we got to know him quite well and amongst ourselves nicknamed him Pozzo because he reminded us of the larger than life fictional character of the same name in the play 'Waiting For Godot' in which I had acted at school. After several hours it began to rain heavily. Arriving in a small town between two and three o'clock in the morning somewhere in the middle of France, we stopped in torrential rain in the main square and dashed into a café that was still open. Once inside, Pozzo bought a round of drinks – Brandy I think. We sat round a table with the rain lashing down outside as the drinks were brought. Pozzo stood up, "A toast, gentlemen!" he declared. We all stood up and raised our glasses: "Fuck 'em all!" he intoned. "Fuck 'em all" we cried in response, hardly able to contain our laughter. And we repeated the toast several times as we sipped our drinks. The tone in which it was offered encapsulated the dogged resolution, defiance and English good humour we all shared and made a firm impression on us that remained with us for the rest of our lives. For years to come, in adversity, we would remember and repeat the toast. Even now, I find that, when occasion demands, repeating the toast aloud or under my breath is a great way of clearing my emotional decks of negative baggage and focusing with confidence and optimism on the way ahead.

Some brandies later Pozzo apologised and said that he was exhausted and felt he would be too tired to continue driving the following day. We thanked him for bringing us so far, for the great time we had shared and wished him goodnight as he trundled off to a soft bed somewhere in the establishment. We remained in the café, dozing fitfully until dawn when we resumed our journey from the rain sodden square, although the rain itself had mercifully stopped.

Martyn and I again started off behind Chris and Derek. We had been walking for a while when we managed to secure a hitch in another British manufactured car, an Austin Standard Eight. It was being driven by a friendly French garage owner who was returning home to his business in the South of France. It was only a small car but he was very proud of it. He considered that British cars which were then prevalent on the continent were well engineered and built. A little further down the road we came upon Chris and Derek and the driver kindly stopped and took them on board. It was quite a squeeze but we managed and the driver didn't mind. I think with a long drive in prospect he was grateful for our company. I remember that high on a ridge somewhere just south of Lyon he stopped and bought us a magnificent lunch. Further along the Rhone Valley he stopped to change a punctured tyre while we relaxed by the banks of the river. He arrived at his destination, a little seaside village called Cassis in the early hours of the following morning. He left us tired but grateful in an open air café facing the sea where we rested and dozed until the café opened for breakfast.

We set off once more in pairs and Martyn and I got a lift in late afternoon from a Riviera playboy type driving a silver open top Mercedes sports car who took us close to Nice. Martyn and I swam in the sea that evening in Nice and failing to get another lift spent an uncomfortable night trying to sleep on the pavement along the Corniche in Menton near the Italian border. The following day having failed to get a lift, we took the train across the Franco-Italian border to Pisa where in an extremely tired and dirty state we were booked into a hotel by a couple of Hong Kong Chinese boys we had met on the train. We did not wake up until the middle of the following afternoon. The Hong Kong boys appeared but we declined their offer to spend time with them. We visited the Leaning Tower and made our way to Livorno where the girls were staying. We were joined later by Chris and Derek. They had virtually split apart towards the end. Chris had also found Derek hard going. But we were all quietly proud that we had achieved our objective and pleased about the memorable experiences we had had on the way. I felt that, in some ways, the week we spent with the girls, though enjoyable was to some extent an anti-climax after the excitement and challenge of the journey. At the end of the week Martyn, Chris and Derek travelled back to England while I took a separate train a day or so later because I had a week more holiday than the others which I planned to use by spending time back in Paris. On the train I started the journey standing in the corridor because all the seats were reserved couchettes. However I fell into conversation with a religious group of female American teachers who loved my 'English' accent and kept asking me to say "smashing!" They were good company and allowed me to sleep in one of their couchettes overnight. Parting company with them on arriving in Paris, one of them who seemed keen to see me again, suggested we meet her and her group under the clock at the station the following day at noon to take the train to Versailles which they were intending to visit. I wasn't that bothered but she was pleasant enough, her companions had been kind and accommodating towards me and I had nothing else planned for that day so I agreed. I was staying in the same hotel in the Place Monge on the Left Bank where I had previously stayed on my earlier school trip to Paris. Unfortunately, overnight in the hotel and un-noticed by me my watch had stopped. This was probably because having gone out the previous evening on my own I had forgotten to check and to wind my watch before going to bed. In those days all wrist watches were powered mechanically by a coiled spring that had to be rewound regularly every twenty four hours or so. I got up and had a leisurely breakfast unaware that my watch had stopped. I thought I had plenty of time to make the projected rendezvous. It wasn't till I got to the station and looked at the giant clock looming over the concourse that I realised that the time was actually three o'clock in the afternoon and I had inadvertently missed the noon rendezvous by over three hours. I didn't think they would have waited for over three hours for me and aborted my journey. I felt sorry and annoyed that they might think that I had not honoured my word but there was nothing I could do. I did not know where they were staying and could not contact them to set the record straight. Would my life have turned out differently if my watch had not stopped that night?

Back in the UK, I was looking forward to taking up my appointment in tandem with Don Holmans as a fully fledged Unattached Officer of H M Customs & Excise based in Harwich Collection. I had previously seen posters on tube trains and buses proclaiming Harwich as the 'Gateway to the Hook of Holland and Europe' and imagined it would be a bustling metropolis, teeming with people and excitement. Alas, having been driven by Ian Holmans in his primitive three-geared 'sit up and beg' Ford Prefect on a foggy September evening through the byways of East Anglia – no motorways then – what we found was a desolate wasteland. Windswept docks and transit sheds lined the river estuary, and the town, named Dovercourt, consisted of little more than a small row of terraced houses on the cliff top, the end one of which served as a faded English seaside guesthouse, where we took up half-board residence. Traffic lights stood for no apparent reason at the point where the road took a sharp right-angled turn before running along the cliff past the guesthouse. The 'Beeching Report' that resulted in the wholesale axing of branch lines throughout the country was still in the future so there was at least a local railway station. That was it. In the guesthouse we shared the dining room with a few other nondescript guests and a wizened, lonely bachelor who had been boarding there for years. At mealtimes he was always last down and meticulously and painstakingly swallowed a battery of pills before picking laboriously and unenthusiastically at his food. He was boring and reclusive. He never spoke to anyone, not even to wish them good morning or good evening. Don tried to cheer him up by playing the odd harmless practical joke on him, including placing over the dining room door a seat cushion that fell on him when he opened it and rearranging his pill bottles on his separate table, but to no avail; he did not react in any way. One day, returning to the guesthouse we learned that he had committed suicide. He had been found early that morning on the beach having taken an overdose of pills. Apparently he had been told by the proprietors that he could no longer stay in his room in the guesthouse. His desperate and depressing presence was hardly a selling point and one could understand the proprietors wanting to be rid of him. Sadly, he had nowhere else to go and nobody else in the world to turn to.

On the work front I remember examining and clearing consignments of brand new Phillips vinyl long playing records in beautiful covers imported from Holland. I also witnessed the smuggling team ripping apart an expensive

Mercedes limousine with an acetylene cutting tool and finding Swiss watches concealed behind the dashboard and wheel arches. Swiss watches were highly prized in this country but as 'luxury' items bore domestic Purchase Tax in addition to Customs duty on importation. Watches together with silk garments, cigarettes, wine and spirits were the principle goods smuggled in those days. Over the years due to fiscal, economic and technological changes, commercial smuggling of such contraband declined as the Department turned its attention to the growing menace of drug smuggling.

Outside working hours there wasn't an awful lot to do. We attended local dances. But by the time I had worked my way round the available female talent and matronly tongues had begun to wag, I decided it was time to seek my fortune elsewhere. I promptly applied for a move back to London. Quite apart from running the gauntlet of prospective mother-in-laws, I was travelling back home each weekend to play rugby for my Old Boys side. These were the days, incidentally, in the Outdoor Service when you not only had to work Monday to Friday but Saturday morning as well. However, with the connivance of my Landing Officer colleagues who lived in the area and without telling the Surveyor, I used to knock off early on the Saturday morning and race to catch the one and only local train connecting with the mainline service to London. I used to see this local train approaching round the bay and calculated the time I had to run from the transit shed to the nearside platform, run the length of this platform, cross the footbridge at the far end onto the platform on the other side and dive into a carriage. By this means I cut to a minimum the chances of being spotted by the Surveyor, whose main function in those days appeared to be to catch out and report on Officers of Customs & Excise, from whose ranks they were exclusively drawn, thereby reinforcing the truth of the old adage about poachers turned gamekeepers. Unfortunately for me, one Saturday morning, with everything timed to perfection, I spotted the train puffing round the bay. I waited until it hit the spot on the landscape which, from previous experience, gave me a bare four minutes to run from the transit shed to the safety of a seat in the second class carriage. It was like one of those black and white western movies. As the train approached, I reached the far end of the platform from the footbridge, when to my horror I saw the looming figure of the Surveyor at the other end of the platform striding toward me. I dived into an open doorway which happened to be a waiting room (British Railways this time not the Customs & Excise version). I was out of breath, heart panting. The engine pulled into the station magnifying the panting of my breath. What to do? I only had seconds to go. I decided to make a break for it whatever the consequences and ran down the platform noticing with considerable relief that there was no longer any sight of the Surveyor. I charged over the footbridge and just managed to jump on the train as it began clanking forward. Fate had come to my rescue on this occasion. Either that or the Surveyor was, after all, a kindly, circumspect, old soul who, seeing my predicament, had done the decent thing by disappearing into the station ticket hall.

As a result of the request I had made for voluntary transfer, I was appointed to London Port Collection on 5 November 1960 and resumed living at home in Morden Park. From Harwich I brought with me my set of the 'Departmental Books of Instruction' issued to me, as to all officers, on a personal basis, on completing basic training. The complete set filled two normal-sized bookshelves. Each volume related to some aspect or other of Customs and Excise law and procedure and was intended to provide 'instructions' - not 'guidance', it should be noted - on every conceivable situation that might arise. Apart from a small number of volumes printed in a bye-gone era in normal book format that were still extant, such as the Silk Drawback Instructions, the rest were issued as loose-leaf volumes, the pages of which were secured in heavy, navy-blue cardboard binders with metal, opposing grate, clip release brackets to enable pages to be inserted and removed and a brass pocket on the spine intended to hold a label bearing the title of the 'Instruction' concerned. When I arrived at Liverpool Street station on my way home I alighted from the carriage with my duffle bag containing my personal belongings in one hand and in the other, a tartan grip I had fitted with string handles to supplement the frayed plastic ones. In the grip I put my complete set of the Books of Instruction. A porter noticed me struggling with the weight of the grip and took it from me, exclaiming as he did so "Blimey mate!...What are you?...A bloody weightlifter or sumfin?".

Unattached Officers were allowed two days Amending Leave per quarter in which to bring their Books of Instruction up to date. By working diligently I could normally complete this task in less than the allotted two full days which meant that I earned myself a little extra free time; the more so when I later enlisted the paid help of my sister. While working in London Port Collection, we UOs were required to attend at Custom House for Amending Leave. Awaiting us each quarter was a cardboard box containing piles of loose-leaf pages with accompanying notes directing which pages to insert and remove, pads of amendments printed on glossy, semi transparent, toilet-style paper listing manuscript amendments to be made, interspersed with pre-printed text for non-loose-leaf books, which had to be cut along dotted lines and pasted into the books concerned, sometimes on top of previous similar amendments thereby creating a paper waterfall effect. The first time I went there for Amending Leave, I found a thick pile of the flimsy semi-transparent amendments in my box, going back several years relating to the Silk Drawback Instructions. The copy of this bound instruction book we had been given was a first-print edition which meant that all the amendments would have to be made to it in manuscript or by cut and paste starting with the very earliest on the top of the pile dating back several years and working through to the latest on the bottom. This would have taken weeks rather than days to accomplish. Fortunately, in the room we were using, which doubled as a training room, a fellow UO who had previously attempted this feat had created a gigantic collage of these amendments which he had stuck to the blackboard and had drawn a huge arrow with large exclamation marks pointing to an otherwise innocuous manuscript amendment in tiny print on the final sheet reading 'Amdt 27/60: Silk Drawback Instructions – Cancel the book of instructions.' I had to smile. Whoever created the collage had at least had the awareness and commonsense to save his colleagues a huge amount of wasted time and effort and had been able to communicate that message in an imaginative and effective way; something the Department, bureaucratically over-reliant, as it was then and throughout most of my career on centrally devised, detailed rules and procedures, found it very difficult to achieve. Fortunately and somewhat perversely, the Department recruited and appointed people to the Outdoor Service who were by and large intelligent, individualistic, self reliant and practically minded who managed to make the whole thing work effectively.

For my first assignment in London Port, I was sent to assist the Landing Officers at Bricklayers Arms International Rail Depot, situated at the junction of the New Kent and Old Kent Roads in South East London. Imported goods, sealed under bond for inland Customs clearance were brought there daily in railway wagons from the continent via the Channel ports. The wagons were identified by ten digit serial numbers and I made a mistake one day when I wrote down the wrong number which resulted in a wagon containing goods that had been selected for examination being cleared without examination. I was suitably admonished. On the lighter side, I remember selecting an importation of unaccompanied baggage from Paris for examination. The consignment was described on the Customs declaration form (Baggage Prime Entry) as a personal importation of **ladies' used sports goods,** not liable to duty or tax. I was intrigued because the normal description given for this type of importation was 'Used Personal Effects' meaning the usual items of attire belonging to travellers, such as clothes and shoes. New sports goods were liable to Customs Duty and Purchase Tax and my 'Revenue Nose' began to twitch. Why, I asked myself, would someone want to import a large suitcase full of ladies' **used** sports goods? When the suitcase was opened for me, I found to my surprise that it was completely full of used rubber Johnnies, otherwise known as French Letters, or more prosaically, contraceptives. There they lay in every conceivable shape and colour'. Indeed, they had all patently been used; as it were. I concluded that the declared description fitted well enough and released the consignment by stamping the documents 'CLEARED AS ENTERED', not unmindful of the sexual innuendo that might be inferred in this instance from the use of this standard official phrase.

I also spent days and some nights working at Hither Green International Rail Terminal near Catford, South East London weighing, sampling and raising duty charges on what we termed 'Perishables'. This was the main Customs clearance terminal for fruit, flowers, meat and vegetables imported from the continent destined for the following day's London wholesale markets. The night attendance, known as the 'goodnight shift', attracted overtime payments to compensate for the twelve hours you were supposed to be on duty but you could usually get your head down and sleep for a few hours on a couch in the office before operations began again, in earnest, the following morning. I oscillated between Bricklayers Arms and Hither Green over several months and although I got to know my fixed officer colleagues quite well, I valued my free time and wasn't generally interested in working overtime. This suited them well enough and I remember them telling me how when they were working overtime, the Surveyor used to pretend he was going home by walking down the street and catching a bus. He would then get off the bus a couple of stops away and double back into the transit shed where he would hide behind packing cases to make sure that the officers were working and doing the job properly. I never experienced this myself but can believe it. Throughout the Outdoor Service, the relationship between Officer and Surveyor grade officials was very much one of 'cat and mouse'.

In December 1960, I went to the Raynes Park school end of term dance to which former and existing pupils, their sisters and female friends were also invited. A couple of years previously I had escorted a girl home who I had danced with during the evening and she had let me kiss her outside her house when I wished her goodnight. It was my first proper kiss. I felt so daring and proud, I couldn't wait to announce to my friends that I had joined the 'I've kissed a girl club'. I had kissed a few more girls following this initiation but had not developed any steady relationship as a consequence. However, that all changed when I asked a good looking blond girl to dance with me that evening. Her name was Ulla and she was Danish. She was a mature sixteen-year old and had come to England to learn the language while working as an au pair for a family who occupied a large detached house off the Ridgeway in Wimbledon. She was planning to become an air stewardess with Scandinavian Airline Systems (SAS) on completing her education. In short, I quickly fell in love with her and found that my feelings were reciprocated. The affair extended beyond the normal two to three weeks relationship and became so serious that, by the spring of 1961, her brother Soren had been dispatched by her parents to support her and, I believe, to wean her away from me, bearing in mind that, at the end of the day, she was very young with all her adult life in front of her. Her brother, who was older than both of us, set himself up in a flat at the top of Wimbledon Hill, close to the common. Ulla moved in with Soren when she finished her stint as an au pair and they both took temporary jobs in Harvey Nicholls departmental store in Knightsbridge. Maybe Ulla had told her parents she intended staying in England to be with me when the family plan had been that she should return to Denmark at the conclusion of her time as an au pair; I don't know. I do know that Soren, whilst amiable towards me on the surface, seemed to be on a mission to gently break our relationship. Our affair lasted until the early summer. I had taken Ulla to meet my Auntie Noll in her convent in Grayshott in my newly acquired car. I worried that Ulla was not as relaxed and warm as usual. A weekend later, on a hot, cloudless June day, I took her in my car for a trip to Cambridge which she had said she always wanted to visit. Her father was a professor at Copenhagen University and had often talked to her about this beautiful English University City. He was a great admirer of England and all things English and had come over for a couple of days at the height of our affair. My mother invited him round to our house for tea while he was here. The trip to Cambridge was perfect but the spark in our relationship was no longer there. When we got back to her flat, sitting in the car outside, she told me that she wanted to remain friends with me but that was all. I went to see her with Soren once after that in my favourite King of Denmark pub near their flat. I was sad that she no longer loved me but I saw no future in a platonic relationship when our mutual feelings had previously been so deep. I never met or heard from her again. Although I was hurt, strangely enough my life with my friends and family took on an unexpected intensity in the immediate aftermath, which I found stimulating and restorative.

My mother and father celebrated their Silver Wedding in July 1961. After Sunday lunch at the George Inn we took them to a lovely country pub in the Surrey hills, aptly called The Well from the ancient well situated in the adjacent garden. The pub had been introduced to me by Terry French after my break-up with Ulla. We sat outside in the garden enjoying the balmy weather and watching the sheep peacefully grazing on the hillside opposite. This was the first time my mother had been to a pub since she married my father. We wanted to show her that pubs had developed over the years and that they weren't the dark, gloomy, dissolute and sometimes violent places she had known in her childhood.

Being now free of romantic entanglements, I applied on 25 July 1961 for a transfer to Dover Collection. I had heard from fellow UOs about the grand tour. This amounted to an exceedingly well paid opportunity to travel round the country in stages, at the Department's expense, starting with the Channel ports in the summer holiday season, moving to East Anglia in the autumn for the harvesting of sugar beat on which there was an Excise duty, and travelling up to Scotland in the winter for the whisky distillery season. The expenses you were paid were apparently enough to enable you to buy a smart sports car with which to charm a string of landladies' daughters round the country. This would be the life for me I thought.

Being a working young man and having left my schooldays behind me, I went, at some juncture, on an Easter tour to South Wales with my Old Boys rugby team. We stayed in the Welsh Valleys in a little town called Tredegar. We played the local side and Merthyr Tydfil and lost heavily to both. We were astonished that spectators were being charged to watch the games and that the Welsh boys were receiving 'boot money' for playing. We were strictly amateurs watched by the proverbial man and his dog if we were lucky. The weather was awful; it rained practically the whole time, coming straight at you over the bare hill tops.

On the Saturday we trooped off to watch England play Wales at Cardiff Arms Park in the Five Nations series. I remember having to temper our support for the England team as we were surrounded and heavily outnumbered by Welsh fans. England were getting stuffed and one of the England Props was buckling badly in the set scrums. At one point the ball, which was of the old leather and lace variety was kicked into the open terrace where we were standing opposite the river Taff end. It was caught by a Welsh youth who refused to throw it back so the game could not continue. There was only one match ball in those days. When at last he succumbed to the protestations of the crowd and threw the one and only match ball back, one of his friends shouted at him "What did you do that for … stupid?" to which he retorted, eyes alight with the gleam of the true zealot "I touched it didn't I!" One evening in Tredegar we got invited home by a couple of girls. Sitting by the fireplace was one of the girls' uncles, an ex miner whose face was scarred by coal flints. He had played for Wales some years previously and was wearing his Welsh International blazer. In the Valleys it seemed that practically every other member of the male population had played for Wales at some time or another. I was making good headway with the better looking of the two girls when John Bray our captain and 'Whigs' Loible arrived. Whigs was a mild mannered, willowy, fair haired, naturally handsome chap who played in the Centre position with me in the team. He later became an accountant, dying unexpectedly in early middle age. The moment he entered the house, the girl I had been impressing immediately turned her attention for the rest of the evening to Whigs. Looking at the record books I find that the tour must have taken place around the weekend of 21 January 1961 not Easter. Although losing

6 – 3, England were not embarrassingly overwhelmed by the Welsh as my memory suggests they were. You have to believe, that the things I am writing about actually happened: of that there is no doubt in my mind. But to paraphrase Eric Morecombe in the classic TV Morecombe and Wise comedy sketch when Andre Previn the famous conductor accused him of playing all the wrong notes of the Grieg Piano Concerto – 'I'm playing all the right notes-memories but not necessarily in the right order!' In similar vein, I recall playing for the Old Boys in Middlesex Sevens competitions, held every year in the spring after the main fifteen-a-side season had finished. It was then the most prestigious Sevens competition in the country, if not the world. All the leading sides entered and qualified for the Finals in the first week of May at Twickenham having disposed of the minnows such as ourselves in the preliminary rounds along the way. In the preliminaries I remember being side-stepped by Bob Hiller, the England Fullback, playing for Harlequins, from fully ten yards away but redeemed myself when playing against Rosslyn Park who were then, like Harlequins, one of the top English clubs. I tackled Ransome head on, the sometime England Winger, bringing him crashing to the ground when he was bearing down on me at a great rate of knots. Having been knocked out in the preliminaries, we always attended the Finals at Twickenham as spectators the following weekend. It was an enjoyable event normally blessed with hot sunny weather. We always took a picnic which we were able to consume in the stand or in the car park outside. It was a great way to bring down the curtain on the season.

In terms of dates, I do know precisely when and where I spent my next summer holiday. I went with Martyn Bond,

Chris Eggleton, and two other old school friends, Dick Foulsham and Fred Crowe in the second half of August 1961 for two weeks to Tossa de Mar on the Costa Brava in Spain. Following the previous years experience in hitchhiking to Italy, we had decided to go somewhere a little more luxurious and relaxing. This was right at the start of the enormous 1960s foreign holiday tourist boom. Martyn, Chris and I travelled by channel ferry and train across France and into Spain. I think that Dick and Fred, whose family was reputed to be fairly well off, actually went by air which we thought was unusual and, in any case, more expensive than we could afford. Changing at the border on to a Spanish train, Martyn, Chris and I were persuaded by a Spanish peasant woman selling her wares from the platform to purchase a bottle of Spanish Brandy. The price was astronomically small compared to the UK. We found prices generally around one tenth of the UK level so our spending money went a long way and you could drink as much as you liked. As the train pulled out of the station we each took a swig of the brandy but it was so cheap and foul tasting we spat it out jettisoning the bottle out the train window, fully expecting it to explode as it impacted with the ground. Apart from this cautionary experience the holiday was very good value and most enjoyable. We all four got on well together and there were plenty of girls around, mainly English some of whom we befriended, sharing sociable evenings together moving from bar to bar in the balmy Spanish night.

One particular bar run by a Spanish family on the left-hand side of a narrow street leading down to the beach became our favourite watering hole of an evening. The proprietor's daughter performed flamenco at intervals during the evening and I was flattered when one night, sitting on a bar stool with my back to the counter to watch her performance, she finished by flashing me a scintillating smile and inserting herself between my thighs with her back pressing against my chest. I put my arms round her slender waist brushing her long black hair with my cheek. She was an attractive girl and we quickly became close. I can't remember whether she spoke much English. I spoke little Spanish. However we agreed to meet when she was not working in the cafe one afternoon in the outskirts of town adjacent to a building site where a new tourist hotel was being constructed. I guess we chose that area because we wanted to be away from nosey friends and family members. When I got there, I was surprised to find two middle aged Spanish ladies dressed in traditional black and grey garb who had seen better days advancing towards me. There was no sign of my young Spanish dancer. One of the ladies grabbed me by the arms and started trying to kiss me. Her teeth were held in place by an ugly metal brace. She said something to the effect that if I wanted kissing and so on she would show me the way and I needn't bother with the café proprietor's daughter. I couldn't believe what was happening. They were obviously related to her and I think they were her aunts. Shocked and disgusted, I broke away from the attempted embrace, looked around and beat a hasty retreat to rejoin my friends on the beach as the two harridans shouted imprecations after me warning me against having any further communication or contact with their niece. They had obviously found out about our developing relationship and secret assignation. In time honoured tradition, Spanish families in those days controlled the process of falling in love and matchmaking in a rigorous and hidebound manner. Young girls were subjected to all sorts of restrictions that did not apply to English girls. Latin girls were only allowed to meet boys with potentially amorous intentions in the presence of a chaperone. Alas, these cultural differences destroyed our budding romance. I never saw my raven haired senorita again.

A photograph of Martyn and I, taken on our last night in Tossa, shows us holding hands with  holidaying English girls in a beachside café, testifying to the fact that I must have recovered with reasonable aplomb from the disappointment of my failed Spanish romance. Funnily enough I knew Christine, the girl Martyn befriended, from St James Youth Club back home; small world! On the way back home, I managed to jump the train as it was slowly circumventing Paris en route for the Channel ports, waved goodbye to my friends and spent an enjoyable week with my brother who had travelled from England by prearrangement, staying in my usual hotel in the Place Monge. The weather was stifling and we barely had the energy to stagger from one café to the next.

Back home finally, I was sent to the London Docks to work. The Port of London as it was known consisted of a myriad of docks and wharves in all shapes and sizes from the gigantic 'Royal Group' located on the north side of the river and the equally extensive timber dock, The Surrey Docks, on the south side to the comparatively diminutive St Katherine's Dock hard by the Tower of London, now a hotel, shopping, entertainment complex and yacht marina. The port extended from the Pool of London, in the short stretch of the Thames that lies between Tower Bridge and London Bridge, all the way down to Tilbury. The dockyards were full of steam ships of all shapes and sizes sporting wooden masts, smoky funnels and even the odd sail.

Quaysides were crammed with musty vaults, Victorian warehouses looming over cobbled streets and courtyards and cranes like giant daddy longlegs towering overhead. Containers did not exist. Ships were loaded and unloaded manually in piecemeal fashion by stevedores, coopers and dockers employed on a casual basis only; 'on the stump' as it was termed. I spent most of my time in the Upper docks and longest of all at Free Trade Wharf at Wapping that is now the site of a luxury block of flats.

The two fixed Landing Officers and I were assisted by dockers called Fred and Alf. Fred was in fact a Cooper which put him in a class above Alf. Their language was amazing; a fascinating patois in which they used the 'F' word constantly but which had a certain rhythm and poetry to it. For all their want of formal education, they were warm-hearted, sensible and loyal Eastenders who addressed Landing Officers, even young ones like me as 'Sir', showing unquestioning obedience to our wishes and deference without compromising their own considerable dignity. The Fixed Landing Officers and I used to lunch in our wharf side office on duplicate samples of imported foodstuffs, cooked for us by the uniformed Watcher, later renamed Revenue Assistant, followed by a game of makeshift indoor cricket in a cleared space in the warehouse where we carried out our physical examinations of cargo consignments.

On one occasion, when I had decided to carry out an examination of a consignment of glass lampshades, Fred and Alf told me that a complaint had been received about breakages that had occurred in previous consignments which the importer implied might have been caused by careless handling by dockers. Fred and Alf felt this represented a gross slur on their honour. To be fair, both Fred and Alf, and dockers in general, were highly skilled in handling goods of all descriptions and although there was inevitably a small amount of unavoidable breakage they were very careful and solicitous in ensuring that, by and large, they reached importers undamaged. "Well..." said Fred "If its damage he's worried about, we'd better make sure he really does have something to fucking complain about." and proceeded to extract several lampshades from their boxes which they goal-kicked forcibly in all directions shattering as they struck walls, pillars and packing cases surrounding the examination bay. I thought it was highly amusing. I felt they had been unjustly accused and sympathised with their reaction. It was no skin of my nose because we got our import duty and tax on the goods anyway, whether they were delivered whole or not.

Fred and Alf never stooped to any serious impropriety that I was aware of but the lay dockers who worked at the wharf were not averse to the occasional descent into organised pillage. When I arrived in the office early one morning Eric Taylor, one of the fixed Landing Officers, told me to scrutinise the dockers carefully as they came on shift and to look closely at their shoes. Sure enough as they trooped past, I noticed that the shoes they were wearing were old with extensively worn uppers and holes in many of the soles. Eric told me to look again when they finished their shift. When the siren went signalling the end of their day's labour, I stationed myself again by the office window. From there I watched the same gang of dockers streaming past, up the causeway and out through the dock gate past the habitually dozing Port of London (PLA) policeman, each of them sporting a brand new pair of shoes. The vessel they had been unloading had brought with it a cargo of Romanian leather shoes. "Look at the River" said Eric and I quickly spotted the old shoes they had worn to work that morning floating gently away in a ragged, bobbing flotilla on the ebb tide.

Free Trade Wharf and the Upper Docks handled a variety of smaller cargo vessels mostly carrying general cargo from European, North African and Middle Eastern ports. The captain of a Polish boat made the mistake one day of consuming too much vodka for lunch prior to departing from the wharf down river on the afternoon high tide. Under his drunken influence, the vessel lurched away from its berth, slammed against one of the jetties in the river supporting some of the wharf's cranes, damaging a wooden pile and decking and careered into midstream where he collided with a string of moored, empty barges which ricocheted against one another emitting loud booming noises like a frustrated pod of mechanical hippopotamuses. On another occasion an importer made a Customs declaration for a consignment of tortoises he was importing from Algeria in North Africa for the UK pet trade. Normally importers or their shipping agents made written declarations known as 'Entries' on large pre-printed forms known as 'Sale ' forms because they were sold by the Department for Customs clearance purposes (no other forms were allowed to be used). These Entries were then lodged with us by importers and agents. We scrutinised the Entry forms and supporting documentation for correctness and selected a proportion of the importations for physical examination to check that the goods were correctly described and quantified. Usually this took place without the importer or agent being present. However when the importer was not sure exactly what was being imported a Prime Entry could be completed which meant that he could attend the compulsory examination of the consignment and complete or 'perfect' the Entry when the exact contents were revealed. In this case therefore the importer was present when I performed my examination. Thc tortoiscs were contained in three or four large Ali Baba type baskets. When the lids were removed, I found that the poor creatures had simply been piled loosely, one on top of another, in higgledy-piggledy fashion. No food or water, cushioning straw or thermal material had been provided. Over half of them were dead and the remainder distressed and disorientated. It was a sorry sight. I couldn't believe the indifference of the importer as he counted up the number of surviving animals so that he could 'perfect' the Entry. To cap it all, he was the spitting image of the tortoises he was bringing from their natural habitat all the way across the sea in such a callous manner. He had a thin lined face, a beaky nose, bulbous eyes and wrinkled neck and the habit like the tortoises of slowly extending and retracting his neck into a stiff shirt collar that was too large for his scraggy physique.

My other memorable encounter with animals was walking to work one dismal morning through one of the docks - I think it was London Dock, where the Surveyor had his office – when suddenly, a dark rat, the size of a medium sized dog emerged from the brackish water, swished silently across the quay right in front of me and disappeared into a gloom-laden warehouse as swiftly as he had appeared. The Surveyor was a tall, ecclesiastical, grey haired man named Phillips. We rarely saw him and he rarely spoke to us. When he did speak it was only on official matters. Despite being of Welsh extraction, he had a steady, uninspiring tone to his voice and a pedantic manner. He was typical of many of the Surveyors of his era, having been promoted to the supervisory rank purely on the basis of technical knowledge and not on any leadership qualities he may or may not have possessed. Eligibility for the grade was tested by written examination, qualification for which took two years of extensive private study, on which Eric Taylor was incidentally embarking, and which only permitted two attempts during the relatively early stages of an Officer's career. The upper limit was something like 34 years of age. Moreover, the time and effort involved unfairly favoured single rather than family men.

My first encounter with Phillips was when walking through one of the square shaped, enclosed docks one morning on my way to Free Trade Wharf. I spotted Phillips on the other side of the dock heading resolutely in the same direction as me. Despite the cover provided by the colonnaded warehouses on all sides he had spotted me too and a surreptitious race developed. I succeeded in getting to the end first where the exit lay which meant that I would arrive at Free Trade Wharf at my Journal Office as it was known and would be able to sign the Attendance Journal before he did. Unlike the Excise, we worked on the basis of fixed timed attendance in Customs stations. If the Surveyor arrived before you he would draw a line in the journal noting the time and adding his signature. If you got there after he had drawn the line and I was usually late by about quarter of an hour in the mornings, you were 'cut out' as the jargon had it. In principle, this constituted a disciplinary offence for being late on duty or 'theft of official time' as it was more prosaically termed. I think on this occasion Phillips gave up the chase. However, some weeks later I was 'cut out' by him. He had left our office by the time I arrived and I was obliged to telephone him at his office to explain why I was late. I did so and gave the excuse of delays on the trains that morning which he seemed to accept. Some weeks later he was on leave and I happened to be assisting for a couple of days in 53 Office where he was based. The local Watcher called me into Phillips' room and showed me the Surveyor's Diary. This was an official document that every Surveyor was expected to keep religiously and was inspected periodically by the Collector. The Watcher told me that he had been cut out on the same day as me, had given Phillips an excuse and heard nothing more about it. "Look" he said "Would you believe it!" He pointed to an entry Phillips had made on the morning in question which read 'Cottee and - whatever the Watcher's name was – severely verbally admonished.' We both laughed. Not once had Phillips spoken to us in any way that justified this statement. In fact he had accepted our explanations and that was the end of the conversation we had had with him. I met him in the flesh shortly before Christmas when he suddenly arrived at Free Trade Wharf unannounced, in the middle of an extended lunchtime session with the warehouse keeper and a couple of his members of staff celebrating the festive season. We were drinking duplicate samples of wine which were strictly supposed to be disposed of 'down the common sewer'. We jokingly translated this to 'connoisseur' as we swigged away. The party was warming up nicely and getting to the raucous stage when Phillips burst in. Everything went deathly quiet. Phillips asked what was going on in his meek voice looking around with clear disapproval registered on his features. Eric Taylor immediately reposted, rather neatly

I thought, by saying that we were cementing relations with the warehouse keeper. Again Phillips said nothing in response. The warehouse keeper and his colleagues in their embarrassment quickly made their apologies and left. In the uneasy silence that followed Phillips sat down and carried out his supervisory documentary checks before departing after about half an hour without a further word being spoken by anyone. No doubt this went down in his Surveyor's Diary as another occasion on which he had been obliged to deliver a severe verbal admonition!

Sometimes in my lunch hour I would go to the Whitechapel Art Gallery or to Tower Hill, if I was in the vicinity, to listen to people like Donald Soper, the nationally renowned Methodist minister, who used to speak on all sorts of subjects but given his calling, mostly on moral matters. He was a wonderful orator who never failed to trump hecklers in the crowd with his enormous intellect, integrity and razor like wit. Jack Dash, an avowed Communist and Dockers' Union activist, was an effective orator in the firebrand mode and I remember him stirring the dockers up with his invective and flowing white hair when a strike was being contemplated at Brussels Wharf. I also remember one afternoon, well after the lunchtime period had finished, arriving at a bonded wine and spirits warehouse in Tooley Street. As I was about to enter, a senior policeman judging by the layers of silver braid adorning his uniform, staggered out into the street, heading unsteadily towards Scotland Yard. The warehouse keeper told me that he was a high ranking officer with the Met Police who had a partiality for enjoying long and relaxing lunch breaks in the bosom of the warehouse imbibing, at the warehouse keeper's expense, glasses of Tigers Milk and Bulls Blood; proprietary

Hungarian wines that were stored there duty free. However, the warehouse keeper reassured me that his self invited police visitor was only served from the warehouse duty paid stock so no revenue offence was being committed. Quite how the police officer reconciled his frequent, free, liquid lunches with the efficient execution of his duties in the afternoon was another matter.

After a while, I started to use my car to drive from home to Free Trade Wharf and back rather than rely on public transport. One day I was driving home along the notorious Cable Street, a long straight cobbled-stoned thoroughfare that in its heyday in the nineteenth century had been the haunt of sailors seeking drink, drugs and prostitution. Many of the buildings lining the street had been demolished except for an isolated section of run-down terraced houses and shops situated about halfway along its length. Suddenly as I approached this section, two women shot out from one of the buildings to my right. They both ended up in an undignified heap in the middle of the road, right in front of my car, scratching, kicking, biting, shrieking and generally trying to take huge lumps out of one another. They were obviously members of the oldest profession in the world trying to reconcile some sort of grievance associated with their trade. Hair, shoes, blood and strips of clothing were flying everywhere. It was both comical and vicious. I have never quite seen a fight like it!

One morning at Free Trade Wharf in early 1962, I received a telephone call from the London Port Appointer. He told me that a vacancy for an Unattached Officer had come up in Dover Collection for which I had applied earlier and that I was now the senior man on the transfer list. Seniority ruled everything. However, he asked me whether, exceptionally, I would be prepared to let the officer next on the list go in my place. This officer apparently had a wife and children living in Dover whereas to all intents and purposes I was unencumbered on the domestic front. I thought about it briefly and concluded that, in the circumstances, it would be wrong to stand in this officer's way. I was naturally disappointed but calculated that another vacancy would come along soon enough. The decision I made not to transfer to Dover at that time and the fact that I was lucky enough to own my own car, changed the course of my life as subsequent events were to prove.

My mother had loaned me the money for my first car, A British manufactured Austin A30 four door saloon, registration RYK 779 which I bought from the local Stonecot Hill Garage around the time of my twentieth birthday in May 1961. I was alone among my friends in being the proud owner of my own car. It cost £405 and served me well over the next six or seven years. It's true that I seemed to be constantly replacing tyres and batteries and other parts like plugs, starter motors, points, leads, distributor caps, water pumps, radiators and hoses. Not being much of a mechanic I nevertheless learned how the engine worked and carried out most of the repairs myself, mainly because it was expensive to get the garage to do it. It was always a toss-up whether the car would start first thing in the morning especially in the winter. Getting the engine to start and adjusting the choke became something of a fine art. At times I would have to set the choke and crank the engine by hand using an old starter handle that you had to insert through a hole in the front bumper. With repeated use the hole gradually became more and more elliptical in shape making it doubly difficult to get a purchase on the engine before turning the handle. All my best efforts in this direction failed to fire the engine after I had driven to Epsom Downs racecourse one summer evening with Martyn, Chris and Tim Biddiscombe, another mutual school friend, who joined the school halfway through, allegedly from Australia but actually from India where his father had been serving as a Regimental Sergeant Major in the British Army. Frustrated but undaunted, between us, we pushed the car all the way home, a distance of some five miles, most of which was, fortunately, downhill.

The traffic indicators that were operated by a switch in the middle of the dashboard were a constant source of amusement and irritation. They were of the semaphore variety, housed in the door column and, after turning the switch, had to be encouraged to spring into their intended horizontal position by banging the inside of either door column with one's fist. When you were trying to steer and change gear at the same time, this wasn't always easy.

Another problem I had to contend with was air leaking into the braking system and forming bubbles in the brake fluid. Alarmingly, this problem only manifested itself intermittently. I would step on the brake pedal and find that nothing happened. I could gradually get pressure back by pumping the brake pedal vigorously, supplemented, in emergencies, by pulling on the hand break at the same time. It was a bit unnerving and I used to dream at night about my struggle to get the car to stop. One day, coming down a long, straight stretch of road from Wandsworth Bridge against a steady stream of oncoming traffic, I saw a stationary milk float several hundred yards ahead of me on my side of the road. I touched the brake pedal to reduce speed but nothing happened. Eventually by pumping the brake pedal and yanking on the hand break I managed to slow my progress sufficiently to avoid slamming into the milk float. Consequently, I became something of an expert at bleeding brakes and replacing lost fluid but could never rest easy that I had affected a permanent cure. Even when the brakes were working properly they were barely able to cope with steep slopes like the abrupt, winding incline down which I found myself driving one summer with my uncle AG and Tim Biddiscombe on our way to the pretty little Thames Valley town of Marlow. There we hired a boat which we rowed all the way to the world famous Henley Regatta and back. In one of the locks on the way to the Regatta, a loud mouthed poseur dressed in blazer and cravat with champagne glass in hand was showing off to his friends seated on a posh motor boat. Standing on the side of the lock as the gates opened, he attempted to jump heroically onto the boat as it moved away. Unfortunately for him, the rush of water into the lock moved the boat a couple of feet further away than he had anticipated and he plunged feet first in the gap between the side of the boat and the lock, glass still in hand. How we laughed; we three men in a humble rowing boat!

I encountered a tricky problem with the engine when in my car my brother and I went for a day driving through the Vale of Evesham in Worcestershire and up the Malvern Hills. We got halfway up the highest peak when there was a loud bang. I immediately lost power and couldn't get any further. I managed to turn the car round and drove slowly with a loud rhythmic hammering noise coming from the engine, all the way back to my Aunt Dorothy and Uncle Graham with whom we were staying for a few days at their home on the outskirts of Birmingham. Graham arranged for the car to be repaired in a local garage. I had no idea what the problem was until they told me that one of the big ends had gone. It sounded drastic but thanks to Graham's influence with the garage proprietor, the repair bill was affordable. The big ends, I learned, were the vital metal joints that translate the downward motion of the cylinders into the rotary motion of the crankshaft that drives the wheels. The fact that I had not been keeping the lubricating oil round the engine properly topped up had not helped. With hindsight, driving up to Birmingham on the newly opened and virtually traffic free M1, the first motorway to be built in Britain, I remembered noticing that the oil warning light kept flickering on and off and had done nothing about it. Chastened by this experience, I checked the oil and water levels regularly after that and topped them up when necessary. However, the engine got progressively more worn and after driving around for months with clouds of increasingly smelly, white smoke belching from the exhaust pipe, it packed up altogether and had to be replaced. Again this was not astronomically expensive. Engines in those days, though far less reliable, were relatively small, simple and easy to fit, unlike the massive computer governed beasts that lurk under the bonnets of today's cars. I saved money by buying my road fund licence quarterly and waiting a further month before renewing. I also drove around on tyres before replacing them that were so bald you could almost see your reflection in them. Needless to say, this was before the MOT test came into being.

Despite the expense and frustration of running a car, it gave me great freedom. As well as using it to get to work,

I drove myself and friends to rugby matches, parties and various social gatherings. One Saturday night after we had been playing rugby, I drove Martyn accompanied by his friend Chris in my car to a house in Dorset Road, Merton Park where we had been told that a party was being held which we planned to gatecrash. We had bought a bottle of red wine to serve as an entrance offering but we didn't really know the people there and were refused entry. Stuck with our bottle of wine and nowhere to go, Martyn remembered that the Casilla Coffee House was not far away in Sheridan Road and suggested we pop round there to drink the wine. Coffee houses were fashionable then but I had not heard of the Casilla Coffee House. Nevertheless we agreed to go. Following Martyn's directions I drove into the adjacent Sheridan Road and stopped outside a three story Victorian house bearing, on a board in the front porch, the name Casilla. Martyn said the Ware family who lived there were welcoming and always happy to have people dropping in for a cup of coffee and a chat; hence the affectionate designation of the Casilla Coffee House. He had been friends from primary school days with Rosalind, the eldest daughter, who Chris also knew from Merton Park primary school. Martyn knocked on the door and sure enough we were greeted warmly and invited in. It so happened that Rosalind, or Ros as she was known, was at home entertaining her friend Marjorie Tolley, known as Chicky. I remember standing in the entrance hall and looking up to see Chicky leaning over the upstairs landing banister before she came down the stairs to join us. Ros led us into the front room where we opened the bottle of wine and consumed the contents sitting round the fire and chatting. Ros and Chicky had met in ballet classes in Wimbledon and become best friends. They were in the habit of spending weekends in each other's houses and it was Chicky's turn to stay with Ros. I quickly became aware that Ros had a sleek physique, fantastic legs and a bum that was the best I had ever seen. She was wearing a short, straight, figure hugging, brown corduroy dress and high heels and spoke beautifully and with assurance. I was impressed. So much so that at one point in the evening when we must have been talking generally for some reason about people getting married, I remember Ros who, at that moment, was standing sideways in front of the fire declaring vehemently to no-one in particular that "I'm never getting married!": humm... I thought we'll see about that! I was aware that she seemed to have eyes mainly for Chris and certainly didn't seem to pay much attention to me but the gauntlet had been thrown down and I was determined to pick it up despite the competition I might face. Coincidentally, this was the first time Martyn had met Chicky and it turned out that he had become as much enamoured with her as I was with Ros. Martyn married Chicky in due course and they lived happily as soul mates and lovers until Chicky died of an undiagnosed brain tumour in 2002.

A couple of months later, I took the opportunity provided by my forthcoming 21st birthday party being held at Morden Hall of inviting Ros, her sister Chris and Chicky along. I was pleased when they agreed to come. I remember Ros wore a light blue satiny dress with a flared skirt over a stiff petticoat and had her hair fashionably dressed in beehive style. I danced and spent time with her and a few days later rang her up and invited her to come with me to a Saturday evening wedding reception being held in the house of one of my tennis club female friends on the edge of Wimbledon Common. It wasn't a terribly formal affair, so I came dressed in my usual post rugby attire, much to Ros' amazement and unspoken disapproval which she only revealed to me some years later. This attire consisted of my blue, V- neck drinking sweater and favourite jeans with a hole in the crutch. Nevertheless as far as I was concerned the evening went well and she agreed to come out with me again. It wasn't long before she came round to my house and got to know my parents, my brother and sister and wider circle of friends.

By the time the summer holiday period came round Ros and I were regretting that we had previously made arrangements to go on holiday with friends. My friend Tim Biddiscombe was also keen on Ros' sister Christine. Unfortunately, she was very unsure of herself at the time and the relationship never blossomed into anything more serious as it might have otherwise done. Ros went off to Jersey with Chicky and her family while Tim Biddiscombe and I went off to Bavaria in Southern Germany via Paris where I met up with Dorothy Dauvissat from my Sussex Club days. We had an enjoyable time with her and lived well, thinking we could afford it. Unfortunately we had miscalculated the exchange rate between the pound and French franc and it was not until we arrived at the Gare De L'Est to change our French francs into German currency before boarding the Orient Express for Munich that we realised that in a mere two days in Paris we had spent well over half the money we had brought with us for the entire two week trip. For the rest of the holiday we had to restrict ourselves to a single evening meal a day which we shared. We were so famished and had lost so much weight by the time we got back home to Hythe where Tim's parents lived that Tim's Dad took us out to an upmarket pub for a slap up meal which I remember devouring with huge relish and relief; not to mention the glass of brandy consumed by the sparkling open fire: or was this at another time? – memory plays strange tricks!

We had flown out from the nearby Lydd airport on a twin-engine, Avro turbo-prop passenger plane. I have always loved travelling by air but remember feeling nervous, not so much because this was the first time I had flown but because we were taking off from a bumpy grass runway dotted with rabbit holes. As the aircraft gathered speed I was wondering if one of the wheels would get stuck in one of these holes and throw the aircraft over before it was able to lift off the ground. Fortunately it climbed a few feet in the air without incident before abruptly shooting over the edge of the coastal cliff at the end of the runway. Suddenly we found ourselves hundreds of feet above the glistening sea heading calmly across the English Channel for Beauvais in northern France from whence we travelled by train to Paris and onward into Germany.

As well as staying briefly in Paris we spent a couple of days in Munich which was gearing up for the October Beer Festival or Oktoberfest before travelling to our intended destination of Garmisch-Partenkirchen in the Bavarian Alps. Garmisch was a lovely, typical Alpine town and. despite our shortage of spending money we had a great time there. The surrounding mountains were spectacular and one sunny day we decided to ascend the Zugspitze, the highest peak in the range. A cable car took us to the summit where there was a restaurant and signs indicating various footpaths. After sunbathing for a bit we chose one path for an afternoon stroll not paying too much attention to the sign warning that the path was closed in winter and in adverse weather conditions. It wasn't long before we realised why the sign had been put there. The path was cut into the side of the rock and was barely a foot wide with a sheer drop on the left-hand side to the valley floor thousands of feet below. At one point, as we descended gingerly, Tim who was in front of me slipped. His legs shot forward from under him. Instinctively he tried to save his camera slung over his left shoulder from falling into the abyss rather than himself. Mercifully, his fall took him straight down the path and he managed to hold onto his camera while at the same time saving himself from plunging over the edge. What had begun as a pleasant stroll, turned from that moment into a serious mountaineering challenge for which we were spectacularly ill-equipped, attired in our Sunday best shiny leather shoes with flat soles and summer slacks and shirts. The descent into the valley took us most of the afternoon and by the time we reached the safety of a reasonably flat boulder strewn area through which a river ran we realised that there was no obvious way out. The valley appeared to be completely enclosed by a ring of mountains including the one we had just descended. We decided to follow the course of the river and eventually came to a rock wall where the river disappeared. To the right we spotted a small tunnel in the rock through which we surmised the river flowed when in high spate and decided to follow it to see where it led. We had to bend double and scrambled in this fashion for some distance in the semi-dark with the sound of tumbling water to our left before the tunnel opened out into a huge gallery through which the river was pouring. We stepped across a few rocks and climbed over a metal rail onto the end of a wide pathway that formed a viewing area at that spot before leading back down the gallery.

Relieved that we seemed to be returning to some semblance of civilisation we walked down the path, passing sightseers who looked strangely at us. After a while we arrived at the lower end where the river burst majestically from the mouth of the gallery into flat, open pasture land covered in long grass and wild flowers. At this point there was a ticket office and turnstiles. We passed through the exit gate noticing that the uniformed official in the office was looking somewhat puzzled. This was a scenic spot for which you had to pay to enter and there was only one way in and out. He obviously couldn't remember selling us tickets and could not work out how we had got in without him knowing and without paying. We finally made it back to our hotel in Garmisch in the fading light of early evening, chastened yet invigorated by our unplanned adventure.

While in Garmisch I recall being impressed at seeing Turkish guest-workers building roads in the town at 10 'clock at night; something that would not have happened in England with the 'nine to five' 5 working day mentality that prevailed at that time. I also remember being surprised one evening when in a local beer hall one of the German guests raised his arm in a Nazi style salute and fellow Germans around him gasped.

Back in the UK, I spent much of my free time round at Ros' house. In October I remember watching with some trepidation the black and white television pictures of Russian cargo vessels laden with intercontinental missiles heading for Cuba and the waiting cordon of United States naval ships. This was the moment of the Cold War when the world came closest to a nuclear holocaust. Everybody was quietly relieved when by skilful diplomacy president

Kennedy averted the crises. I was also round at Ros' one Sunday afternoon just over a year later watching television when the dreadful news of Kennedy's assassination came through and the world seemed to catch its breath. He had promised much with his youthful looks and fresh approach and it was terrible to see him cut down in an act of meaningless violence. Fortunately the fresh approach he promised, dispensing with the sterilities and arcane formalities of the post war years, was not lost and was unleashed, independently of the tragedy, by young people themselves mainly through the 60's development of fashion and pop music in which British bands such as the Beatles and the Rolling Stones played a leading part. I do also remember much earlier at the start of the Cold War watching black and white cinema newsreels of the Berlin airlift and, for most of my adult life, never expecting to see the Berlin wall, erected shortly afterwards, coming down. I also have sombre, black and white memories of watching the funeral processions of George VI and Churchill on television when, for a brief moment, the whole of the British nation drew in on itself, uncertain of its future direction and purpose.

By the time the 1962/3 rugby season got under way, Ros and Chicky started to come to watch me and Martyn playing for the Raynes Park Old Boys at Claygate, sometimes helping with the preparation of the aftermatch food. Luckily for me, Ros enjoyed the sport for itself and by the end of the season had acquired a greater knowledge of the intricacies and the rules of the game than most players. The Old Boys Society owned the land on which we played and on which the clubhouse stood. The land was sold for a tidy sum in the 1970s to make way for the construction of the A3 Esher Bypass under which it now lies buried, unheeded by the traffic swishing over it en route for the M25 (London Orbital Motorway). The money we received still subsidises the Annual Old Boys Reunion Dinner which I attend most years.

The clubhouse was not very grand. There were no showers just a single copper bath we shared with the opposing team into which we all sunk after the match. Last-in usually found the water tepid and muddy. But the traditional rendition of well loved rugby songs and a few beers made sure that everyone enjoyed a good time before leaving the clubhouse; some later than others. Sometimes we would go for a curry afterwards at the Rawalpindhi in Wimbledon High Street, an Indian restaurant also frequented by the harum-scarum actor Oliver Reed who we would see there or in the neighbouring pubs from time to time. Indian restaurants were just coming in to vogue and multiplying though there was no such dish as Tandoori or Balti on the menus then; just plain Biriani, Madras or Vindaloo.

Sundays always passed pleasantly starting with a trip to the pub with Ros' father Frank and brother Dick. We normally went to the King of Denmark which I had discovered when going out with Ulla. It was a small hostelry on Wimbledon Hill with a public bar separated from the small, main lounge bar by a tiny off-licence. It also had a small room at the back that served as a secondary, more private, lounge bar that we invariably used. The latter led through French style windows into a tiny, vine covered garden at the rear, containing a cheerful, caged canary, where you could sit in summer. I loved the smell of the whole place. It was unique in my experience and is difficult to describe. It had a faded, sour, sweet, polished quality that I found subtly disarming and the beer –what is now called Real Ale – and was then known simply as Bitter was well kept by the proprietor and made a highly tasty appetiser for the ensuing Sunday roast-lunch cooked by Ros' mum Kathleen. I drove in my faithful A30 and I always stopped on the way back at a local newsagent where Frank would by a block of ice-cream for dessert which came wrapped in newspaper to prevent it melting; Ros' family not then having the benefit of a refrigerator. Later on we were often joined on these forays by Bob, Christine's boyfriend then fiancée. Somehow, although he enjoyed greater financial security than the rest of us put together, he invariably contrived to get away without buying a round. Re-visiting the King of Denmark many years later shortly after Ros' mum died, I was disappointed to find that the discrete bars had been knocked into a single wraparound bar as in so many other pubs these days. The old homely atmosphere and special smell had long since disappeared; replaced, in an attempt to mask the pervading, anodyne corporatism masquerading as 'character' by 'old' photos and 'quirky' prints on the walls: Where before I parked my car directly outside the pub or failing that, no more than twenty yards away in the little road running down the side, the whole area is now covered by a residents only parking permit scheme and the nearest place I could find to park my car was over a quarter of a mile away. Such is progress!

The winter months of January and February 1963 were the coldest since 1740. I walked from home to Ros' house and back several times as the roads were too icy to drive in my car. Nobody had central heating. My parent's house was always a cold house at the best of times. When waking in the mornings, I recall seeing icicles inside the bedroom windows as well as hanging outside from the eves in foot long stalactites. It took a great effort of will to get out of a cosy warm bed in the winter. Ros' house always seemed warmer. The external and internal walls were thick and they had a strategically placed oil heater in the main part of the house which supplemented the coal fires. Although this was an exceptionally cold spell when temperatures remained below freezing, there is no doubt in my mind that, in general, winters were far colder in my childhood and early manhood than they are now. It snowed every year just after Christmas and we were able to have snowball fights and build snowmen in the garden. I remember Terry French and me, on a visit to London one winter, dropping snowballs from the top of St Paul's Cathedral on to unsuspecting city types striding like purposeful bowler-hatted ants across the cathedral precincts far below. Now in 2007, as I write, we have roses in bloom in January and squirrels who no longer hibernate dancing round the garden.

The first time I can ever remember the weather being warm in winter was one Saturday afternoon in Bracknell in 1969 standing around with other players gathered together outside our clubhouse for the afternoon's ruby match. I was able to wear a sweater and jacket and not feel cold; which is saying something for me because I have always been a cold morsel, no doubt due to the fact that I have a slow heartbeat – the same as Roger Bannister, the first man to run the mile in under four minutes – good for stamina sports but not so good for normal circulation. I only found this out from my local doctor when I was in my sixties.

The other winter problem we had to contend with was fog; or more correctly smog, a dirty, orangey-coloured mixture of fog and the acrid smoke that poured from millions of domestic and industrial coal fires into the still, cold night air. In the worst of these smogs, you literally could not see your own hand outstretched in front of your face. Walking down the London Road towards Ros' house during a particularly nasty one, I remember seeing a car travelling slowly towards me, oblivious to the fact that he was heading up the wrong side of the dual carriageway. Before I could react, he had passed like a ship in the night and was swallowed up in the enveloping gloom.

After separate holidays in 1962, Ros and I decided to take our 1963 summer holiday together, galvanised into going somewhere sunny after a very cold evening when we went to watch Cliff Richard in the cheery, heart warming film 'Summer Holiday' with the catchy theme tune 'We're All Going On A Summer Holiday' at the Odeon, Worcester Park. It was a calm, clear night when we came out of the cinema but extremely cold. It took ages, with the starter handle cranking the engine, to get the car started, while Ros sat inside wrapped in the car blanket, shivering. We booked to go for two weeks to Tarragona in Spain. Naturally, I had to book two rooms because it would have been unthinkable then to go on holiday and share a bedroom with a member of the opposite sex to whom you were not married. Before we departed, my mother said that it was a good test and that if we were still together when we came back it would mean that our relationship would last. She was right.

We journeyed by train overnight across France before changing trains at the Spanish border for the fast train to Barcelona. On the final leg south from Barcelona to

Tarragona we clattered slowly along a single track in carriages, reminiscent of the American West, which had wooden shutters for windows and a veranda at each end. At one point, in the stultifying heat of the early afternoon, the train stopped in the middle of nowhere for what seemed like an hour. Wc concluded that the driver must have been taking his siesta. We eventually arrived in the early evening in Tarragona to find engine sheds on the beach. Tarragona was very much a commercial town that happened to be by the sea rather than a pleasure resort as such. Nevertheless we had an enjoyable stay in the Hotel Europa a traditional establishment in the grand hotel mode that was well situated in the main street leading to the seafront promenade. We fell in love with the cute, well behaved Spanish children who were allowed to play under their elders' supervision on the promenade in the evenings at a time when children of their age in England were asleep in bed. We mixed with the locals on the bus that took us to the beaches adjacent to the town and shared the hotel lift one afternoon with the 'top of the bill' bullfighter who was staying in our hotel. He was dressed in his full matador's costume, yellowy-gold in colour and splashed with ornate beads and embroidery. Later we saw him perform in the bullring. I like watching bull fighting in Spain. It dramatically and honestly conveys the fundamental Spanish preoccupation with death and while it is 'not fair' in the English sense, because the bull always gets killed in the end- that is not the point. The bulls are reared in special estates and have a wonderful life up to the time that they reach their prime of life and are ready to compete in the ring. They are magnificent beasts and admired by Spanish aficionados just as much as they admire the bull fighters themselves. The contest is not entirely one-sided as the bullfighters themselves are frequently injured, sometimes quite seriously and the bulls die bravely, fighting proudly according to their natural instincts. Is this any less cruel than the factory farming practices commonplace in the UK where, for instance, chickens are reared in battery huts, never seeing natural light or fresh air before they are slaughtered mindlessly and mechanically in their millions to provide cheap food for our table?

I remember arriving back at Waterloo Station at the end of the holiday wearing a rather fetching broad-brimmed hat I had bought in Tarragona, the first of many such hats that I have bought over the years on my travels. I could see my mother who was waiting to greet us registering the fact that Ros and I were in good spirits, comfortable in each other's company and still very much together. She said nothing on the subject but in that moment I knew that she had accepted that our relationship was built on firm foundations and was unlikely to be broken. I think she thought that Ros was well mannered and brought up from a good family and that although she wore too much make-up, she spoke beautifully, as was indeed the case and that I was unlikely to be parted from her. Of all the girls with whom I went out, my mother's favourite was the one I liked least. Fortunately, my sister met her on the bus one day on the way to Morden while I was away from home working at the Sussex Club and told her that "I've seen Norman's new girlfriend and she (Barbara Achenbach – a beautiful, blond, German girl) is very nice!": neatly saving me the bother of breaking off the relationship myself on my return.

Cheese and wine parties were popular in the 60s. Small cubes of bog standard cheddar and pineapple chunks on cocktail sticks were laid out on plates and washed down with white or red wine of the chateau plonk variety by the guests attending. After one such party at the local Cranleigh tennis club, Ros threw up as we were sitting in the kitchen over a cup of coffee back at Casilla and I quickly followed suit. At a slightly more sophisticated house party one Saturday night, I over imbibed, quaffing too many gin and oranges before foolishly climbing into a hammock, the swinging motion of which quickly brought on the inevitable nausea. I have never touched gin since. A trip one evening to the famous Prospect of Whitby pub in Wapping left Ros feeling ill, partly due to the large schooner glasses of sherry she was drinking and partly from being seated next to a huge roaring open fire and then emerging suddenly into the cold night air. In a curious way these shared, ignominious experiences strengthened the developing bond between us – in sickness and in health – as the Common Prayer Book has it.

Shortly after first getting together with Ros, I withdrew my application for a transfer to Dover Collection, thereby forgoing my opportunity to go on the UO grand tour and applied for London South instead. In October 1963, my application for transfer to London South from London Port came through. My last few months in the Port had been mainly spent assisting the fixed officers in Cutler Street Warehouse, a huge bonded warehouse complex built originally by the East India Company in the eighteenth century. The high ceilinged Surveyor's office on the ground floor just inside the main entrance was reputed to have been used by Clive of India himself who allegedly made occasional visits in ghost-like form usually after the witness in question had been over-indulging in a few waxers

(Customs slang for free drinks taken from warehouse stocks). The complex was split into various sub-warehouses managed by specialist companies. On the ground floor there was an opium warehouse guarded by a sleeping policeman, his senses dulled by the pervading sickly-sweet aroma of the drug that you could distinctly smell as you approached the entrance. Opium was imported for use in medicine. There was no revenue duty on opium. But it was, then as now, a restricted substance because of its addictive, narcotic properties and therefore subject to Customs licensing controls. Next door was a gloomy vintage port warehouse containing elegant long tapering casks known as 'port pipes' presided over by a lugubrious Liverpuddlian Departmental Clerical Officer of large menacing physique who was invariably drunk by the time afternoons came round and apt to become violent. Next was the carpet warehouse containing the most fabulous and expensive Chinese and Persian carpets I have ever seen. These were liable to a specific duty based on square yardage and the fixed officer was responsible for measuring them and verifying the declared revenue charge. Also on the ground floor and above was a wine and spirits bond run by Stowells of Chelsea. At the top of the building was the Tobacco Floor. I assisted the fixed officers in all these areas apart from the opium warehouse but spent most of my time on the Tobacco Floor. Our office was a twentieth century addition built onto the top floor of the warehouse. It had a glass ceiling, a linoleum covered floor and little insulation from the cold in floor and walls. In the winter, as our first task of the day, we would often have to scrape overnight ice from the office floor. The Cuban, Romeo & Juliet cigars that Churchill smoked passed through here and the whole floor exuded a mature and exotic aroma. For revenue purposes, we had to weigh the cigars allowing a deduction for the weight both of the boxes and packets in which they were contained and also the wrappers and bands enclosing the better quality brands. I enjoyed the work a lot.

Occasionally we went for lunch at the aptly named Dirty Dick's pub in the nearby Bishopsgate Road, opposite Liverpool Street station. One day an officer named Ottway who had been sent to the Tobacco Floor for disciplinary reasons and who I had never seen in all the time I had been working there, turned up half an hour before pub opening time one morning and regaled us with amusing observations and jokes before inviting us to join him at Dirty Dick's. He lived in Southend and said he felt he ought to put in an appearance occasionally to comply with his punishment. I was amazed at how he managed to get away with it and couldn't help but admire his charming bravado. I never saw him again. I suspect he had private business interests and was stringing out his employment in Customs & Excise for as long as he could.

In the Bonhill Street Bond which I seem to recall was an annexe of the main Cutler Street warehouse, we received the remnants of the raw tobacco leaves used in the UK manufacture of cigarettes and pipe tobacco. On deposit in the bond, the UK manufacturers received a refund of the duty paid on the imported raw leaf depending on the type and weight of the remnants. The refund was known as duty drawback and was classified according to the different types of remnant consisting of stalks, offal and snuff. Each deposit had to be separately recorded in a huge warehouse register with an identifying rotation number before being weighed, spitted and the contents analysed for adulterants before being sent for destruction on a landfill sight to the east of London. I was sent to Bonhill Street for a few weeks to 'officiate' while the transfer system found a replacement for the previous fixed officer who had left on health grounds. The place was in a shambles and I quickly devoted my effort to sorting things out and made considerable progress before realising that the rotation numbers on the bags in the warehouse, apart from the ones I had personally taken in and assessed for drawback, bore no resemblance to the bags shown in the register as awaiting disposal. I decided that in order to bring matters under better control, I needed to personally supervise every aspect of the work including the physical receipt and disposal of bags by the resident Watcher who I quickly realised suffered from poor eyesight and had largely been left to his own devices by the previous fixed officer and officiating UOs. I listed the discrepancies and when the Surveyor paid a visit and asked me how I was getting on, I explained the situation to him and gave him my findings. You could commit rape or murder in Customs & Excise in those days and get away with it but let a single penny of revenue slip from the Treasury's maw and you would be burnt at the stake. All hell broke loose. In the following days Inspectors from the Chief Inspectors Office arrived and went through everything with a fine tooth comb to determine whether there had been any malpractice or revenue loss including visits to the landfill sight to ensure that the remnants had been securely buried and were not being reconstituted into cigarettes or pipe tobacco. I think they found that the bags were not being properly buried but there was no evidence of removal from the dump for improper use. They also found no evidence of deliberate malpractice by Departmental staff. This confirmed my view that this was a case of bungling incompetence rather than anything else. I didn't find out what happened subsequently to the half-blind Watcher.

Almost my final act before leaving London Port was to take a document for signature rescinding the Customs approval of St Katherine's Dock and after signature by the Dock owner, returning it to the Cutler Street Surveyor in his 'Clive of India' office. For me this was a historic moment as it signified the beginning of the inexorable process of progressive closure of the mighty London Docks that had supported the home country and an Empire for over two centuries, before being rejuvenated and transformed some years later into the modern residential and commercial Docklands area we know today.

# UNION OF TWO HOUSES

Ros and I became engaged to be married after I proposed to her in the kitchen at Casilla shortly after Martyn and Chicky had announced their engagement. I think my words were “How about it then?” not very romantic I admit but I’ve never been one for schmaltz. I had to ask her father’s permission which he gave and we celebrated in a lovely little restaurant at the top of Wimbledon Hill on 6 June 1964 where, during the meal, I placed on her finger a topaz and diamond ring she had chosen and I had bought at Halfhides the jewellers in Wimbledon. We reckoned that our engagement would last for around two years to allow time to arrange the wedding and for us to save for the honeymoon and a deposit for a home of our own. Ros said she wanted to get married in the first week in September because the weather was always good then so we settled on Saturday 3rd September 1966 as the date for the happy event.

To help save money for the wedding, we holidayed together in Devon and Cornwall with my brother and his girlfriend Christine in the summer of 1964. As custom demanded, Roger and I slept in one room and the girls in another. We spent the first week in Seaton in Devon staying in a guesthouse that was advertised in the Automobile Association Handbook as having a sea view and car parking. When we got there we found that the car parking consisted of the public car park some five hundred yards away for which you had to pay and the sea could only be viewed from a top floor landing as a tiny triangular patch of blue in the gap between neighbouring rooftops. The guesthouse was run by a mean-minded, middle-aged landlady whose invalid husband slept overnight in the breakfast room leaving stale air and a lingering body odour mingling with the toast, eggs and bacon. The hot water was not turned on until 5.30 pm in the afternoons so after a day on the beach you had to wait before you were able to wash and prepare for the evening. I complained to the landlady but got nowhere. Moreover, she insisted that we enter our names in a register in the hall showing when we came in and went out which I flatly refused to do. I was amazed when we left to find that other guests had written complimentary comments in the guest book. I did not follow their example. I put down exactly what I thought of the place – in short, awful. When I got back home I wrote to the Automobile Association telling them what I had found and how disappointed we had been with their recommendation. I never received a reply but noted with some satisfaction that in the following years Handbook this particular guest house no longer featured. For the second week we stayed in a typical Cornish farmhouse situated between Helston and Porthleven which was idyllic. The farmer wore tweeds and brown brogue shoes in the evening, his wife and two rosy cheeked daughters were warm and friendly and we ate hearty breakfasts in a sunny room with cows poking their heads through the open window to complete the rustic atmosphere.

Again, the following year we economised on our summer holiday by joining my mother and father on a trip to Normandy and Brittany in France. Again the sleeping arrangements meant that I shared a room with my father while Ros roomed with Mum. We drove in my father's Morris 1100 and would have ended up in Moscow if I had not been there with them to navigate. Especially in Brittany, English was not widely spoken. My father spoke no French. His recourse when he could not make himself understood was to talk more slowly and loudly in pigeon English until he was almost shouting. This proved mildly embarrassing on a few occasions but we got on well and had a good time visiting Dinard, an old haunt of my father's from his pre-marriage days and the D Day beaches. I remember one evening at a small seaside resort called Le Treport, going for a late evening walk along the cliff outside the town. Perched on the top was a café. The proprietor was packing up as we approached and had just turned the lights out. It must have been nearly 11 'clock on a calm mid-summer night but as soon as he spotted us heading towards him he turned the lights back on and removed the chairs from the tables inviting us to sit down which we did. We apologised for the lateness of the hour but he didn't turn a hair and despite the fact that we were the only customers, he was genuinely delighted to serve us with the nightcaps we ordered. Quite a contrast we all thought from the prevailing attitude amongst English proprietors of catering establishments who expected you to fit in with their narrow convenience rather than the other way round. In Brittany we stayed for a delightful week in the Hotel du Commerce situated at the very end of the bay in a lovely fishing village called Erquy with seven beautiful sandy beaches. In the late afternoon we would sit outside the hotel admiring the picturesque view of the harbour and fishing boats as we sipped our drinks. Suddenly the idyllic peace would be shattered as the local fishermen, joined by the local mayor, invaded the bar area and started conversing and playing cards in typically exuberant, noisy Gallic style; good fun!

On the work front, I was being paid subsistence and travelling expenses in addition to my salary which helped with our savings. I was now working locally, travelling around in my own car, assisting and officiating for the fixed officers in my home Collection of London South. I flitted about between a variety of General Excise Stations located at Wimbledon, where I had spent my Waiting Room days and which was now located in the Merton, South Wimbledon area, Putney, Sutton, Kingston, Croydon, Peckham, New Malden, Walton on Thames and Wandsworth. Gradually I began working up a fair amount of expertise in the brewery, distillery and wet warehousing regimes and found myself spending longer and longer spells, not just assisting fixed officers but increasingly officiating for them and covering unfilled vacancies: Watney's Mortlake Brewery, Gordon's Wandsworth Distillery and Linklater, Mackie Todd's Merton Abbey Bonded warehouse eventually became fixed stars in my Unattached Officer firmament.

At Wimbledon Excise late one morning I got stuck with an overweight, recently widowed mother of five children who had come to the office during our public opening hours to obtain a Grant of Probate in relation to the estate of her late husband who had died intestate; that is without leaving a will. In those days Excise officers were empowered by the government to grant probate for a small administrative fee to people who could not afford to employ a solicitor for the purpose. She began to weep uncontrollably asking me how she was supposed to cope with her five children and what would become of her. I sympathised with her but it got to the point where I couldn't stop her wailing. The time had passed when we normally closed the front door to the office and she was still crying her eyes out. I felt helpless. Fortunately one of the fixed officers who was wondering why the front door was still open saw through the glass panels at the top of the interview room that I was struggling and was able to intervene, pointing out that we were now closed for lunch and ushering her out into the street, much to my relief. On another occasion when I was dealing with a probate case at Sutton Excise, I forgot to administer the oath that applicants were obliged to swear on an officially provided copy of the Bible. I had to take the bible and documents round to the person's house that same night and administer the oath there. I remember I had planned to go out with friends that evening and was unable to do so; the more so as my car broke down on the way back prompting me to utter an oath of a different, non-sacred kind.

At Walton-on-Thames Excise, where, in wintertime, the first job of the day was to bring the coal in and light the fire in the main office, I went one day on a 'cautionary' visit to a still user. Cautionary visits were paid without prior notification to businesses and establishments handling or selling alcoholic spirits and related equipment under licence. The aim of the survey was to check that the alcohol and the associated equipment with which they were dealing was being used for commercial purposes, according to the licence provisions, and not for the drinks trade thereby evading the excise duty on spirits produced for human consumption. We also paid cautionary visits to pubs to check that they were not selling illicit spirits and that they were not boosting the alcohol content of their beer by adding sugar to the barrels stored in the cellar. Contrary to popular belief we were not responsible for checking the measures they sold: this was the responsibility of the Weights & Measures Division of the Board of Trade. The rationale for cautionary work was always a bit tenuous and I suspect some fixed officers who found the concept rather embarrassing and a waste of time from a cost-effective point of view, recorded in their survey books cautionary work they had not actually performed. This was known as 'stamping'. On this particular occasion the 'still user' turned out to be a smart Catholic Girls school run by nuns. To say that I found this episode embarrassing would be no understatement. I arrived at the school entrance via a long tree-lined drive around 11 am on a sunny morning and was ushered into the presence of the Mother Superior to whom I had to explain my sudden appearance and purpose of my visit. She arranged for me to be escorted by one of the nuns to the school chemistry laboratory where the still was apparently located. When we arrived at the lab, I found that a lesson was in progress. The nun escorting me knocked on the door and we entered. All eyes turned in my direction as my escort explained to the nun conducting the class what I was there to do. A deathly silence descended, cloaking suppressed giggles as I moved to the other side of the room by the window where the still was mounted on a work bench by a sink. I tried not to look but could feel the eyes and pigtails of the serried ranks of young girls in their smart grey and white uniforms following me round the room. I tried to assume a professional air while I examined the still which turned out to be a small, innocuous, glass contraption producing pure distilled water for chemical experiments in the lab. Becoming increasingly conscious that the girls were casting admiring glances at my backside and legs, I asked the nun in charge of the class the obligatory questions about the use to which the still was being put, evoking further suppressed giggles. I apologised for interrupting her class, thanked her for her assistance and left. I thought at the time that this was my most embarrassing moment. And if you forgive the play on words, I **still** think this represents my most embarrassing moment.

I got stuck into a concerted spell of cautionary work at Wandsworth Excise for want of anything better to do while the fixed officer was away on holiday for three weeks. He had not left me any instructions and I thought that in the circumstances I had done him a favour. Apparently not; because he rang me at my next station on the Monday morning, furious that I had completed all his outstanding cautionary work in three weeks which he had planned to extend over twelve months. Excise stations were staffed on what was known as the Units System whereby visits and administrative and clerical duties were each given a time allowance negotiated by the Federation, the Union representing the Officers of Customs & Excise and the Official Side representing the Board of Customs & Excise Commissioners. By a combination of these agreed and often generous allowances coupled with a degree of creative accounting many stations although nominally schemed on the 1600 annual working hours basis were in reality lightly loaded. Many excise officers had hobbies they pursued and others ran businesses in parallel with their official duties. In scooting round in my Austin A30 mopping up all his cautionary in three weeks I had exposed the underlying lightness of his station and he was not best pleased.

Embarrassment of a different kind came at the end of a visit to a purchase tax trader one afternoon while I was at Wimbledon Excise. One of the discretionary checks was to examine the Annual Accounts and Nominal or Private Ledger containing information about the assets and financial status of thc business. We had no legal right to examine these records but could ask to see them. I noticed from the record of previous visits to this business that this check had not been performed for some while so decided to ask the proprietor for the documents in question. I asked politely and was subjected to an angry tirade and blank refusal. I managed to calm the man down after a while and he eventually agreed to let me see the records. It turned out that he had been incensed by the rude and officious manner adopted by the last visiting officer attempting to perform the same check and after all that time was still seething about his behaviour. When I got back to the office I discovered that a Mr Newsome, the previous Surveyor, nicknamed 'Nuisance' because of his habit of needlessly riling traders had paid the visit in question from which I had felt the still reverberating aftershock.

At Kingston Excise I was embarrassed by the sheer volume of drawback claims on large shiny official forms which came pouring out like a waterfall from the olive green standard issue Stationary Office metal cupboard when I opened the door. When I told the Surveyor about the contents of the cupboard, he told me he was aware of the problem and not to worry, so I piled the bills back inside and quickly shut the door. Apparently, the fixed officer was on sick leave suffering from mental problems. I must admit I was a little surprised that the trader who had submitted the claims was not making more of a fuss about getting his money back, although traders were very indulgent and deferential in their dealings with our Department in those days. Moreover, the Department itself was much more lenient than would be the case nowadays in the attitude it adopted towards its officers found to be suffering from stress or the ever present occupational hazard in wet warehouses of habitual drinking and alcoholism. In Merton Abbey Bonded warehouse specialising in the importation of South African 'Dry Fly' sherry, where I spent a number of months, I got used to drinking regular tots of sherry, wine and brandy with the fixed officers at intervals during the working day. So much so that when at Christmas my father offered me a glass of sherry I downed it in one or two well practised gulps. He was obviously shocked at how quickly I had emptied the glass and made a comment that made me realise just how much my regular drinking habit at the Bond was surreptitiously extending my tolerance beyond acceptable limits. I resolved to be a bit more guarded in future bearing in mind the numerous stories that circulated about warehouse officers who were drunk for most of the working day including the officer in Metropolitan Vaults, London who had to drink a beaker full of brandy before he could sign on in the morning and the officer who was so drunk he had to be hid upright in the office cupboard whenever the Surveyor or Inspectors called. I remember one afternoon at Merton Abbey when the Surveyor appeared unannounced in the office as the two fixed officers were finishing off a tot of brandy from a measuring jar. The Surveyor who was a mild mannered and quietly spoken Irishman sat down at the desk opposite Mr Bennett the senior fixed officer. The atmosphere was tense and I was waiting for the Surveyor to say something whereupon Mr Bennett coyly pushed the measuring jar towards the

Surveyor as an invitation to partake, which, to my surprise, he did, struggling to raise the heavy glass jar in both hands to his trembling lips before nervously taking a sip. Mr Bennett offered the Surveyor a toast, to which he meekly replied, sealing his complicity. Mr Bennett's perennial maxim was that you should only take alcohol out from the bond inside your own stomach, on the rather dubious moral grounds that you could not then be accused of stealing and that consumption was confined to officially drawn samples which were in any case due to be disposed of as waste down the sink after testing. I survived an extended period working there without slipping too heavily into the drinking routine. Towards the end of my time there, I was engaged by the Collector to reconcile the triennial stocktaking that had taken place over one weekend. I spent several weeks reconciling the differences between the physical stock in the warehouse and the book stock in the warehouse ledgers, whittling the difference down to a very small number of bottles. However a total reconciliation proved impossible to achieve. I got to the point where I felt I was trying to reconcile the irreconcilable and the Collector agreed, commending me on the work I had done.

At Watney's Mortlake Brewery the 'provided' office was palatial and located at the top of the brew house affording a magnificent view of the River Thames where the University Boat Race finished each year. I took Ros there in 1965 for the boat race where we mingled with various local dignitaries and the brewery management, who were allowed, for the purposes of this one occasion only, to reclaim 'our' office. An enormous window and external balcony ran the forty foot length of the room providing an unrivalled grandstand view of the finish of the race.

The brewery was 'coursed': that is, the two fixed officers worked shifts because brewing went on round the clock seven days a week. I covered one of these two posts for several months before the fixed officer was eventually appointed and arrived. Each day the brewer would deliver two quart bottles of freshly brewed beer for our refreshment throughout the day, a gift for which we were grateful but never abused. I became expert in the brewing business and greatly enjoyed my time there. John Drysdale, the other fixed officer, was a real gentleman and I greatly respected his integrity and enjoyed his companionship. I only blotted my copybook once at the brewery when helping the Surveyor, Horace Pett to reguage the 'drip' at the bottom of a collecting vessel by omitting, on the five bar gate system, to count one of the copper jugs full of water that we had emptied into it. I was annoyed with myself and apologised to Horace for letting him down and for the extra work we had to do starting all over again from the beginning. He was obviously disappointed that I had made a mistake through a lapse in concentration but graciously accepted my apology and we swiftly got the job done without more ado. I never made a mistake calculating the 'presumptive' charge. This was a calculation using a complicated formula which enabled us to calculate the quantity and strength of beer which would normally be produced from the declared raw ingredients. It was a sort of double check supplementing the physical checks we made on the unfermented beer or 'wort' as it was known in the trade. We had a strange hand operated machine to help us perform the calculation which was affectionately known as the Mortlake Wurlitzer. It was composed of cogs, rotors and levers and was operated by a small handle at the side that had to be variously and vigorously rotated clockwise and then anti-clockwise or vice versa a specified number of times in order to reveal the answer, which was then displayed on numbered, typewriter-style keys.

I finished my course one afternoon having parked my car outside a riverside pub adjacent to the brewery to find that the river had risen above the embankment and my little vehicle was up to its axles in water. I managed to wade through the small lake that had formed around it and get it started. Needless to say I didn't make the mistake of parking there again. Foolishly, I had overlooked the fact that the tidal effects on the water level at certain times of year can be quite pronounced even as high up the Thames as Mortlake. The effect of the tide is only finally neutralised at Teddington – hence the name 'Tide Ending Town'.

The vacant post was eventually filled by an Unattached Officer transferring on first fixity from one of the Scottish Collections. The delay in filling the vacancy was partly due to the fact that he had hoped to secure a fixed post nearer his Scottish home but mainly because vacancies in Scotland were highly sought after and all vacancies were filled on a seniority basis. He was unsuccessful and had to accept the residual Mortlake post. I spent a couple of weeks with him showing him the ropes and commiserating with him about the domestic and financial difficulties he was encountering in moving himself and his family down to the London area. That mission accomplished, I bade a sad farewell to Mortlake Brewery and served the remainder of my days in London South Collection some miles downriver at Wandsworth Distillery.

The distillery occupied a riverside site, producing on an industrial scale virtually neat alcohol from molasses, a derivative of sugar cane, shipped there by specially adapted barges. The spirit, once it had been produced, was sold, duty paid, to the London gin houses such as Gordon's where it was reduced (diluted) with liquor (water) and rectified (re-distilled) with flavourings such as juniper berries before being bottled and sold to the public. The waste fractions from the distillation process known as 'feints' were collected and held in an open air tank immediately adjacent to the main entrance and public road. The odour from this tank was nauseating and, driven by the prevailing winds, tended to waft over a nearby block of Council flats. Talk about feeling faint from the feints! This sort of environmental spoliation would, quite rightly, never be permitted today. It was undeniably the dirtiest and smelliest place in which I had ever worked but there were compensations.

The provided office was an old Georgian house which stood like a faded, yet still elegant oasis in the middle of towering still-houses, spirit warehouses and general industrial rubble strewn about the site. With the exception of the young and likeable Surveyor who died suddenly of a brain tumour, the cast of characters making up the Station complement were like something out of a Dickens novel. There was the comparatively young fixed officer who always won at darts in the office. He lived locally and played football for Wimbledon one of the leading amateur teams of the day. He was a highly talented, naturally gifted sportsman who could have easily played at professional level but alas in those days his salary in Customs & Excise vastly outweighed the wages he would have earned by belonging to a professional football club. There was Kemp the most miserable man I have ever come across whose creased, down-turned, features mirrored his demeanour but who occasionally revealed a dry sarcastic wit. There was Bob Holt who had transferred to Customs & Excise from the Colonial Office who drank himself to death on the raw spirits he smuggled in sample bottles from the still-house in the pockets of his white cotton coat that we all had to wear when surveying the plant. He would retreat into the office toilet where he would remain for some time downing his tipple before emerging with his face pulsing with a ruddy glow induced by the alcohol he had consumed. It seemed a far cry for him from the days of the sundown gin and tonics he had no doubt imbibed on the colonial verandas in the disappearing years of the British Empire. He thought no-one knew what he was up to and tried to maintain his dignity with us. But of course everybody knew and found it rather sad. There was the ex RAF officer who was so intelligent he could multiply multiple digit numbers in his head and write down the answer on one line. There was the ghoulish, greasy black haired, bulging eyed individual who professed a smirking affinity with the rats that could be seen at night scampering around, feeding on molasses stuck to gangplanks and stairways. He travelled to and fro between the distillery on a pre-war motorbike and side car. He used the side car to transport lumps of wood and other flotsam and jetsam he personally fished from the river for a garden shed he was constructing at his private house. When questioned about this somewhat odd and unbecoming practice he could barely contain his glee, telling us how much money he was saving himself.

I shall never forget the day when I witnessed one of the workers engaged on the construction of a new still-house fall from the surrounding scaffolding after it had been hit by the moving jib of a crane. He fell about forty feet and landed face down in an area strewn with metal parts and building materials. It all seemed to happen in slow motion. Someone in the office immediately rang 999. We were all convinced that he must have been killed or at least severely injured in his fall but miraculously he had landed in a small, clear patch of soft earth and the only injury he had suffered was a broken wrist.

At the end of 1965, the 'Parker Reorganisation' finally rang down the curtain on the old style Department, full of independent minded, eccentric characters and judged by today's standards, laughable inefficiencies and prejudices. Since joining the Department in 1960, as an Unattached Officer, I at last had the chance to apply for my own fixed station. Because of my relative juniority, I only managed to secure my 75$^{th}$ choice out of 77 fixed stations in my chosen Collections and was appointed from 1 January 1966 to Notting Hill Excise in Praed Street, London, close to Paddington Railway Station. Notting Hill lay in the North Kensington area of London. It shared the same Regency and Victorian stock of housing as its sister borough of South Kensington but unlike the latter had become very seedy and rundown. It was unpopular for this reason as an area in which to work and also because there had been race riots there not long before. The Surveyor, a lovely man named Ray Williams who was the spitting image of Charlie Barlow, a popular character in the TV cop series of the time called Z Cars, had the name changed after a couple of years to the more upmarket Bayswater to make recruitment easier. I remember complaining to Ray one day that I couldn't see how I could afford the house, car and children that went with married life but he told me not to worry and that we would manage somehow, adding that he had experienced the self-same doubts before he got married and it had all worked out well in the end. He had a bubbly laugh and a great sense of humour and I came across him from time to time throughout my career.

Before engaging in the tortuous and expensive business of searching for and purchasing a home of our own, Ros and I had been waiting to find out where I would get fixed. The price of property where we lived was beyond our reach. Ros was working in the City of London for a petrochemical construction company called Lummus and with my appointment to Notting Hill, we decided to search for somewhere within commuting distance of Paddington Station. At the time, the Western Region Division of British Rail was offering commuters big discounts on monthly season tickets. This prompted us to extend our search westwards outside London. In Berkshire at Arborfield Cross, south of Reading an attractive terrace of four houses was being built. We liked the look of the design and the specification which included three bedrooms, an integral garage, central heating and gardens front and back. And, importantly, we could afford the asking price of £4750. We drove over and inspected the site which was situated in a short length of road named Chamberlain Gardens in a predominantly rural setting and decided to put a deposit down on the end terrace plot bordered by long gardens stretching back from a collection of Victorian properties on the main Eversley Road. Chamberlain Gardens contained no other houses and came to a dead end where our future house was under construction. Out of curiosity, I went back to our old house recently when I happened to be in the area and was saddened to find how much the immediate surroundings have degenerated over the years. The Victorian gardens and what had once been open land opposite have disappeared, replaced by closely packed houses of little architectural merit. Chamberlain Gardens, which ended where our house stood, is now a through road, giving a gloomy, claustrophobic feel to the place. However this was all in the future.

The house was finished in time for our wedding – just. We paid the required deposit of £1000, representing the legal obligatory minimum 20% of the purchase price, which we saved over the two years of our engagement and took possession of the keys arranging at the same time for the modern Scandinavian designed furniture we had seen and bought at the Ideal Home Exhibition to be installed along with the electric cooker and the clothes tub. I was now the proud holder of a mortgage which I had obtained from the Civil Service Building Society who, unlike the other lenders we tried, allowed me to borrow up to three times my salary rather than the, then, standard two and a half times. Without this additional flexibility we would have struggled to complete the purchase. As it was, we could not afford a television, telephone or carpets. We had a fridge. Also, instead of a washing machine, we had a more rudimentary 'Baby Burco' tub for washing clothes which boiled over, flooding the kitchen floor with hot water the first time Ros attempted to use it. But we were more than happy to make small sacrifices such as these for the privilege of becoming home owners in our own right.

On Saturday 3rd September 1966, we were married in Ros' local church, St Mary's, Merton Park. We had worked hard in the months and weeks leading up to the ceremony to make sure that everything would run smoothly on the day and so it did. Waiting for her to arrive in the church on her father's arm, I remember thinking that I was sitting on the same spot on the front pew where Lord Nelson had sat before departing for the last time from his home in Merton to join the fleet off Cape Trafalgar. As the church filled with our respective families and friends, I was stirred by the towering, tumbling torrent of organ notes reverberating round the ancient church as the organist played Bach's Toccata and Fugue in D Minor – one of my all time favourites that we had asked to be played while the guests took their seats. The organist insisted, rightly, in playing the whole piece, including the sublime and dramatic conclusion, even though this meant keeping Ros and her father waiting outside for a few minutes. It was a fitting introduction. She looked fantastic. I had no doubt that I wanted to marry her and affirmed my marriage vows loudly and clearly. It was a great day and I enjoyed every moment. The weather was beautiful as Ros had predicted and everything went smoothly.

The reception was held at the Crown Inn in Morden and I remember driving away in my Austin A30 suitably decorated with foam, confetti and an old tin can tied to the back bumper rattling on the road behind us as we took our leave of friends and family for the first time as a newly married couple. We drove to our new house in Arborfield where I cleaned the car thoroughly, removing the foam, confetti, tin can and a smelly kipper that I found on the engine when I opened the bonnet. That evening we drove to Frimley Hall, a very posh restaurant in those days where we had made a booking for dinner. On the journey there, I could still hear a rattling sound coming from the underside of the car despite the fact that I had removed the trailing tin can. As we approached the restaurant, set in a large park with a lake and long gravel drive, the rattling sound became worse and I was getting embarrassed as we slowed to a halt in front of the main entrance. I can't remember whether it was then or later that evening that someone told me that the noise was caused by coins in the hub caps which clattered around at slow speed when not held by centrifugal force. I removed the hub caps and - lo and behold – found coins our friends had put there. I thought it was a pretty clever wheeze.

That night, in our new house, we slept in the same bed together for the first time and drove the following day to London Airport at Heathrow to catch our flight to Majorca for our honeymoon. When we got to Heathrow, the terminal building was packed and after saying goodbye to family members who had driven over to wish us well, we were ushered through the waiting crowds by airport staff so that we would not miss our flight. The aircraft was a four-engine, propeller driven Bristol Brittania, nicknamed 'the whispering giant'. We sat at the back one row in front of another honeymoon couple who were heading for the same resort and hotel as we were. The noise from the engines, far from whispering, rose to a deafening crescendo as the aircraft struggled to surmount the Pyrenees Mountains. However, we landed safely and travelled across the island by single track electric train to the terminus at Soller and then by tram to our hotel in Puerto de Soller, set in a horse-shoe shaped bay on the west side of the island.

We had an enjoyable two weeks and returned to start our married life proper in our new house in Arborfield Cross. Both sets of parents were disappointed that we had moved so far away, to a part of the country, virtually unknown to them. Neither really appreciated the economic constraints that led us to put our own roots down in Berkshire but I have never regretted moving away from the area where we both grew up and would not wish to return even if we could afford it. Initially I continued playing rugby for my school old boy's side at Claygate near Esher and most weekends we would drop into see one or other set of parents for Sunday lunch. However the journey used to get a bit tedious just to play a game of rugby and the following year I joined Bracknell Rugby Club which was a lot closer. I thoroughly enjoyed my last three years at Bracknell playing the game I loved. I enjoyed playing for once with a pack of forwards who could produce decent ball for a set of backs who were pretty tasty, I may say, myself included. After joining the club and starting in the lower sides I was spotted by a leading official of the club and quickly promoted to the first fifteen. He was a lovely man and gave me some very good advice about running lines and offensive kicking. It was a very friendly club and we all got on well together. The clubhouse was a hut standing across the road from the main pitch and from the present day double storey clubhouse behind the Running Horses Pub. Led by our well spoken but down to earth and friendly captain, Jim Monk, a former army officer, we were virtually unbeaten for the three seasons that I played for them.

We still saw our families of course and friends from Merton and Morden and sometimes they ventured out to visit us at the weekend. I put a lot of work into building a back garden from scratch, complete with patio steps and retaining walls on fairly steeply sloping ground and was pleased with the finished effect. We grew some colourful plants, shrubs and trees on both front and back gardens. The old boy that lived with his aged sister in the Victorian house whose garden bordered ours was always pottering around in his extensive vegetable patch. He was Berkshire born and bred and spoke with a wonderfully rustic Berkshire twang referring once to a jet aircraft flying overhead as 'one of thum thurr new fungled corntrarrptions'. He sported a walrus style moustache and always wore a flat hat and striped collarless 'grandfather' style shirt, with waistcoat, pocket watch and chain. Often we would come home from work to find that he had left vegetables from his garden on our back lawn for us. The garden and his vegetables were his great love. Ros would make him an apple tart in recompense which he always greatly enjoyed. Appropriately, he died in his beloved garden one day, while we were both at work in London.

After one of my last games for my Old Boys side, playing in my favourite position of outside centre, before joining Bracknell, where I also played in the centre and occasionally on the wing, my brother Roger and his girlfriend Ann, who he was later to marry, drove back to Arborfield in procession in our respective Austin A30s, in order to spend the remainder of the weekend with Ros and me. Before leaving the clubhouse Roger and I had drank the usual post-match four pints of bitter: this was before modern drink-drive legislation was introduced enforced by breathalysers. It was of no concern to us therefore that we were over the alcohol limit as it is understood nowadays. However when we fell behind a police car on the long winding narrow main road from Virginia Water to Wokingham I became increasingly uneasy because the police car was going so slowly and the four pints I had drunk were rapidly working their way through my bodily irrigation system and Roger's system also I presumed and I could not overtake without breaking the speed limit which was an enforceable offence. Had I overtaken, I also ran the risk of losing Roger and Ann behind me who had not driven to our house before and didn't know the way. So we were stuck there both of us with the strain of ever bulging bladders becoming increasingly unbearable. But there was nothing we could do except drive with patience and decorum. Finally after what seemed like a lifetime of growing torment we reached the market square in Wokingham where we had to turn off onto a by-road for Arborfield Cross. Fortunately the police car continued its stately progress on the main road heading for Reading. I knew, although Roger didn't, that there was a grimy public toilet located in an old Victorian brick-built civic building in the middle of the square and as the police car faded at last from view, I screeched to a halt, leapt out of my car and hurtled across the road towards the 'Gents' toilet hopeing that it would not be shut. My brother instantaneously screeched to a halt behind me, leapt out of his car and dashed after me. Mercifully the toilet was still open. Neither of us said anything but our relief was indescribable. The girls were highly amused. Ann brought the subject up recently when she visited and was still laughing about the incident some forty years later.

We had a lovely little pub called the Bull at Arborfield Cross just round the corner from our house where we used to take friends and family when they were visiting. The landlord was a generously proportioned man named Frank. He and his wife had twin daughters and had come to this part of Berkshire from the Midlands. There was the usual relatively large public bar at the front and a small saloon bar at the back where we used to drink complete with open fire and separate serving hatch. Frank's wife was a statuesque lady of great charm who he betrayed having conducted an affair with the bar maid appropriately named Rosie to match her healthy ruddy complexion. A local lass born and bred, she was no match for Frank's wife in terms of personality and business acumen but had other assets which were often displayed to enticing effect in white frilly open necked blouses contrasting the broad belts and tightly fitting black skirts and high heels she habitually wore.

Walking down the road away from the pub towards the pretty and peaceful area of Swallowfield one Sunday afternoon with friends, we passed a local farmer who had been out shooting pheasants. We said hello and he promptly gave us a brace of pheasants to hang and cook. It was a spontaneous and friendly gesture and I graciously accepted the unexpected gift. I hung the pheasants in the garage for a few days meaning to pluck them and cook them but was put off by the smell and regretfully decide to consign them to the dustbin. It was another small example of how friendly and accommodating the indigenous members of the largely rural local community were towards people, like us, moving in from urban areas and how accommodating they were towards the housing and other infrastructure developments that were being brought in our train.

Shortly after we started living at Arborfield my mother went through a disturbing phase, probably caused by psychological strain from the onset of the menopause, my leaving home - I was her favourite - and the prospect of my brother and sister also moving away in due course, leaving her with my father in his fast approaching retirement. His often stated purpose in retirement was to do as little as possible, a prospect that didn't fill my mother with great enthusiasm or excitement. Anyway, in addition to becoming embarrassingly paranoiac about my sister's male friends, she demanded I return my house key and subsequently accused Ros of stealing her gold wristwatch. As a newly married couple this was the last complication we wanted or foresaw. The whole episode was quite surreal. In the end Ros' father wrote to my father who wrote to me and we all met in a restaurant in London. No mention was made of the accusation. Relations improved thereafter, eventually normalising, thank goodness. I suspect that, subliminally, she blamed Ros for taking me, her first born, away from her. I believe she later found the watch in the garden where it had probably fallen off her wrist while she was gardening. But again, nothing was ever said. I loved my mother and still do. I was angry with her at the time but this feeling quickly passed.

Before we got married my mother had agreed to loan me the money to replace my ageing Austin A30 but when we visited them on our return from honeymoon my mother told me that my father had ruled against it. She was sorry that she couldn't help but I accepted the situation. I was disappointed that my father had adopted this attitude because I had religiously paid back the loan my mother had made to me to buy the A30 in the first place and there was no question of me defaulting this time round. I remember driving back to Arborfield Cross that night thinking as we passed along the Staines By-Pass that Ros and I were really on our own now and we had to stand on our own two feet. In a way, I was glad that my father had forced this attitude on us and I never resented it afterwards – well only a little bit anyway. The upshot was that I had to continue running the A30.

I have owned several cars over the years, including a Morris 1000, Ford Cortina and a string of Hondas, all purchased second-hand with the aid of financial loans from Frizzells the insurance company who provided preferential rates to civil servants. My only brand new car was a leather-seated, olive-green Simca saloon, to which I treated myself when I picked up my first substantive promotion. I currently drive a Honda Insight Hybrid which I bought with savings from my retirement pension lump sum. I have enjoyed owning and driving all these cars but my little grey Austin A30, evokes my fondest memories despite all the hastle of maintaining and keeping it on the road, which I did myself, adjusting and replacing oil, water, tyres, batteries, water pumps, radiators, hoses, bulbs, brake cylinders, brake fluid, exhausts, tappets, points, gaskets and sparking plugs which unlike today, seemed to wear out every few months. Though I am not mechanically minded or fond for its own sake of tinkering around with cars, I became, by necessity, relatively knowledgeable and proficient in car mechanics. I grunted and groaned over and under my car. Despite all my attention, life with my little grey RYK 779 was never without incident.

There was the time before we got married when Ros and I with Martyn and Chicky early in our developing relationships, drove down to the South coast in my little car. We had been on the beach and I was driving back along a particularly winding stretch of road across the Romney Marsh when I played the gallant by attempting to swat a small sand beetle that was buzzing around having become ensnared in Ros' mohair jumper. Unfortunately I took my eye off the road for too long, missed the bend and ended up with the car, passengers and beetle perched on a concrete fence post having felled the previous three. The sheep in the field continued grazing and appeared completely unperturbed. I felt such a fool. I can't remember how we got home. The car was stuck on the post. The engine had died and could not be restarted. I guess we must have walked to my friend Tim Biddiscombe's parent's house in Hythe who, after putting us on a train to Waterloo and thence back home, kindly organised for the car to be recovered and repaired. My main concern was that the sheep would stray onto the road through the gap in the fence I had created, causing further accidents and possible loss of life. In the event, and much to my relief, this didn't happen and a week or so later I was able to return to the area to collect the car after it had been restored to its old self. I had apparently and not surprisingly cracked the sump underneath the engine and lost the engine lubricating oil in bouncing over the posts. I was assured that no sheep or passing motorist had been killed and the fence had been restored. I counted myself lucky. I can still picture my little car perched on the last post with a sad but proud smile on its face.

In the last three years of its life, when I should have replaced it for safety's sake but couldn't afford to, it never ceased to surprise and frustrate me. For our first holiday after we got married, I drove it uneventfully all the way to Cornwall and back, spending sunny days lying on the beach at Prah Sands, consuming locally baked Cornish Pasties for lunch and staying at the farmhouse outside

Helston where we had enjoyed such a pleasant time on summer holiday three years earlier. My brother and his then girlfriend, Christine, shared this holiday with us; Roger driving his own Austin A30, a black, slightly later version than mine, but not nearly so quirky and lovable, as far as I was concerned. The following year Ros and I again drove down to the West Country for our annual holiday which we spent with Roger and his new wife Ann who came from Ottery St Mary in Devon. They were teaching in local schools and living in Kentisbeare while they were saving up to buy a place of their own. They had rented a self contained flat in a farmhouse occupying the whole of the first floor. Driving there, I had my usual intermittent problem with the car hooter. Sometimes it would work when I pushed the button, housed in a plastic cap on the top of the steering column, and at other times, for some strange and perverse reason, nothing would happen. I could often remedy this fault by twisting the plastic cap until electrical contact was restored. However, this time I couldn't get it to work no matter which way I twisted the cap and it fell off the steering column altogether. Disgusted with it, I left it lying in the foot-well, where it had fallen, until a few days later when we were going out one evening to a local pub for a drink with Roger and Ann. For the short journey to the pub and back, I thought it would be better to replace the cap on the steering column. I didn't want to invite attention from the local police for driving around without a functioning hooter and then have them quiz me about my alcohol consumption. We had a pleasant evening which passed without any police intervention and returned to the farmhouse. I parked in the usual place in the farmyard, turned the engine off, removed the ignition key and locked the car before we all trooped upstairs to the flat. We had been sitting there for about ten minutes when suddenly, the car hooter started sounding. I looked out the flat window not knowing quite what to expect. I couldn't really believe what I saw. My little car was sitting there, in serene isolation, exactly as I had left it, with the hooter emitting a monotone beeping noise, breaking the rustic peace of a beautiful summer's evening. I dashed downstairs into the farmyard, unlocked the car and managed to stop it sounding. I then cello-taped the cap in the position it was in. The hooter worked for the remainder of the holiday and journey home, reverting only later to its more familiar intermittently unreliable state. The farmer and his family were as amused as we were by the weird quirk of nature we had witnessed.

Ros and I were also amused one day when I left the car in the garage at our house and returned a little later to find the garage empty. I sensed something was not quite right and looked around. Across the street, upright on some wasteland on the other side of Chamberlain Gardens where houses now stand, was my little car. The hand-break never worked particularly well. While I was in the house, the car had rolled, in reverse, out of the garage, down the relatively steep slope of our front drive, across Chamberlain Gardens, surmounting the pavement on the other side and coming to rest on tufted grass and low brushwood on the open ground. Fortunately no cars or people had been coming along the road as it glided silently across.

Driving in summer was one thing but with the onset of winter in 1968, journeys became ever more hazardous and uncomfortable. I had holes round the jacking points where the bodywork had crumpled and rusted. These I repaired, more from a cosmetic point of view than load bearing. I also had a growing hole in the front foot-well on the passenger side which was covered with a piece of carpet to keep the cold air and road water out; not altogether successfully. The heater was unreliable and generated very little warmth. Ros whose feet were placed either side of the hole would wrap her feet and legs in the car rug in an effort to keep warm. But this was particularly trying on long journeys. Added to these deficiencies the steering joints and suspension were heavily worn. At any speed above 30mph, the car would go into an uncontrollable shake if I hit a large bump or hole in the road. I knew every crack and sunken manhole cover on the way to and from our parents in Merton and Morden Park who we visited regularly at the weekends and was able to steer round them. In January of 1969 I took my car for its first MOT into a garage in Twyford where we used to catch the train for commuting to London where we were both working at the time. I fully expected to return after work that evening to find that it had failed principally because of the loose joints. However, it had been a freezing cold day. The joints had frozen solid and the garage could detect no excessive play between them. Ros had carried on working after we got married partly so we could save up for a new car. We were still saving so I carried on avoiding bumps and holes in the road until a few weeks later when I became really alarmed about the cars behaviour after a long drive back from my brother's house in Ottery St Mary where he and Ann were now living. Reluctantly in some ways I decided to get rid of it and received the princely sum of £5 for it in part exchange for a second-hand, front wheel drive, Morris 1100 with hydrolastic suspension. About a week later, at home one evening after dinner, there was a knock at the door. I opened it to find a local policeman standing there who asked me if I was the owner of Austin A30 registration number RYK 779. I replied that I had been the owner up to a week ago but had sold it to the garage from whom I had bought my new car. I asked him what the problem was and he told me that my little car had been found abandoned with wheels and tyres missing at Bourne End. I felt really sorry and pictured it in my mind lying there bereft of dignity. In another way I suppose it had never failed to surprise me and this final act of it's over timely death at a place aptly named 'Bourne End' seemed oddly fitting.

In the summer of 1969, we drove in my new Morris 1100 to Garmisch-Partenkirken in Bavaria with my school friend Tim Biddiscombe and his wife Jenny. Later, when Tim was working for the European Union and living in Brussels, Jenny eloped with a delegate from Custom & Excise who eventually became a Commissioner. However on our trip together they seemed happy in each other's company and subsequently produced two children, Rupert to whom I was godfather and Alice before they divorced in due course. I was interviewed by a Military Intelligence Officer as part of Tim's vetting for the Brussels appointment and felt obliged to disclose that in the early 60s Tim and I had attended the Ban The Bomb March protest meeting held in Trafalgar Square but that neither of us had strong leanings in that direction politically and went along for amusement and to experience an interesting day out as much as anything.

On the way down, we stopped in Munich. We found a hotel for the night on the Garmisch side of Munich and decided to pop into town in the evening to show the girls some of the sights and to visit the famous Hofbrauhaus beer hall for 'a swift half'. Ros was pregnant with Simon at the time, so we agreed we would not stay out late. We had our drink and were just about to leave when we got talking to a Jewish lad from Scotland who was sitting at the adjoining table. He bought us a beer and we bought him one and the next thing I remember was standing on the table with him and Tim singing Jerusalem and Rule Brittania at the tops of our voices to an empty beer hall. It was late and everyone else had left. Our audience consisted of two security guards dressed in semi-military uniforms and peaked World War II type caps who seemed benign enough, although they clearly wanted us to leave so they could shut up for the night. Very amiably inebriated, we acquiesced and in the street outside haled a taxi to take us back to our hotel, whose name we had inconveniently forgotten. We did eventually find our way back and went up to our respective bedrooms via an enormous staircase which I was having difficulty negotiating – two steps up one step back – that sort of thing – amidst much barely suppressed giggling and finger to mouth shoooshing - so that we might not awaken the other guests. I spent the first half of the night lying in bed watching the ceiling revolving and fighting the urge to go into the bathroom to unburden myself of the evening's pleasures. Eventually I succumbed; much to Ros' relief who had remained stone cold sober throughout. Her only consolation was that despite losing some hours sleep to my groaning and moaning, she was considerably fresher than Tim or me as we ate our breakfast in the morning sunshine on a pretty little terrace with views towards the Bavarian Alps where we were heading. We had a good holiday, playing badminton on the veranda of our chalet and hiking in the mountains.

Back home, Ros and I continued our early married life together at Arborfield Cross. It wasn't always easy. Looking back I used to say, partly in jest, that the first three years were the worst as we adjusted to living with one another. I don't think we will ever achieve complete, undying harmony. I regret the disagreements and rows, fortunately, greatly outweighed by good times, passion and shared values. I will never fully understand her. But I'm surc I'm not the only man on the planet that finds members of the female sex both fatally alluring and utterly perplexing at the same time.

We became friendly with a number of people through the rugby club and local church and enjoyed the company of Yvonne and Bill who lived on the other end of our terrace of four houses. He was a Captain in the army and worked as a lecturer down the road on the outskirts of Arborfield itself where there was a sizable army camp housing the regiment of Royal Electrical and Mechanical Engineers. I started playing squash with Bill after my last year playing rugby. We haven't seen him and Yvonne for years but we still exchange Christmas cards. We still see my old school friends Robbie Stevenson and his wife Margaret. I used to play tennis with Robbie in my youth and we both attended the St James Youth Club in Morden where, on a very windy day in the summer of 1963, he got married, with me acting as his best man. Our families have grown up together and are part of our extended 'family'. Similarly, from those pre-married and early post married days, we have retained our friendship with Terry French and his wife Vicky whose eldest son Richard, is my godson. Ros also met Brenda one of her sister Christine's school friends when doing the weekly shop in Wokingham. Although we both moved away from the Wokingham-Arborfield area subsequently, we have remained in touch with her and her husband Del and get together a couple of times a year. The same might be said about Martyn Bond and Chicky but the effort to stay in touch mainly came from our side. I am godfather to their eldest son, Morgan. This culminated in their unexplained failure to turn up for Ros' sixtieth birthday celebration when I had hoped that Chicky as Ros' longest standing friend would say a few words. Ros had spoken to Chicky a week previously when she had told her that she was looking forward to being there. The next real contact we had was about a year later from Martyn inviting us to Chicky's funeral. She had recently been diagnosed as having cancer and had quite suddenly died of a brain tumour. Whether that was the reason for their non-appearance or some family crises had suddenly erupted – Morgan was going through an unpleasant separation from his ambitious Welsh wife at the time – we shall never know.

Wedding Day at St Mary's Church, Merton, 3 September 1966

13

'Sheridan', 36 Chamberlain Gardens, Arborfield Cross – Our First House

14

1970 Bracknell Rugby Football Team (standing far left)

15

Simon's Baptism in 1970

16

Infant Phillip in 1973

17

Family Night Out - summer holiday in Callela, Spain in 1981

18

Night Out in 1987 as Chairman of London Airports Customs Rugby Club - fraternising with French colleagues at 2 am in the morning in the official apartment of the Collector Paris

19

Attending HM the Queen's Garden Party in 1990

20

Phillip's Graduation Bournemouth University 1995

21

In 1999 with Simon and Theresa Dining at the Blue Haven, Kinsale

22

Snorkelling over the Great Barrier Reef, Queensland, Australia in 2003

23

Second House, 18 Barn Drive, Maidenhead in 2004

24

# NEW SHOOTS

My rugby career as a player ended in early February 1970, when halfway through a game at Bracknell, I was tackled, receiving a severe blow to my left thigh. This was really the only serious injury I had suffered playing the game. The member of the opposing team who inflicted it was intent on causing physical injury. He was the only malicious player I came across in my playing career. I was not the only player on our side he targeted. He tried tripping our fly-half in a particularly nasty fashion and broke his own ankle in the process which was some consolation for the vicious thump I had received. With hindsight, I should not have carried on playing for the remainder of the game. My thigh swelled up and was so heavily bruised that I was eventually persuaded by Ros two or three weeks later to go round to see our local doctor. By this time, I could not bend the leg and he referred me to a consultant at the Royal Berks Hospital in Reading who in turn referred me to a specialist at the Middlesex Hospital in London. The specialist and his assistant examined me and with a grave intake of breath turned their backs and started muttering to each other. Feeling that I might be a terminal case, I asked them what the problem was. The specialist reluctantly turned to me and grudgingly blurted out the single word, "haematoma". "What's a haematoma?" I not unreasonably asked – it was, after all, my leg - at which point he became more sympathetic and communicative. Apparently, the blow I had received had ruptured the main artery in my left leg. In the absence of immediate medical treatment, the bleeding inside my leg had congealed trapping the main leg muscle against the thigh bone which had then partly grown over the muscle thereby preventing me from bending my leg. The specialist arranged for me to undergo a course of radio therapy designed to disperse the congealed blood and free the muscle so that I might recover as much movement as possible. The treatment largely worked. I was able to bend my leg again although not quite as freely as before. Unfortunately also, in view of the several weeks that had elapsed since the original injury, the blood vessels had adopted different internal pathways for circulating the blood. Consequently, I have had to live with slight discomfort in this leg ever since: a sort of bubbling, prickling sensation, punctuated occasionally, usually with the change of seasons, by sharp, mercifully short, stabbing pains. Most of the time, I don't think about it. But when I do; like now, writing about it, I can feel it. I think of it as my 'old war wound'.

The only other war wounds I bear are scars under my chin, over my left eyebrow and in the middle of my forehead. The former resulted from being pushed into the long jump pit in the junior school at Morden Farm and hitting the underside of my chin on the wooden border of the pit as I fell forward: assailant unknown. The latter resulted from standing too close to a junior school friend of mine demonstrating with a new cricket bat how he played the hook shot, the tip of the bat cracking, at the extremity of its arc, into my admiring forehead. I also cut my eyebrow when I failed to commit to a tackle, playing on the wing for my Old Boys side in 1965. The opposing winger was big, fast and sported a ginger beard which gave him the appearance of a wild Viking. I got the back of his boot on my head for my troubles as he swept past me. This was the only match in which I failed to throw myself into the game with my usual gusto and commitment. I was performing as the Dame that evening in the Merton Park Parish Players Christmas Pantomime and I took to the pitch thinking to myself that it would be a disaster were I to get injured and become unable to appear on stage. That was altogether the wrong mind set for a contact sport like rugby. What I hoped to avoid, happened. Fortunately, the wound was not too deep. I was taken to the Nelson Hospital Accident Unit where I had the cut stitched and was released just in time to get made up and into my costume; the makeup lady using all her art to skilfully disguise my wound and stitching.

While undergoing the course of radio treatment, I hobbled around with a stiff leg like Long John Silver. Driving the car presented a bit of a problem. I had to lift my leg into the car and lift it manually onto and off the clutch pedal while operating the gear lever. I found that by reversing the ratchets on the driver's seat, I was able to create sufficient space to enable me to drive effectively and safely. It was in this condition that around 10 o'clock on the morning of the 7th April 1970, I drove to the maternity hospital in Wokingham to find out how the final stages of Ros' pregnancy were going. I had taken her into the hospital the previous evening after she had begun to experience contractions. However, after a while in the hospital, the contractions subsided and ceased. The mid-wife who examined her said she would keep her in overnight but didn't expect anything to happen until the following day and suggested that I come back then. The following day I parked the car and walked into the reception area where a nurse told me that Ros had given birth to a baby boy in the early hours of the morning, weighing some

7llb or so. This had all taken place when her contractions unexpectedly restarted less than an hour after I had left the previous evening. I had stipulated that I wished to be present at the birth. However, we did not have a phone at home – we could not afford one. Mobile phones had not been invented – so the hospital had been unable to contact me. I was disappointed that I had missed the birth of my son and had not been there to help Ros through her ordeal. They explained that there had been some difficulty with the birth but my baby son was now fine. He had been placed in intensive care for the time being as a precaution. I was asked if I wanted to see him and was taken to where he lay in a plastic cot. I marvelled at how perfectly formed he was; complete with real hair, eye-lashes, fingernails and complete set of toes. I left and went to see Ros who was recuperating in a separate ward. I discovered that she had not seen him at all. The reason was that the nursing staff had encountered a serious problem in the immediate afterbirth. After making his first appearance in the world, he had failed to start breathing. Having unsuccessfully applied their usual remedies in such situations, they had become increasingly alarmed and had requested an emergency transfer to the Royal Berks Hospital in Reading. An ambulance had been dispatched and our local GP summoned. Finally, in desperation, the midwife had placed a strong substance on his tongue which mercifully caused him to suddenly swallow, sucking in his first draught of air. He had then been whisked into the intensive care nursery for monitoring; forgetting after the emergency was over that Ros had not seen him. In fact, she says it wasn't until my evening visit that same day that she was allowed to see him in the special nursery. In all he was kept there for 48 hours before being released into her tender care, thankfully progressing normally.

As I said in my address some 36 years later, when he got married, life with my eldest son Simon Francis, for so we had decided to call him, was never straightforward. I was convinced as I gazed at him lying, face upwards, in his little cot, he was saying to me "Well nobody told me to breath!" Fairly laid-back you might say. And you might well be right. Simon has always done everything in his own time. For instance, had he been born on the 2nd of April as expected instead of the 7th, I would have been able to claim a whole year's child tax relief; a not inconsiderable sum in those days and very welcome. The tax year ended on the 4th April, so the delay in his appearance beyond that date meant that we lost the lot. Regretfully, I had to cancel the order for the silver spoon to put in his mouth.

Ros was in the maternity hospital for a week. When she returned home with our new bundle, I was able to take a few days maternity leave from work to help her. By then I was a member of the newly formed Regional Investigation Unit of Customs & Excise, based in Soho in West London. I had been selected for this work after identifying and helping to investigate a number of purchase tax and betting duty frauds in my own area in Notting Hill District where I worked for two years in 1966 and 1967. I believe I was, certainly in the region, if not in the country as a whole, the first officer to identify this type of fraud as a result of routine audit work or 'control visiting' as it was known. In the Investigation Unit we were based in an office in Berwick Street in the heart of Soho, which was a colourful area then as now. This was the highlight of my career from a personal point of view. I found the challenge of the work exciting and the path-finding success we achieved in the field of fiscal fraud extremely satisfying. I enjoyed my time at Notting Hill too. This was my first Fixed Station and I was responsible for everything of a revenue nature that went on there, legal and otherwise. I delighted in the responsibility and the freedom I enjoyed to organise myself and the work. I also remember with some fondness the quirky characters I worked with there. The office was above a social security office in Praed Street not far from Paddington Station which was very handy for my home to office journey. Friday afternoons were often laden with drama. Claimants, usually of Irish extraction, would spend all their weekly allowance in the pub in the afternoon before returning to the benefit office just before closing time shouting, swearing and demanding more money to enable them to get them through the remainder of the week. Sometimes they would try throwing the furniture around but were thwarted by the fact that the chairs and tables provided in the public area had been chained to the floor to prevent such acts of violence. There was also a lady of some breeding, judging by her appearance and manner, who used to appear sporadically, wandering up the staircase to our floor, mouthing a stream of the most vulgar obscenities to anybody she could find; or in the absence of a corporal body, to the thin air. We used to hear her coming and locked all the doors leading to the stairway. We christened her the Mad Lady of Bayswater; for mad she certainly was: she had a furious obsession that she was being followed by MI5 and the Special Branch to whom she referred in the most deprecating terms imaginable. Most of the officers in the District were young, newly appointed, like myself as a result of the Parker Re-organisation, with the notable exception of one, well spoken, old boy, named George Ward. He lived locally in Bayswater and had worked in the Praed Street office for many years. However, we rarely saw him, except occasionally on a Friday lunchtime when he would pop into the office briefly and then repair to the pub on the corner where he would swallow two pints of bitter one after the other without seemingly pausing to take a breath, before disappearing again into the busy street. Of ruddy complexion, he possessed a rather faded 1930s Bohemian aura somewhat at odds with the militarish brush type moustache he sported, through which he appeared to filter his beer. He rarely spoke to anyone but had an engaging twinkle in his eye. He was believed to be running a property business in the area and treated his official duties as something of a sideline, providing a steady stream of income, for little outlay of effort or interest on his part. He memorably told a visiting Collector who asked him if he had any hobbies that he was interested in economics. "Ah!" said the Collector sensing that he might be on to something to explain George's frequent absences from the office "Any particular branch of economics?" to which George replied "Yes – ancient Greek economics!"

Given the freedom we had with the Units system to organise our own work, I used to try to complete as much as I could between Monday morning and Friday lunchtime. This meant that I usually had time on Friday afternoon to do the weekly shop in the local supermarket situated in the Edgware Road. I remember that if we were entertaining at the weekend I would spend significantly more than usual. I would buy prawns, for example, which were expensive for the standard starter dish in those days of prawn cocktail. The total bill would come to around £4.50; normally around £3.50. I crammed all the items I purchased into my tartan grip with the string handles and holes in the base. I would stagger with it back to the office until it was time to carry it down to Paddington Station to link up with Ros at 5.30pm for our end of the working week journey back home to Arborfield. One Friday afternoon when Ros and I were due to be entertaining over the weekend, I bought a large joint of meat which I put into the grip with the rest of the shopping. We boarded the train and found seats in one of the compartments. Each compartment consisted of two banks of five seats facing one another. We chose our seats and before sitting down I placed the tartan grip with the shopping in it in the string netting of the luggage rack above the row of seats opposite. The compartment quickly filled. The train pulled out of the station and the habitual somnambulant silence descended on the occupants as it gathered speed. The journey usually took 37 minutes and was non-stop to Twyford, our destination station. The only sound in the compartment came from newspapers being rustled. This was in the days before mobile phones and iPods. After a while, with the train batting along at a tidy lick, I sensed that one of the passengers opposite, who happened to be seated directly under my grip, was exhibiting signs of unease. Nothing was said: nobody ever spoke to anybody else in these compartments – it just wasn't done. He had really caught my attention though and I tried not to stare because of course nobody ever stared or even looked directly at anybody else in these self-contained universes; it was the unspoken etiquette and custom that everybody always politely observed. And nothing wrong with that, I may say. Eventually I noticed that he was squirming in his seat to avoid drops of blood that were seeping from my tartan grip above him. With some embarrassment, I realised that the joint of meat I had taken from the cold cabinet in the supermarket some three or so hours earlier had thawed and blood from the meat was now seeping through the bottom of my bag onto the passenger beneath. Nothing was said and we were soon approaching our stop at Twyford. As the train pulled to a halt, I rose from my seat retrieved the bag from above the passenger's head and left the compartment with Ros. The look on his face suggested that he thought I must be a murderer and that my bag contained sawn off human body parts. I am sure he regaled his family and friends later with lurid tales of the 'Murder on the 5.30pm from Paddington'.

From the work point of view Notting Hill Excise Station was a slightly forbidding, yet intriguing area to cover. The Excise Station for which I was responsible formed a roughly triangular shape, bounded by the Great Western railway running east to west at the base, Ladbroke Grove running south to north and the Harrow Road lying in a north-westerly to south-westerly direction completing the triangle. It consisted mainly of rundown Georgian and Victorian residential terraced housing interspersed with the odd small warehouse and manufacturing plant, capped by a huge gas works overlooking the railway at the apex of the triangle. I had to visit the gas works once a month to check the usage of oil for which the Gas Board qualified for a duty refund provided usage in the gas making process could be verified. To do this I had to measure the volume of oil in the holding tank. This tank was cylindrical in shape, rising at least one hundred feet into the air and was closed with a domed roof. I say closed because, between the top of the access ladder mounted on the side of the tank and the dipping point, in the roof, there was a hole created by corrosion, about a half a metre in diameter, around which I had to gingerly step before I could reach the dipping point. Perched on a small platform, I then had to drop a weighted steel measuring tape through the dipping point until the weight reached the bottom of the tank before rewinding the tape to observe and record the point at which it had been cut by the liquid contents. This was a tricky operation particularly when it was windy or raining. To me this was part of the excitement of doing the job. I enjoyed not being stuck in an office all day. However, when Ray Williams, my Surveyor came out with me on one of his accompanied supervisory visits, he was appalled at the state of the tank roof and the lack of proper safety handrails. Ray, bless him, was absolutely right technically, from a health and safety point of view, and back on terra firma, immediately took the matter up with the Gas Works manager. Ray was genuinely concerned for my safety and I felt grateful to him that he made me appreciate that I had been putting myself and the Department at unnecessary risk. To be honest I felt I had been pretty stupid in not seeing the wider picture and felt in some measure that I had let Ray down. But he was such a sensitive and kind man that he did not offer a single word of criticism: he didn't need to. He was a great mimic and a wonderfully humorous man who was the spitting image of a famous TV actor (Charlie Barlow) in a popular police drama at the time, and was frequently stopped in the street by strangers and asked for his autograph. I was saddened a few years later to learn that a week after his own retirement, shortly before he and his lovely wife were due to fly out to stay with their eldest daughter living in Canada, he collapsed and died of a heart attack after delivering a speech at a colleague's retirement do.

While I was at Notting Hill, Betting Duty was introduced. Treasury Ministers were nervous about the outcome, largely because, years earlier under the Churchill government, a previous attempt had failed and they recognised that bookmakers didn't exactly enjoy a universal reputation for probity. Licensed betting shops suddenly sprung up all over the place like daises in spring. I had several in my patch almost all of which were individually owned and run by the bookmaker himself. After a few years these independent sole proprietor shops were all bought out by one or other of the large chains. I got to know each of my bookmakers personally and visited them regularly for control purposes in the initial phases. Although the bookies were all pleased about the fact that they could now operate legitimately, few of them realised that unlike the Inland Revenue who they had been fiddling for years, we didn't just sit back and accept what they said. I quickly found that three of my bookies were suppressing bets. I notified the newly formed West London Regional Investigation Unlit of my suspicions and together with them investigated and successfully prosecuted the miscreants. To my knowledge these were the first Betting Duty frauds successfully investigated and prosecuted in the South east of England, if not in the country as a whole. I do believe that one of the bookmakers, who unusually owned two shops in my patch, was straight: he probably had to be because he couldn't be in two places at once and only a fool trusts employees in a business based on receiving large quantities of cash. At any rate, on a routine visit to his main shop, just before Christmas, he asked me if I would care for a festive drink. Thinking that he meant to offer me a glass of whisky or sherry or some such drink, I accepted. I was nervous about doing this, but relationships are important and as I say, at the end of the day I was fairly sure that he was honest and wasn't on the fiddle. He led me down into a basement room and opened a cabinet. But instead of pouring me a drink, he thrust two large unopened bottles of whisky into my arms. I was somewhat taken aback and probably should have handed them back at once, but mainly through embarrassment at having accepted his invitation in the first place, I could only summon up a hasty 'thank you', before swiftly leaving with my prize. Nothing ever came of it on either side. I am sure that if I had found out that he was fiddling, he would have accepted his lot without trying to exert any leverage on me and I think he recognised that I would not have held back if I had found anything wrong. Still, it did show me how easy it is to slip from traditional hospitality into corruption per se.

The bain of my life were two Jewish soft toy traders. One was a lovable rogue name Wally Leffman and the other a distinctly unlovable rogue named Sucher, alias Leslie, alias Harrison; and these were just the aliases I knew about! Neither of them ever paid their Purchase Tax on time at the end of the quarter. Wally was the worst offender in that regard. More than once I had to go round with a distraint order to his shambolic premises in Beethoven Street that had once been private housing. His office was upstairs in a front room overlooking the street. The other rooms on this floor were used for storing bought in items and material, referred to in the trade as 'plush' that was used for stuffing the teddy bears that were put together by a motley crowd of women on the ground floor. At one point, he managed to buy up a huge stock of 'gonks', the day after their brief popularity expired forever. These were small, plastic, Scandinavian troll-like creatures with exaggerated facial features and long, luridly coloured hair. Bless him, he never gave up trying to find a buyer; he's probably still trying! One afternoon, armed with a final tax demand, I went round without prior warning to Beethoven Street. Wally could be elusive if he knew in advance that you were chasing him for money and was adept at finding ways of frustrating the bureaucratic procedures involved. When I arrived, the front door to the entrance hall and the downstairs work rooms was open, as it habitually was, so I entered and went straight up the stairs hoping to find Wally in his office. There were no doors on any of the rooms upstairs or downstairs and as I passed the room on my right at the head of the stairs where the plush was stored, I saw Wally lying face down on top of one of the woman from downstairs, a generously proportioned lady of Caribbean descent, engulfed in plush, with his trousers round his ankles, evidently enjoying himself in time honoured fashion. I quickly moved on into his office and waited. No sooner had I done so than somebody from downstairs came into the office, apologising to me for Wally's absence and explaining that Mr Leffman had been briefly attending to other business and would be with me shortly. When Wally appeared, looking somewhat abashed and flushed, a couple of minutes later, it was difficult to keep a straight face and to concentrate on the matter in hand. For once, and only once, I felt I had the advantage over him. Yet for all the difficulties he created for me and the Department, you had to admire his optimistic spirit and I could not help liking the man.

Sucher's premises consisted of a couple of ground floor rooms in a similarly run down former residential property. He employed a prim, smart, statuesque female secretary, who was intensely loyal to him and who provided the perfect shield for him in his dealings with officialdom. She was the only means of contact I usually had with him other than on the telephone. I think I only contrived to meet him once, in person. I was obliged to examine his accounts and documentation in an unheated dark room with a hole in the floor, while his secretary enjoyed a single bar electric fire in her separate niche. His accounts and records were never in order, deliberately so, I suspected. And his secretary was the perfect foil and filter for any awkward questions I might wish to raise with her boss. I tried hard to find out more about him and his business but never succeeded in pinning him down or proving any deliberate misdeclaration.

I did succeed in identifying one purchase tax fraud after I noticed when walking about my area that there appeared to be far more ice-cream vans bearing the livery of one of my purchase tax traders, an Englishman named Avery, than he had disclosed to me in his declared accounts. He made ice-cream and lollies from premises in Golbourne Road that had been partly converted from residential accommodation into a public counter and manufacturing plant and store rooms. Avery lived in a flat with his wife on the top floor. Again, I believe that this was the first purchase tax fraud in the country to be identified, investigated and successfully prosecuted at local level as a result of routine control visiting.

With the experience I had gained in identifying and investigating fiscal fraud in my own Excise area, I was invited to transfer to the West London Regional Investigation Unit which I joined on 1 January 1968. I remained there for four exciting and happy years, achieving vetting as a Specialist Investigator, followed by notional promotion after a couple of years from Executive to Higher Executive Officer when the Department changed to the standard

Treasury grading structure. In 1972, partly as a result of my success in the Investigation Unit and as a prelude to the Department assuming responsibility for the new European Union Value Added Tax (VAT), I was promoted to Senior Executive Officer, or Surveyor, as the Grade was still titled in the Department. I left the Investigation Unit in May of that year to take up my duties in the higher grade which entailed a period of unattachment before I was eligible to apply for appointment to a fixed District of my own. I was proud and pleased that I had obtained such rapid promotion but never stopped looking back with fondness on these formative years at Notting Hill Excise and in the West London Investigation specialism.

I often recalled, later in my career, the raids we conducted on illegal gambling dens in Soho and the alarm provoked in one case where the premises were shared with a strip club. Naked girls flew in all directions as we entered with a search warrant. On another occasion, we lost the evidence we had collected, which we had passed to one of our less experienced and proficient investigating officers, named Gethin, to place in a bag. Unfortunately due to a lapse in his concentration, the bag was deftly removed from his charge by one of the offenders and removed via the back door, which he was supposed to be guarding. The bag was found the following day in the neighbouring area of Hyde Park; empty of course! He was referred to thereafter as 'Back Door Gethin' a nickname he accepted with good humour. Such surprise visits to obtain evidence were known in our investigation specialism as the 'knock'; that is a knock on the door and in we all go. In Betting Duty cases we had the support of a search warrant but for Purchase Tax we had to rely on persuasion to gain entry, although technically we did have power of entry into premises in the form of an ancient document, known as a writ of assistance that the Surveyor held and issued when required. In addition, we enjoyed extensive historical powers listed in the personal commission that each officer carried. When I retired I was presented with my commission, duly cancelled, and mounted in a large wooden frame, showing the dates of my service 1960 to 2000. This now hangs proudly on my office wall and is a tangible reminder of my life as a Customs & Excise officer.

The Investigation Unit office in Soho overlooked a brothel and one day, when, for once, we were not too busy, we undertook a survey to find out how long the gentlemen visitors spent inside. For those who might be interested in such social ephemera, the average time worked out to be fourteen minutes. The girls would sometimes wave at us and we would respond in kind.

Everybody who lived or worked in Soho knew Rosie. He was an inebriate, yet cultured man, besotted by the demon drink who everybody in the village loved and cared for. He was so named because, no matter how drunk and dishevelled he looked, he always took the trouble to wear a fresh rose in his lapel each day. He was funny and harmless, rather like a music hall drunk and when he died everybody turned out for his funeral. His funeral bier was bedecked with roses and many ladies of the night, local traders and shopkeepers shed a tear at his passing.

On taking up my position on promotion as an Unattached Surveyor, I was sent to officiate in vacant Districts in several places. Surveyor vacancies had arisen as a result of

Departmental modernisation and restructuring flowing from the introduction of VAT. In Southampton I was sent to take charge of a newly formed Customs District which brought together uniformed, anti-smuggling staff formerly known as 'Waterguard', re-titled 'Preventive' and civilian-dress, personnel responsible for safeguarding the revenue on imports and exports of cargo, titled Outdoor Service Landing Officers. On arrival I was told by the Assistant Collector that the Preventive staff, although technically part of my District, would be unlikely to bother me and I should not bother them. There had been a great deal of barely concealed opposition to the integration of the two service strands, not only in Southampton but also in other large traditional ports round the country. Waterguard officers had enjoyed a strong quasi-militaristic esprit de corps but were generally inferior in rank to the civilian-dress Landing Officers. Integration had brought this difference in status into high and unwelcome relief for them. Sure enough, I never encountered any of the Preventive members of staff while I was there but I didn't see any ships either. This was in the days when the great ocean passenger liners and general cargo ships no longer sailed the seas. The transit sheds in the Western Docks which comprised the District I was overseeing were vast yet largely empty. The Landing and Preventive Officers between them had virtually nothing to do. Anyway, I had been told not to 'rock the boat', as it were, so I didn't.

Actually, I did briefly see some Preventive staff when I paid a supervisory visit one afternoon to Eastleigh Airport, just outside Southampton. As well as the Western Dock area, the airport was part of my District. As I strode into the Customs Channels, passengers from a Channel Island's flight were streaming through unhindered with not a single Preventive officer in sight. Surprised that the channel had been left completely unattended, I looked around and spotted a group of Preventive officers in an adjacent office playing cards. I advanced towards the office and as I did so, they saw me and scattered belatedly and rather shamefacedly into the channels to check the remaining passengers.

After Southampton, I spent a month working in a benighted area of Stratford in East London at the London Overseas Mail Office or LOMO as it was known which handled postal packets and parcels arriving in this country from overseas. The place was riven with union inspired 'Spanish Practices' designed to minimise the postal workers effort and maximise their earnings, including overtime. Not much has changed in over thirty years if recent disputes in the Post Office are anything to go by. Quite why Maggie Thatcher, having privatised practically everything else, never privatised the Post Office is a mystery to me. From LOMO, I was posted to Burton on Trent to manage the Excise staff working at the huge Charrington's brewery in the town centre and other surrounding breweries. I had arranged suitable digs in advance. When I arrived at the address I had been given, the landlady was very pleasant but she had not received the booking communication from our Departmental Appointment Office and all her bed and breakfast accommodation was taken. Everywhere else in the town was full except for a cheap doss house frequented by workers from the local steel plant. With no alternative accommodation available, she arranged for me to stay there. I spent one evening and night there before returning to plead with her to find me somewhere else. I am not a prude or a snob but this was the bed and breakfast from hell. Everything about if was awful.

The men were unkempt and crude in their conversation and manners. I had to sleep in a room with six or so of these sweating, belching, farting and snoring labourers in bunk beds. The food and cutlery was disgusting. Everything smelt of gherkins and pickles and I just couldn't face staying there another night. She saw how distressed I was and very kindly arranged for me to stay with her sister in her pleasant house not far away, despite the fact that her sister was not in the bed and breakfast business.

At 7am on 30 October 1972, my second son, Phillip Ross was born, in the same Wokingham maternity hospital as Simon but without any of the complications attending Simon's entry into the world. When he was born I was still working as an Unattached Surveyor holding down a vacant post in the so-called Bench District in the Custom House London designed by Sir Christopher Wren. This time I was present at the birth. It all happened so quickly. I remember the umbilical cord. I was surprised it was so colourful and dry. It appeared to me just like a multi-coloured telephone cord. Phillip looked like a cross between a walnut and a little old man. But again, the abiding miracle was that everything was there and in place; eyelashes, hair, fingers and toes complete with tiny nails, not to forget his little willy; amazing! While Ros was recuperating in the maternity hospital, I looked after Simon with some help from my mother in law. For practically the only time in my life I had to change dirty nappies: and true to form, Simon chose this particular week to contract a severe bout of diarrhoea which made the experience even more trying.

The Bench District took its name from the King's Bench where in the seventeenth century importers and their agents would pay their dues to the King's officials sitting upon their eponymous bench. There was no longer any bench as such but the people for whom I was responsible still worked in the magnificent, long, high-ceilinged hall known as the Long Room, accepting and checking shipping entries and duty deposits. My office was a magnificent palatial room immediately adjacent to the Long Room. It boasted enormous sash windows affording a splendid Canaletto style view of the hustle and bustle of ships, boats barges and lighters plying their busy trade on the river. One sunny afternoon, after lunch the humming of the boats and the lapping of the water had a particularly soporific effect and I fell gently asleep for a good half hour before I came to. Nobody troubled me in my office and the job was not one of the most challenging or burdensome I had ever encountered. Nevertheless I felt guilty when I regained consciousness. As well as my palatial office, I enjoyed another unique privilege. I had sole use of the Queen's toilet, for which I held the only key. The toilet had been upgraded for an official visit to the Custom House by Her Majesty some months previously, should she wish to 'spend a penny' during her tour. I don't know whether or not she did actually avail herself of the little room while she was there but I certainly used it and was amused every time I went in there by the blue foam upholstery on the toilet seat, put there to cushion the Royal posterior.

Before I was appointed to the Bench District, I spent a month seconded to the Chief Inspector's Office as a member of an inspection team. The team was responsible for examining and auditing the work of selected Outfield managers and officials and reporting back to the Chief Inspector with recommendations for change and improvement where appropriate. I went on two inspections, each of which was led by the same Senior Inspector, a ruddy faced, bluff, slightly militarish, conscientious, middle-aged man, who was demanding but straightforward and good company. On the first inspection we went to the West Country. We found a few things wrong. I remember that one individual manager seemed to have been pin-pointed in advance for some searching examination. Some shortcomings were identified and I believe he may have been moved subsequently. The best part was staying for the duration of the inspection in a hotel in the centre of the Royal Crescent in Bath. For the second inspection we descended on the London area. Because of the experience I had as an Unattached Officer working in breweries and distilleries, I was asked by the Senior Inspector to pay an unannounced visit, one morning, to a brewery on the South side of the River Thames from London Bridge. When I got there I carried out a full survey and found that in every case the brews had been under-declared by the brewer, both from the point of view of alcoholic strength and the volume of liquor held in the collecting and fermenting vessels. The brews had supposedly been checked by the Officer and Senior Officer safeguarding the revenue at the brewery but their records showed that they had accepted the brewer's declarations without challenge. Although there were only a couple of inches and degrees difference between my findings and the brewer's declaration in each vessel, the amount of revenue at stake was considerable. At the end of my survey, I reported my findings to the Senior Inspector who was horrified. He instructed me to undertake a further unannounced visit the following day and to carry out another full check of all brews. The following morning, early, walking down the road leading to the brewery,

I suddenly noticed the Senior Inspector accompanied by an Inspector in front of me hurrying towards the premises. The Senior Inspector appeared more flushed than usual and was clearly alarmed at the apparent deficiencies I had uncovered. I caught up with him. He explained that since I had spoken to him the previous day, he had reflected further and decided that in view of the potentially serious nature of the shortcomings in official surveillance, he needed to see for himself, exactly what was going on. Together we found further evidence of the same pattern of under-declaration and acquiescence by the Excise Officers in relation to the latest brews. I was pleased because the Senior Inspector had greeted my initial report to him with a dash of incredulity and I felt vindicated that he himself had confirmed my findings. The Senior Inspector notified the Chief Inspector who promptly raised the matter with senior management in the area. It transpired that the Officer in immediate charge of the brewery had been promoted only recently and transferred to this particular vacant post in London from his native Northern Ireland where he had served for many years in a menial job as a Revenue Assistant on the Irish Land Boundary. Had it not been for the opportunities created by the large expansion and restructuring of the Department in order to accommodate the new Value Added Tax, he probably would have remained as a Revenue Assistant on the Land Boundary for the remainder of his career, which given that he was well over fifty years of age, did not in any event, have long to run. He was short sighted and had been given no training in performing the duties of his new Executive grade, or in the technical aspects of brewery control work. His immediate superior, who was also expected to perform practical work and checks at the brewery, had been transferred under the same Departmental restructuring from the Forestry Commission, with no previous experience of Customs & Excise work. He had similarly been given no training either in brewery work or more generally in our Departmental ways and suffered from a disability which meant that he could only see out of one eye. Between the two of them it is little wonder that they were meekly accepting whatever the brewer told them and that the brewer felt he could take advantage. Disciplinary action was taken against the Divisional Manager for failing to recognise the potential danger to the revenue and to provide adequate training or checks to ensure that the two individuals directly concerned were able to perform their duties correctly and were effectively carrying them out. I was not told what form the disciplinary action took but I believe it was quite severe.

With Phillip's birth, Chief Inspector's Office kindly arranged for me to work closer to home and I was transferred from Custom House in London to take over the Thames Valley Investigation Unit based in Reading. When I arrived I found a lot of uncoordinated activity and lines of enquiry being pursued by the previous manager that were floundering and unlikely to produce significant returns. Potentially more rewarding enquiries were being ignored. I immediately put a stop to the wasteful amount of effort being expended on surveillance in a futile attempt to identify alleged disposals of minor quantities of duty free liquor and tobacco from the United States airbase at Upper Heyford. Instead, I instigated and helped to successfully conclude the first ever purchase tax fraud in the Thames Valley Region. This was followed by further successful purchase tax and betting duty fraud cases. Before redirecting resources away from Upper

Heyford, I paid a visit to the base and entered another world. I had never thought of Americans until then as foreigners but although they spoke a version of the same language as us, they were in all other respects completely different. We were shown into the Security Administration Office on the base where we were greeted by a loud voiced, brash type with a large badge on his short sleeve, open necked shirt stating that he was ;'Michael J Foster Jr. – Office of Special Investigations'. To be fair, he was very helpful to us and when we politely asked him whether he would mind awfully if we could interview one of the US air force personnel on the base, whose name we gave him, he picked up one of the several phones on his desk and having contacted the individual concerned, growled into the mouthpiece "Schutzmeier – Git Your Ass Over Here!": This was not how our military personnel would have reacted in similar circumstances, but there you go. Schutzmeier promptly appeared, a seven foot crew cut Texan wearing an open-necked shirt and brothel creeper type shoes. It was like being transported for a moment into a real life version of a Hollywood movie.

After two months in charge of the Reading Investigation Unit, I was appointed to my first fixed post as a Surveyor. On 18 December 1972, I took charge of an Excise District located in Hayes Middlesex, within sniffing distance of the Nestle instant-coffee factory. The District was housed in a two storey building of World War II vintage, attached to a large ground-level storage warehouse where the Inland Revenue kept their tax records.

The building was separated from the road, appropriately, if somewhat prosaically called Nestles Avenue, by a six foot wire fence enclosing a wide turfed area. A concrete path led from the road across the turfed area, passing, halfway along its length, through a World War II air raid shelter before reaching the front door of our offices. In wet weather, rain water collected in the dark interior of the air–raid shelter making the path almost impassable at that point. It wasn't exactly providing easy access or a warm welcome to members of the public and traders who needed to call at our office. One of my claims to fame during the seven happy, formative years I spent there as an operational manager was to have the shelter demolished. I fully expected World War II skeletons to be unearthed when it was finally dismantled and must admit I was slightly disappointed when none were found. The building and the land was owned by the Property Services Agency who I later discovered were the most incompetent and old-fashioned government department I ever came across throughout my career. The building is still there, unchanged since my days. I am amazed that it has not been bulldozed and the land sold for development. The site must be worth millions of pounds and is crying out for commercial or residential redevelopment. In fact, my staff and I shared the building with a second Excise District headed by David Admans, an ex Royal Navy Officer, whose daughter was an Olympic swimmer. We also played host to the Divisional Manager who was based in the building and whose office was adjacent to mine and David's on the first floor. His name was Ken Moll. He was a tall, well-built, grey haired Yorkshireman who had a reputation for being somewhat austere and pernickety which was, in part, true. At various times during the day, he would spend hours of our valuable time regaling us with seemingly endless sagas, including the minutest details of his home life and summer holidays.

At four o'clock, he would wish us 'good afternoon', would doff his hat and depart for home, leaving us with a mountain of work to attend to. Nevertheless, although he was at first aloof and cold and could be very boring, I gradually grew to like and respect him. He for his part, eventually warmed to me, boosted by a trip with him for some reason to his house, one afternoon, when I met and clearly impressed his wife. He became a valuable mentor to me and was instrumental in giving me projects to undertake in his Division to aid my development and raise my profile within the region. One, which I undertook towards the end of my time at Hayes and which he greatly valued, involved a wholesale review of the Divisional structure and office locations.

He recommended me for a special management course at our Departmental Training Centre in Southend which I found useful although some of the managers who attended from other parts of the country found the format disquieting not to say disturbing. For instance, on the first morning when the course started, the trainers entered the room, sat down in front of us and said nothing. The silence went on for some time. It transpired that this was a deliberate ploy on their part to see what response it would elicit. I didn't mind the lack of structure and psychological pressure they put on us but others felt uncomfortable. Sitting beside me throughout the three week course was an older, traditional style manager from Southampton Docks who did everything by the book. We got quite friendly and went to the cinema together one evening. He and others found that his view of himself and the way he had been managing others was under challenge. He didn't speak much during the sessions yet at the same time displayed no overt signs of anxiety. I was shocked to learn shortly afterward, that on returning to Southampton the afternoon the course ended, he had committed suicide by walking in front of a train. Not long after this, and perhaps understandably, the Department pulled the plug on this particular American inspired psychological approach to management training.

I have fond memories of the all the people I worked with at Hayes. There was an active social element there which I encouraged. I remember an enjoyable evening spent in a curry house in Southall (Little India in West London) to which Ros and other spouses were invited. Speaking of Southall, I remember organising a small team of my officers to pay an unannounced visit to the Southall greyhound track one evening during a race meeting. The visit, known rather decorously, in our departmental jargon as a promiscuous visit, was designed to ensure that the bookmakers present at the meeting were accounting for betting duty correctly. The plan was to mingle with the crowd, remaining incognito initially, to observe what was taking place, before later approaching the bookmakers to check on their records. However the moment I entered the stadium with my team, wearing my prized camel hair coat, one of the on-course bookmakers who I recognised from my days as an Excise Officer at Notting Hill, instantly recognised me and shouted at the top of his voice so that all the other bookies could hear, "Good evening Mr Cottee, I suppose you've come to pay us a visit to check that we're all being honest and paying our betting tax correctly." He was a wily, yet likeable, old bird. I was surprised that he remembered my name and face but had to admit that he had effectively scuppered the main purpose of our carefully organised visitation.

My appointment to Hayes Excise was timely not just from a career point of view, but also because Ros and I now had two young children. It provided Ros and me with the opportunity to move, with the aid of a 'Crown Transfer', from Arborfield Cross to a larger house closer to my new office. To qualify for the 'Crown Transfer', under which solicitors, estate agents fees and additional mortgage payments were partially reimbursed and a fixed sum provided for new curtains and carpets, we had to find somewhere to live that would reduce the time taken to travel to and from work by over a half. We had been happy at Arborfield Cross. In the seven years we lived there, I never grew tired of that moment when the train from London would emerge from a long cutting west of Maidenhead to a beautiful rural scene with open fields on either side as we approached Twyford. The first day we caught the train from Twyford into London after we got married, we were practically the only passengers on board and we could sit anywhere we chose. By the end, we were lucky if we got a seat because the train was so packed with commuters, many of whom had, no doubt, been encouraged, like us, by the special discounted commuter fares that British rail then offered to commuters living a distance outside London. This dramatic change, demonstrated to me, albeit in a small way, how quickly the population in the Reading, Wokingham, Arborfield area had been growing in those few years. Partly for this reason and partly as a result of the general inflationary economic conditions prevailing at that time, house prices were soaring and within a matter of four or five weeks, in the early winter months of 1973, we managed to find a buyer by sticking a hand-written 'For Sale' notice on our garage door. Apparently, a friend of a young couple, looking for a property in the Arborfield area, had spotted my hand written notice and the couple themselves came one dark evening to view our humble abode. Inside, the house was well decorated and furnished. Also, I had put a lot of work into creating an attractive and interesting back garden but they didn't even bother to look at it: I thought it would have been a great selling feature! After a cursory tour of the inside of the house, they decided then and there that they wished to buy; at the agreed price. We had bought for £4750 in 1966 and sold for £12650. We let them store their furniture in our garage before completing in the early spring when we moved out.

Ros had given up paid employment when Simon was born having continued with Lummus & Co in London for three years after we got married so that we could afford to replace my Austin A30 car. With the money she saved, we bought a white Morris 1100 with hydrolastic suspension. It was a joy to drive after the old bone-shaker that my A30 had become. My elevation to the Surveyor grade in 1972 set in train the whole moving house process, and, for the one and only time in my life, I felt financially well enough off to buy a brand new car; an olive green French manufactured Simca saloon with beige leather seats. I must say it was almost worth the money spent for the sheer pleasure I enjoyed of savouring that new car smell whenever I eased myself into the driving seat and I was pleased by the admiring glances of friends and neighbours.

Ros, who was now a mother of two young children and a housewife without a house went to stay with my brother Roger and sister-in-law Ann at their house in Wimborne in Dorsetshire for a couple of months while I continued working at Hayes, staying with my parents at Wolsey Crescent and travelling down to Wimborne at the weekend. While all this was going on, we found a new detached four bedroom house on the western outskirts of Maidenhead that we liked and that we could afford, given that the location of the house in relation to my new workplace at Hayes allowed us to qualify for financial assistance under the 'Crown Transfer' arrangements. The purchase price was £18500. At the very last moment, just as we were about to complete and move in, the Conservative government under prime minister Ted Heath, introduced a mortgage freeze as part of Phase Two of its anti-inflation programme. The programme also included limits on pay rises, which of course tended to impinge more effectively on those like myself who worked in the public sector. Fortunately, after a couple of weeks delay, during which Ros, the two boys and I stayed with our friends Brenda and Dell at their house outside Newbury, it was decided that the freeze applied only to new mortgage applications. We were permitted, to continue with the purchase because our contract negotiations had begun before the freeze came in and, indeed, were very near to completion. Consequently, we were at last able to exchange contracts and moved in to our brand new house at 18 Barn Drive in June 1973, where we have remained ever since. Simon was old enough to appreciate the change in scene and for a long time afterwards wanted to go back to our old house at Arborfield Cross. Phillip, who had been a nightmare while we had been staying with Brenda and Del, quickly settled into his new surroundings.

I can't leave Arborfield Cross without mentioning 'The Pram Incident'. Apparently, and I say so advisably, since I have no personal recollection of the incident, I am told that, one morning, I was pushing Simon and Phillip in their pram beside the local main road, when I allowed the large radius wheels that prams had in those days to slip over the curb, which had the unintended effect of tipping the pram over and depositing both my young sons in the road in the path of oncoming traffic. As I say, I have no recollection of such an incident occurring but, over the years, it has become an apocryphal fact among the rest of the family, the truth of which may not be gainsaid. More seriously, I do very much recall receiving a telephone call from Ros at my Hayes office one morning, shortly after I had taken up my appointment there, telling me that she had taken Simon to the doctor complaining of a stiff neck. The doctor decided that he should be referred to hospital as a suspected meningitis case. I immediately dropped everything and sped home with the sympathy of colleagues ringing in my ears. Ros and I drove him to the hospital and had the heart rending experience of explaining to him that we had to leave him there. He was only two years old bless him and I'm sure he didn't really understand why we were abandoning him in a strange place. He was upset and whimpering as we left, standing there in his little pyjamas. It nearly broke my heart but we didn't have an option but to leave him in the capable hands of the hospital staff. Fortunately, it quickly transpired that he had not contracted meningitis and we were able to bring him home within a couple of days. The general consensus was that he must have strained his neck when I had taken him swimming the previous weekend at the indoor pool in Reading.

While on the subject of toddler illnesses, I remember a fraught few days on holiday in Perranporth in 1971 where, together with Ros' parents, Kath and Frank and her sister Jacquie, we had rented a holiday chalet for two weeks in the summer. It was a relatively small chalet and we were all packed in closely together, although occupying separate bedrooms with flimsy walls between. Firstly, we nearly lost Frank, when he was almost swept out to sea by a sudden rip tide. Fortunately, I was in the water with him at the time and was having my own difficulty contending with the current. I saw him struggling to stay on his feet and to regain the shoreline. Between us we managed to help one another to the safety of the big wide sandy beach that is such a feature of Perranporth. For the first few days on this same beach, Simon seemed determined to plough furrows in the sand with his nose. We tried to divert him by involving him in other exercises such as building sandcastles, not altogether successfully. The upshot was that he caught a nasty germ from his nose-digging exploits and spent the remainder of the holiday keeping everyone on tenterhooks and in fitful sleep patterns at night with his whining and crying. Mind you, the previous year, to be fair, when Simon was only a tiny baby, we went to stay with Robbie and Margaret in their house at New Milton on the South Coast for our summer break and he gave us no cause to feel embarrassed or concerned. When children are so young, before they are able to speak, it is always worrying when they are unhappy because they can't tell you what is wrong with them. And with the first-born you are always doubly anxious.

Before we left Arborfield for good, both Simon and Phillip had been christened in our local church. Neither have religious faith and neither wished to be confirmed when they reached their teenage years. I can't argue with that.

Indeed Phillip, in particular, has developed a strong antipathy towards the church not only in terms of its liturgy but also as an institution. Nevertheless, they both hold strong moral views based on Christian and Humanist principals.

I should also mention that, around this time, my father reached the age of 65 and retired from work. He was now an old age pensioner and about a year after we left Arborfield, he and my mother, spent a short time living with us in our new house at Maidenhead before they moved down to Bradpole, just outside Bridport in Dorset, where they had bought a bungalow with the proceeds of their sale of the old family home at 25 Wolsey Crescent, Morden Park. This effectively cut my direct links with the scenes of my childhood and youth.

# MAIN OF LIGHT

I was now thirty two years old and entering middle age. I had a wife and young family, a new detached house, in a sought after part of the country and a new job that brought me within the managerial cadre in my chosen profession and a new car.

Our new house formed part of a recently completed private development comprising some fifty properties, mostly detached, on the edge of the village of Cox Green, west of Maidenhead. The gardens at the front and back were small like most modern developments at that time and since. But the garden at the back of the house we had chosen was south facing and sunny and not overlooked, which we felt was important. Barn Drive was, effectively, a three pronged cul-de-sac. Consequently, due to the absence of through traffic, it was both quiet and also relatively safe for the children. At the back, we overlooked school playing fields and Windsor Great Park in the distance. The only disadvantage was that the main Western Region railway line lay between the end of the garden and these open spaces. However the line was sunk in a cutting. We quickly got used to the intermittent sound of passing trains and most of the time we are not conscious of them speeding past. Other advantages were that the house was situated within walking distance of the local primary and secondary schools, the doctors' surgery, local shops and a nice little pub called The Thatched Cottage. We also had good connections with Maidenhead Bus and Railway Stations and the emerging motorway system. The M4 ended at the Thicket Roundabout on the A4 Bath Road in those days and it was only later that it was extended to Reading, Bristol and South Wales. We were close to a particularly beautiful stretch of the River Thames running from Windsor in an upstream direction through Maidenhead, Marlow, Henley, Wargrave and Sonning. To the south and west lay attractive open arable land and to the north, National Trust land comprising the wooded Maidenhead Thicket area and the more open Pinkney's Green into which we were free to ramble, to play outdoor games and to picnic. There was also a decent rugby club linked to the town which I joined as a non-playing member. Over the years we have never formed any burning desire to move away. In addition to the beauty of the Thames Valley as a whole and to the surrounding countryside in particular, we enjoy easy access to major towns like Reading, High Wycombe, Slough and, of course, London, where we can take advantage, from time to time, of the many cultural, sporting and shopping opportunities they have to offer.

We settled quickly and made friends with other young couples with children of a similar age to ours who moved into Barn Drive over the next couple of years or so. The baby sitting circle that the wives organized and ran was very efficient and brought us even closer to some of the other families in the street; most notably to John and Irene Rees and their two daughters, as well as to Tony and Jean Harris and their son. These relationships were strengthened when our respective children attended the local 'Wessex' Primary and 'Cox Green Comprehensive' Senior Schools. Like us, John, Irene, Tony and Jean still live in Barn Drive and we remain close friends, frequently socialising together.

John and Irene's younger daughter Allison who is now in her thirties still remembers when I used to her hold her upside down by her ankles and pretend to drop her in our dustbin. I also recall the night when we all attended a social evening at the Community Centre and the fire alarm went off. I don't say that people panicked but there was a certain amount of consternation in the air and rushing to get to the exits. John Rees who was always fairly laid back and I couldn't smell any smoke or detect any indications of a fire. Slightly amused by the general kerfuffle while I shouted helpfully "Fire!" as a joke, we waited until everybody else had left. I was impressed with John's sense of calm. Needless to say it was a false alarm and we all trooped back in again a few minutes later and continued with the evening. I like to think that in a real crisis like the sinking of the Titanic, I would act calmly in the same way, though possibly, without indulging in the schoolboy jocularity to which I had stooped on this occasion.

Before starting school proper, Simon went to playschool at the age of three. This was situated in premises along the Bath Road, later transformed into the prestigious Redroofs Theatre School. Phillip followed him to the same play centre, also at the age of three, but when it closed, after the Principal contracted cancer, he transferred to a new playschool facing the cricket field at Littlewick Green. It was through this play group that Ros acquired our first family pet. I was away from home at the time on a residential training course and when I returned, I found that our family circle had been widened to include a male black and white kitten that Phillip had christened 'Whiskers'. I must admit that I never warmed to this animal. I think it was because I was not involved in the decision to take him into the family which was pretty mean-spirited on my part. I am not against cats as such and indeed have been very fond of the two later male cats for whom we later provided a home; William and lastly, most especially, Charlie. I am sure that there is some deep, pre-historical, psychological reason why I never liked Whiskers. However, I still feel ashamed that I didn't treat him as well as I should have.

In the summer of 1974 with Phillip still only a toddler, we spent our family holiday with my parents in their new bungalow in Bradpole. The bungalow only had two fairly small bedrooms so it was a bit of a squeeze and when the boys got older my father and I had to sleep on put-you-ups in the lounge. Left to herself, my mother would have spent every day on the local beach at West Bay but we did persuade her to venture further afield for part of the time to the picturesque seaside resorts of Charmouth and Lyme Regis. My father, who had vowed to do nothing in his retirement, true to his word, usually stayed at home watching cricket on TV although he joined the local bowls club, as had my mother, and he occasionally went to play at the club in the afternoon. In the evening we would sit round the dinner table listening to my mother's stories and anecdotes and playing cards for matchsticks which my mother greatly enjoyed. Simon and Phillip also joined in when they were older. On one such evening when we were all seated round the heavy oak dining table my mother had brought with her from Morden Park, the conversation turned to the subject of television programmes. I remarked in passing that I thought Kenny Everett, a former disc jockey and whacky comedian, who had a popular programme on the BBC at the time, could be very funny and gave as an example the occasion when he wore a US generals uniform whose epaulets suddenly sprung up revealing a battery of canons while he intoned "Bomb the bastards!" Everyone started laughing except my father who completely lost his temper and began shouting at me. The boys had to swallow their giggles and my mother, Ros and I sat there open mouthed at his sudden and unwarranted outburst. That was the end of that. You could have cut the atmosphere with a knife. Presumably my father did not like Kenny Everett. Or perhaps he disliked the fact that I had uttered a swear word. Or perhaps he was uncomfortable with the political connotations of the sketch. I can't say. It was embarrassing to say the least and the boys have never forgotten it.

Despite this hiccup, we spent our summer holidays in 1977 with Mum and Dad. In 1978 we again stayed with them for a week, having passed the preceding seven days with Roger and Ann who had moved to Minehead in North Devon where my brother was teaching. On one of these holidays we nearly lost Simon when we went with my mother to Lyme Regis. It was a beautiful hot and sunny day and the beach was packed with holidaymakers. Ros, my mother and I were sunbathing on the sand within sight of the stone chine that juts out into the bay. The boys were pottering around and I remember seeing Simon wandering onto the famous stone breakwater known locally as The Cob. I expected him to explore it and return to our spot on the beach. When I next looked up to check on his movements, I couldn't see him anywhere. I raised the alarm with Ros and my mother and dashed on to The Cob. On the far side, the water was over six feet deep with rocks beneath. I anxiously peered into the green-blue water below, thinking he might have lost his footing on The Cob and fallen in. But he was not there. I double checked and rushed back to our spot on the beach. We all then started searching. It is difficult to recall one's feelings at moments like this. Perhaps optimism mingled with anxiety best sums it up. Thank goodness, after a few worrying minutes, I spotted him walking towards us from the opposite end of the bay from the Cob, calm as you like, along the water's edge, looking for us. He had returned from the chine back onto the beach and had understandably lost sight of us, given that the beach was so crowded. Although he was yet a child, I admired the way he had not panicked and had chosen an effective strategy for finding us again.

Until their deaths, we visited my parents at Bradpole regularly every few months, staying for a couple of days or so at a time, generally enjoying ourselves and their company. We broadly followed the same routine although sometimes in the evening, Ros and I would slip away for a couple of drinks in the quaint old Dorsetshire village pubs at Loders or Uploders, leaving my mother and father to babysit. We also left Simon and Phillip with them one spring for a week and they got on reasonably well together. Unfortunately they were constrained in getting around because there had been heavy flooding in the area and the local river had burst its banks almost cutting off the village from the outside world. Phillip suffered from homesickness but Simon adopted a fatherly role and looked after him well.

Dorset was and remains a lovely part of the world to visit. My mother always used to say that she had no need to go abroad for holidays because she had everything she needed at hand. Up to a point, this was true for us too. We were able to go there for holidays, as a family, at little expense, which was an important consideration when raising a young family in those days.

In 1975 just before Simon started school at Wessex Infants, we spent our summer holiday with Ros' parents, Kath and Frank. We hired a family villa for two weeks in Erquy in Brittany where we had stayed ten years previously with my own parents. The plan was to drive there and back in my French manufactured Simca. I bought a roof rack and fitted it on the car where it was secured by two brackets clamped at either side to the roof guttering. I loaded the heaviest suitcases onto the rack and fixed them with straps and stowed the remainder of our combined luggage in the boot and car interior. We all climbed in; four adults and two children – no seat belts or child car seats in those days - and off we set to catch the cross channel ferry from Weymouth to Cherbourg. Such was the weight on the wheel axles, the tyres were scraping the wheel arches whenever I had to drive over large bumps in the road surface. I drove carefully therefore but even so, as I accelerated away after negotiating a sharp right-angled bend in the by-pass round Dorchester town centre, some ten miles or so from Weymouth, the roof rack became dislodged. The next thing I knew, roof rack and contents were sliding off the roof, gracefully tobogganing down the boot, landing in the road behind and coming to a halt in front of a following car. Frank and I retrieved the load and managed to replace it on the roof where we secured it more firmly with the aid of additional strapping. Fortunately, despite the inauspicious start, the rest of the journey passed without mishap, apart, that is, when, having arrived in France, I had a close encounter with the French traffic police. Coming up to the brow of a hill, I inadvisably tried to overtake a slow moving lorry and found myself crossing double white lines before I could regain my side of the road. As I came over the hill, I saw a police car parked on the opposite verge and two policemen looking at me in horror and beginning to wave me down until they spotted the GB sticker on the back of my French car, whereupon they gave a Gallic shrug of the shoulders as if to say "What do you expect from the mad English!" and I sped on my way, relieved but feeling a little embarrassed and foolish.

Erquy and its seven magnificent surrounding beaches had lost none of its charm. We were blessed with mainly fine weather. Frank particularly enjoyed the day we spent along the coast at Dinard where, in his youth, he had spent pre-war motor-cycling holidays. We all got on well together, although my mother-in-law irritated me when she got annoyed with the French for not providing everything she was used to in England. I remember her making a silly fuss about the fact that the local shops did not stock Kellogs Corn Flakes. Like many English people abroad she made absolutely no allowance for being in a different country with a different culture and cuisine. She got her just deserts when she, Ros and I went out to dine one evening in a local restaurant. I guess we left Frank behind in the villa babysitting. Anyway, she ordered crab from the menu expecting it to be served, as in England, as a loose compote of crabmeat ready to put it into her mouth. Imagine her surprise when her plate arrived with a large crab on it and a pair of nutcrackers. To be fair she did see the funny side as we helped her crack the shell and extract the meat inside, discarding the poisonous bit: but it didn't endear her any more to the French way of doing things. I have always been a Francophile but like my mother-in-law, my sons Simon and Phillip unfortunately take a more jaundiced view of our continental neighbours.

The following year we again holidayed with Frank and Kath. This time we travelled to Pembrokeshire in South Wales where we had hired a cottage in the pretty little village of St Florence outside Tenby. We again travelled there and back in my olive green Simca saloon, loaded down to the gunnels, tyres grating against the wheel arches which made me feel distinctly nervous but we made it there and back.

In June 1977 the country celebrated the Queen's Silver Jubilee. Like many other local communities up and down the land we marked the occasion in Barn Drive with a street party. I am no royalist but it was a fun day, recalling the lost years of wartime solidarity among neighbours and friends. I was a member of the organising committee and if it had not been for me and Jean Harris who was also a member, nothing would have got done. One of the main features was a fancy dress parade for the children. The theme was patriotic in keeping with the day. Simon decided he wanted to go as Richard The Lionheart and he looked splendid in his crown, chain mail, Cross of St George surplus, shield and silver painted wooden sword. We dressed Phillip as Sir Walter Raleigh and he really looked cute; he was only five years old with blond hair and blue eyes. We made him a Tudor style hat, doublet, cloak, hose and slippers. We also gave him a neat pointed moustache and beard. To complete the effect, he carried one of my pipes in one hand and a potato in the other with a duelling sword hanging from his belt. The costumes on show were humorous and interesting and all were homemade. After the grand parade, the judges awarded the first prize to Phillip. He just looked so winsome. Simon was naturally disappointed but accepted the outcome gracefully. This was to be a pattern of events that was repeated several times as the boys grew older, Phillip winning accolades and succeeding while Simon, who was equally talented, for one reason or another, perhaps lacking Phillip's drive and determination, never attaining the same level of public recognition for his efforts. Simon to his credit never became jealous of the success of his younger brother and as the older brother always looked after Phillip's interests and fiercely defended him when needed. This being England, we had just about completed the fancy dress parade and judging, when it started to rain. Fortunately we had anticipated this possibility and made arrangements with Black and Decker who at that time occupied the commercial estate on the other side of Canon Lane to use their canteen area for the remainder of the festivities.

The boys differed in other ways too. If they had been really naughty we would send them to their bedrooms. Simon's reaction would be to come straight out again; we could only keep him in there with great difficulty. Phillip on the other hand would defiantly shut himself in and would stay, barricaded in his room for hours if we let him. We would only be able to prize him out with considerable effort! Still, I think they both got the message when we resorted to such measures. When Simon was older, I remember one occasion when Ros had sent him to his room, when he uncharacteristically started shouting at her in an abusive manner. I got annoyed that he should treat his mother in this way and stormed upstairs to remonstrate with him. However as I shot up the stairs he shot past me down them and ran out into the street. I turned and ran after him intending to give him a swipe when I caught up with him but for the first time in his life and mine he outran me and I couldn't catch him. That was a mini watershed moment for me; to be outrun by my own son.

In the autumn of 1977, I took Simon down to Maidenhead Rugby Club and he joined the Mini-Rugby Section. He became a talented rugby player and represented his school side when he was at Cox Green Senior School. His best position was Centre and his master said he had the potential to play in that position at County level and beyond. The Cox Green side of which he was a member was highly successful and beat all the other schools around including rugby orientated public schools. However, although rugby was my first love and I consequently gave him every encouragement, Simon preferred football and switched to that game when he reached his early teens. He was a good left footed footballer but was probably a better rugby player. However much I would have preferred him to stay with the fifteen-a-side game and the rugby club, there was little point in trying to persuade him to change his natural affinity for the round ball game. He grew up supporting Chelsea Football Club and has loyally supported them through thick and thin over the years. Phillip grew up supporting Liverpool, which, in the 70s and 80s, in his formative years, was probably the most high profile and successful British soccer team.

In January 1978 Phillip followed Simon into full time education at Wessex Infants School. Phil prospered throughout his school years, gaining a clutch of Ordinary and Advanced level academic qualifications and excelling in sports. He was Berkshire County champion in the 100m sprint and played rugby and cricket for the County. He was also selected for and attended residential England Rugby training weeks at under 15 and 16 level but injury on both occasions meant that he never quite made the very top level by representing his country. Unfortunately he tended to be injury prone, partly because of the competitive and uncompromising way he entered into the spirit of the game. Simon was always more circumspect and rarely got injured. Academically, Simon was as bright as Phillip but lacked his application and determination to succeed in the subjects he was taught, apart from History that is, in which he had a strong personal interest and where he benefited from a sympathetic History master who knew how to get the best out of him. The Parents' Evenings we attended to discuss Simon's progress were invariably a nightmare. He would somehow contrive to get into trouble with the teaching staff just before the event and the common refrain from most of his teachers was that he had the ability but did not apply himself. Phillip's Parents' Evenings by contrast consisted of unstinting praise across the board. When he followed Simon at Cox Green Comprehensive School, I think it took Phillip some time to live down his older brother's bad reputation. Simon left school as soon as he could at the age of sixteen, convinced that he would succeed without paper qualifications and that he would be a millionaire by the time he was twenty. Phillip went on to University at Bournemouth where he graduated with a 2.1 degree in Business Administration.

Once the boys took up mini-rugby, it was not long before I became involved in the coaching of the youngest age group at Maidenhead. After a couple of years I took over as

Chairman of the Mini Section and in due course became Chairman of the Junior Section. During this time I gained an official coaching award from the Rugby Football Union. I eventually became Director of Youth Rugby on the reconstructed Management Board of the club and then spent an enjoyable year refereeing junior games before becoming Director of the Senior Playing side of the club, ending up as Director Playing Administration. This was a difficult time for the club. We had to adapt to the introduction in 1995 of professionalism while preserving, not only our amateur ethos and values but also our standing in the leagues and our financial future. Despite being unable to attract a major financial backer we managed to remain among the top one hundred clubs in the country. Bearing in mind that there are at least 1200 clubs in England, this was no mean achievement. When I stood down from the Management Board of the club in 2002 I felt that all the objectives I had helped to set had been achieved. By then I had been involved, one way or another, in the fortunes of the club, the players and its supporters for nigh on twenty five years. I consoled myself with the knowledge that I had done my bit and put back into the game I loved all that I had got out of it as a player. There were occasions when the responsibilities I had were demanding, not just in terms of the considerable amount of my free time I devoted to the club, but on the people management side also. Nonetheless it represented a relief for me from the stresses and strains of my paid job in Customs & Excise and I became friends with a lot of people through the club and through the social activities that we enjoyed together. I met Rick Smith at the club when his son was playing mini-rugby in Phillip's age group and we started playing squash together on Friday nights at the local leisure centre. That was around 1978.

We have continued playing each other and socialising most Friday nights since then although we have gravitated from squash to racket ball and now badminton as my leg joints and muscles become stiffer and less pliable with advancing years.

Phillip's two strongest friendships were forged with Cox Green school classmates, John Hadley and Stuart Williams who played rugby with him at Maidenhead. Simon's friends by contrast were largely fellow football players or fans such as Lee Carberry and the Milligan brothers. As the boys grew older Ros and I between us would ferry them to and from football as well as rugby matches at weekends not forgetting cricket and athletics in the summer and cubs when they were younger. At times we felt as though we were providing a free taxi and child minding service and looking back I don't know how we found the time to squeeze in all these activities taking into account the other demands we had of running a house and garden and going out to work. Still it was all worthwhile, even when we found ourselves having to take Phil to hospital to sit with him in the accident and emergency clinic for hours waiting for one of his sporting injuries to be treated. One Sunday morning at junior level, he got tackled in the process of scoring a last- minute, match winning try and was knocked unconscious. This did not involve a hospital visit fortunately because the game had ended and he quickly came round in the changing room but for hours afterwards kept asking us and anyone in the vicinity whether the conversion kick had been successful. The reply would be the same – '"Yes" - only for him to ask the same question two or three minutes later. He did eventually recover his full wits. It made me recall the time when Robbie Stevenson and I cycled to play an away game for the Old Boys on a ground opposite Richmond Park. I was knocked out playing at full back when I brought down an opposing player in a last-ditch tackle. His knee struck the base of my scull behind my left ear. I was resuscitated with the usual sponge of cold water and carried on playing, more by instinct than real awareness of what was happening. A little later in the game, I again found myself having to put in a last-ditch tackle and feeling groggy, again had the cold sponge treatment. When the final whistle went, I realised that I could not remember how we had got to the ground and on which peg I had hung my clothes in the changing room. I remember feeling anxious that I was unable to remember such straightforward things but in the bar afterwards my memory gradually returned and I cycled home with Robbie in the way we had arrived. While it lasted, it was a weird feeling.

I remember Phillip's last game of football. He played for a successful local side based in Burnham and was one of their leading goal scorers. It was a grey damp Sunday afternoon on a windswept muddy pitch in the Slough area. It was a cup final and I can't remember who won – I think they may have – but this was virtually irrelevant, such were the arguments, swearing, shouting and fighting on and off the pitch between players, parents and referee that Phil walked away at the end, vowing never to play in a soccer match again so disillusioned was he with the bitterness and anti-social attitudes that all too often permeate the game. He preferred, as I do, the social side of rugby and the general culture of the game where you try to knock seven bags of shit out of the opposition on the field of play but enjoy a drink and friendship with them in the bar afterwards. He carried on playing rugby for Maidenhead up to and including Colts level and he played at Bournemouth for the University 1st XV until finally having to retire through injury - what else - when he snapped the tendon in his finger.

Once the boys had started playing mini-rugby, and I became a non-playing member of the club, I was able to get tickets again each year for Five Nations Internationals at Twickenham. I remember taking Ros and the boys in the late 1970s after an absence of eight or nine years and being struck by how much faster and open the game had become since I had last attended an international game; it seemed like basketball by comparison. On one of these occasions when England were playing Ireland, I recall standing with Ros in the lower enclosure of the old West Stand, just in front of three Irish lads. The lad in the middle was virtually unconscious with drink and propped on either side by his mates to keep him from sinking into a heap on the ground. Every so often he would raise his head, half open his eyes and utter the slurred imprecation "Put your backs into it Ireland!" before slumping back into his semi-conscious state. On another occasion when we were with the boys in the West Stand ring seats, I remember Phillip being highly amused by the wit of an England supporter behind us at an England versus France game, when during a stoppage for attention to be given to an injured French player lying prone on the thick, lush Twickenham turf, shouting out in the relative quiet, "Why don't you just bury the bastard!" The banter at rugby matches was and largely remains, good natured, the fans happily mixed together in the same seating areas, remaining silent while kicks at goal are being taken and applauding outstanding play by either side. Simon reminded me recently of the time when he, Phillip and I were sitting in the old South Stand for an

England versus Australia match. At half time the England players were standing in a huddle on the half way line for their oranges and half time pep talk from the captain Billy Beaumont when suddenly, from almost immediately in front of us a young lady ran onto the pitch, bare to the waist, displaying the most magnificent pair of breasts you could ever wish to see. The crowd erupted, cheering and applauding and even Billy Beaumont, when he realised what was happening, gave up his earnest team talk to admire her capacious and perfectly formed bosom. Her name was Erica Roe and she became famous overnight. This game was remembered not so much for the fact that despite losing at half time England eventually won but for Erica's magnificent half time exploit and the rapturous reception from both spectators and players alike that she received. For years afterwards it was referred to as 'The Erica Roe Match'.

Every year in May at the end of the season we went as a family with other young families from the rugby club to Twickenham for the finals of the Middlesex Sevens Competition which in those amateur days was the most prestigious Sevens tournament in this country if not in the world as a whole. It was always a great day out and the weather was usually hot and sunny. Considerable quantities of food and drink were consumed over the course of the day and everybody behaved very civilly despite some unlicensed and generally amusing horse play from time to time, particularly in the extended interval preceding the grand final. One year, frightened by the introduction of government legislation designed to end football hooliganism and violence – never part of the rugby scene – the Twickenham authorities restricted the bar opening hours leading to long queues and good natured frustration. At one point, a spectator appeared who had patiently managed to negotiate the queues. He was walking along the edge of the pitch in front of the South Stand where we were sitting, carrying a large square metal tray, supporting several pints of beer for him and his mates to consume back in their seats. Holding the tray and its precious contents triumphantly aloft balanced on the upturned palm of one of his hands like a professional French waiter, his taxing mission almost accomplished, he smiled broadly like a Cheshire cat and gesticulated with his free hand towards the cheering and jeering crowd, when to everyone's amusement, somebody in the stand with a well aimed thrust of a broom handle at the underside of the tray, knocked the whole lot over. Crestfallen and soaked in beer, he quickly saw the funny side too.

Somehow or other, as well as the sporting activities in which we were involved, we managed to fit in visits with the boys to theme parks and museums, walks in the countryside and parties and dinner parties. Simon particularly enjoyed the visits we made to various places of interest and museums. I remember him covered in soot, scrambling enthusiastically over the tracks and climbing on and off steam engines at an open day one Easter at the Didcot Railway Museum. None of us in the family will ever forget the look on his face when leaving the Childe Beale Wildlife Centre in Pangbourne one Sunday afternoon he offered a peacock a lick of the ice cream cornet we had just bought him, whereupon the peacock snatched the whole cornet from his hand and ran off with it. Unfortunately the park had closed and the ice cream van had packed up so we were unable to buy him another ice cream to replace the one the peacock had so unexpectedly and deftly stolen from him. He laughed and we laughed. We had to admire the bravado and opportunism of our splendidly feathered friend.

By 1979 I was driving a Sahara beige Ford Cortina family saloon and went in it to France for our first foreign holiday together as a nuclear family. It was a camping holiday which we all very much enjoyed. We spent the first ten days in the Vendee on the coast and the final few days in Brittany and were surprised at the quality of the tented accommodation and the facilities of the campsites generally. Returning on the ferry, I encountered an old school friend, Fred Crowe, with his family. He was driving a rather sumptuous Volvo saloon and I felt somewhat ashamed at the model I was driving which was beginning to rust on the top of the off side wing. Nonetheless when I later sold the car to replace it with the first of the several Hondas I have owned, both Ros and I were convinced that it was silently shedding tears that we were abandoning it: silly I know. It was only a lump of metal after all but it really looked so sad and forlorn. It must have been on the afternoon of the day we were due to embark on this holiday that I popped into Maidenhead at the last minute to return and renew some library books when I locked the car keys in the car. I had parked outside the library and was beginning to panic as time was short and we had to be leaving to catch the car ferry from the channel port that evening. As I stood there wondering what to do, a man walked past and asked me if I was in trouble. I explained what had happened and much to my astonishment he plucked from his pocket a huge bunch of keys, the second of which he tried in my car door released the lock and I was able to retrieve my keys from the ignition. The holiday was saved and I thanked my lucky stars. Was he an itinerant car thief or what? – I don't know but his fortuitous appearance got me out of a tight spot.

The following year we borrowed my brother-in-law Peter's Volkswagen Camper Van for a summer holiday in Scotland. Unfortunately the weather was wet. In Edinburg I experienced true 'Scottish mist' for the first time. It was a peculiar mixture of fine rain and spray. When the sun did shine, which was usually when we were travelling, the scenery was breathtaking. I have vivid memories of Glencoe and Loch Lomond in this respect. We spent five days in a campsite at the foot of Ben Nevis which we hoped to climb but were prevented by inclement conditions. We got as far north as Loch Ness but did not see the famed monster. One evening at the campsite, the boys were playing an informal game of football with another couple of young Scottish boys when suddenly they heard Simon and Phillip talking to one another and in a tone of amazed disgust opined "Are you English?" I had never reckoned with the idea that the Scots and for that matter the Welsh and Irish had anything but unqualified friendly feelings towards their fellow English inhabitants of the British Isles. A lot of history and Celtic national pride burnt in that casual remark spat out in such distaste. Nevertheless they carried on playing football together. Before we returned home we vowed that the following year we would seek the sunshine abroad and apart from an ill-fated two weeks in York in the summer of 1985, which Ros and I both enjoyed and the boys, who were both in their teens, hated, our remaining family holidays were all spent on the continent. The redeeming feature for them in the York based holiday was the day we crossed the Pennines to watch an England Test Match at Old Trafford. The boys insist that we saw Ian

Botham batting but all I remember is that we were waiting with huge anticipation for him to come in to bat once the next wicket fell; but it never fell.

Random recollections of these continental holidays in the 1980s call to mind Phillip learning to swim on the water as well as under it in the hotel pool in Callela Northern Spain in 1981 and the look of astonishment and delight on his and Simon's face at a family evening at a local night club when they were each presented by the waitress with a cigar. I also recall playing crazy golf in C'An Picafort in Majorca the following year, when both the boys played better than I did and in 1983 in Westendorf in Austria when Simon won the skittles evening and downed his prize which consisted of glasses of schnapps leaving him decidedly tipsy on the way home. A couple of evenings later, I also got pretty tipsy on a group excursion to a restaurant-wine cellar in the mountains. On the way back to the hotel on the tour bus, I took over the commentary at the invitation of the official guide. Whenever I get a little tipsy I often think, misguidedly perhaps, that I become rather amusing. Anyway, I just let the words and observations flow as we hurtled down the mountain, mimicking the usual tour guide speech and had everybody falling about laughing as we reached the bottom. In Agde in the South of France in 1984 my ears were opened to the music of Spandau Ballet which Simon played constantly on his portable radio. One evening we were sitting in the garden area adjacent to our caravan where we had been eating our evening meal when an enormous brightly coloured cicada with bulging eyes suddenly flopped onto the table. Simon, Phillip and I immediately jumped to our feet in alarm, knocking over our chairs, while Ros remained seated wondering what all the fuss was about and mocking our manly cowardice – quite rightly – as she gently brushed the mighty insect to one side. This was the first of a series of four mobile home holidays that we took with the same provider, switching to a beautiful site near Agay in Provence for the next three years,1986 to 1989.

These holidays proved excellent value, giving controlled freedom for the boys within the campsite area and offering excellent facilities and enjoyment for Ros and me. After the first year, Simon, who had left school in 1987 with a single O Level qualification in History, the only subject he had really loved, started taking his holiday separately from the rest of the family. To compensate, Phillip took a school friend with him for each of the next three years. For the first of these years, Phillip took Luke Sale. Phillip at that time was about half as tall again as Luke. This frustrated Phillip who looked big enough and old enough to gain admittance to the campsite night club in the evening while Luke was barred as too young looking; although I believe they found a way round the problem.

On one of these holidays Phillip, though comparatively tall for his age was still fortunately small and lithe enough to climb through the sun roof of my red Honda Accord to retrieve my car keys which I had stupidly left in the ignition before locking the car doors. With the help of a friend from a neighbouring caravan we were able to insert a broom handle inside the flap style, off-side, rear window of the car and were able to engage the sunroof opening and closing button so that Phil could gain access. It was a triumph of luck, ingenuity and athleticism that meant I wasn't going to be lost after all in deepest France, as I initially feared. We all thought that Phillip was going to continue to be one of the tallest pupils in his class and that he would probably grow to be a six footer like me but shortly afterwards he stopped shooting upwards and was outstripped by most of his friends including Luke. Of the different friends he took, John Hadley was the best company and I shall never forget the struggle John had to contain himself one evening as I hit my head for the fourth time on the metal frame of the caravan door and let loose with a string of repeated F.... words "If I hit my F....... head on that F...... door one more F.....time" etc, etc. Poor John was red in the face and almost burst his ample girth with suppressed laughter.

We were disappointed that Simon had not made more of his academic opportunities at school particularly because everybody agreed, including Simon himself, that he was intelligent and had the ability. Unfortunately from our perspective he had fallen in with a crowd who although decent individuals in themselves were not academically inclined and had no ambition in that direction. Simon thought that loyalty to his friends and common sense was more important to him than qualifications. Unfortunately for him there was an economic recession in the late eighties and early nineties and he went from casual job to casual job ranging from fork lift driving, retail selling, financial advising and carpet fitting without making any real progress. He was out of work at times but never failed to look for employment and to contribute to the running of the home. He steadfastly refused to draw the dole and his friends were very loyal to him and supported him through this difficult period. It was eventually through these friends that he had the opportunity to obtain a permanent position at Mars in Slough. I shall never the forget the rainy night when

I sat in my car outside the Mars building waiting for Simon to return from his final recruitment interview, praying that he would not be rejected. Mars have always maintained high recruitment standards and jobs with the company are highly sought after. I was so proud of him and relieved when he came back and told me that he had got through and I felt so pleased for him that he could now look forward to a career of substance, where at the price of shift working, he would earn good money and would be able to make progress within the company according to his own merits and to his performance on the job.

The same year that Simon left school we had an extension built on the house. I sit here now writing this story in what was originally the garage and is now a study. We built a new garage on the driveway forward from and interconnecting with this additional room and linked it in an 'L' shape with the existing living room which increased that area by half. At the time we debated whether to move or extend and chose the latter course which I have never really regretted. The boys were adamant that they didn't want to move away from the area and their friends. While the extension was being built Ros and I went on holiday on our own as a couple for the first time since we had the children. I took Ros to Paris, a city I had always loved since my youth but she had never visited. That year I had received a fairly substantial and unexpected bonus at work and decided with little hesitation to spend it on this trip. Much as we love our children it was wonderful for Ros and me to spend time in each other's company without having to worry about their immediate needs. Simon was old enough to look after Phillip and we felt confident that they would come to no harm in our absence. The following year, having received a second and last bonus before the scheme was withdrawn, Ros and I went to Venice on the same basis. However, to return for a moment to the Paris trip, we found, when we got back home, the house was still standing and the boys had coped pretty well in our absence. Nevertheless, there had been 'an accident'. Nothing material in the house was broken but Simon had lost his front tooth. We asked how it had happened and both he and Phillip came up with explanations which seemed strange and vaguely improbable but from which they could not be shaken. They were evasive but when pressed, they said that Simon had stepped on the end of a plank covering part of the unfinished extension and the other end of the plank had hit him in the mouth dislodging the tooth. Knowing where the plank was lying I found it difficult to envisage from a purely mechanical point of view how this could have happened. It wasn't until many years later that we discovered the truth.

For Simon's eighteenth birthday we agreed that he could organise a party for himself and his friends using the new spare room-study as the venue. Arriving at our front door his friends were welcomed and ushered through our main living room into the party room which had been suitably decorated for the occasion. Once everybody who was expected had arrived, we let Simon close the door into the spare room so they could enjoy themselves without troubling us old fuddy duddies. Ros and I finished what we were doing and after a relatively short interval settled down with Phillip to watch a Barry McGuigan championship boxing match on the television. Just before the fight was due to start imagine our surprise when the door into the spare room opened and a large policeman in full uniform suddenly appeared before us in our living room asking us whether we were aware of the fight going on outside. We felt pretty stupid and embarrassed, to say the least, and had to admit that we were aware of the party going on but not of any trouble developing. Apparently members of the notorious local Holyport gang had got wind of the party and a battle had ensued with Simon and his friends sallying back and forth through the interconnecting door giving access through our new garage to the street outside where missiles including beer cans were being thrown. The people who lived on the corner had apparently had beer cans land in their garden and, being the kind of stuffy couple they were, had rung the police to complain. We were blissfully unaware of the turmoil outside in the street and, after receiving a dressing down from the police inspector about parental responsibility, were left feeling chastened and unsettled for the rest of the evening.

That summer we stopped overnight on the drive down to Agay at Vallon Pont D'Arc, intending by prior arrangement to meet up with my brother and his wife Ann who regularly spent a few weeks in their caravan in that part of France. They were both teachers and Francophiles and could afford an extended break. This was in the days before the advent of mobile phones and though we waited by the predetermined spot at the appointed hour and beyond, they never showed up. The following year we agreed even more precise rendezvous details and were relieved when they arrived at the hotel where we were staying (The Auberge de Die) to join us for dinner in the evening. It was a delightful meal which we enjoyed sitting outside in the hotel garden in the warmth of the Provencal dusk. I was relaxed, taking the opportunity to exercise my communication skills and thinking, honed over the years in my management capacity at work. I talked a lot and the conversation flowed. However, on reflection, shortly afterwards, it struck me as strange that my brother had not entered the conversation at all throughout the evening. He seemed to be quizzically observing from the sidelines not entering into the spirit of the occasion as he normally did. I concluded that perhaps he had not been feeling well and forgot about it. Several months later after we had not heard from him, I recalled this incident and it crossed my mind that they might have been experiencing marital problems, difficult though this was to believe, because they always seemed so close and, unlike Ros and I, never argued between themselves. Ros decided to give Ann a ring. Ann was in a terrible state. Roger, who was headmaster of a local middle school in Mansfield had been seeing another woman, a teaching colleague and headmistress of a similar school in the area. They had been co-opted from their schools to conduct an educational project and their relationship had developed from there. Roger had continued living at home and had kept the affair secret until Ann discovered what had been going on after a hotel where my brother and this lady had stayed overnight sent an earring she had inadvertently left in the bedroom through the post addressed to 'Mrs Cottee'. Roger and Joan, for such was her name, had obviously signed themselves in as Mr & Mrs Cottee. Ann was understandably devastated and reluctantly accepted that the marriage was over though Roger at first refused to leave the marital home. My mother was there supporting Ann when Roger finally, reluctantly, quit and was appalled by the vindictive and cruel way he behaved towards his wife of so many years and the mother of his two children. As a consequence my mother wrote him out of her will but did not tell him. This meant that when my mother died in 1993 that duty fell to me. Roger tried his utmost to squeeze every last penny from Ann as part of the divorce settlement and in the circumstances, my sister and I who were the main beneficiaries, felt that the provisions of my mother's will, making a small behest in Ann's favour and excluding him should be honoured. My mother after all had made it abundantly clear that she did not want any of her money going to Roger's new partner –"That woman!" Roger never once rang me or spoke to me to explain what had happened or to express any regret at the outcome. After he moved into a house in Laxton that he and Joan had bought, he did ring me out of the blue to tell me that "We (he and Joan) are very happy" and to give me his new address and to tell me that we could pop in at any time. He seemed to think that we could just switch over to his new situation as though nothing had happened. When I tried to explain how we felt and to try and reach some accommodation with him and with his changed circumstances, he became patronising and schoolmasterly in tone, talking to me as though I was a small boy. I had always considered him to be my best friend and was disappointed by his self-righteousness and pomposity. Before I could make any further progress with him, he swore at me and put the phone down.

I heard nothing further from him until we received an invitation from Joan to attend his combined fiftieth birthday celebration and retirement do in a hotel in the area where they lived. Ros and I, my sister Sue and her husband Ken accepted in the hope that we could begin repairing the relationship between us and consequently drove all the way up there armed with cards and presents including a present from my mother. He took the cards and presents and although Joan made desperate attempts at welcoming us to engage us in small talk, Roger basically cut us dead. He adopted the same approach when we met at his daughter Nicola's first wedding and it wasn't until she re-married in 2007 that he acknowledged us and engaged, at my initiative, in an extended conversation. I asked him how he was getting on and we covered quite a lot of ground on the subject of his life and pursuits but he was clearly not interested in anything I had to tell him about my life. But at least we were back on speaking terms. Apparently, even now he blames Ann and us for the breakdown and the day after the wedding, made disparaging remarks to Ann to that effect with a vindictive look on his face. Ah well – so be it!

# APOGEE

During my time at Hayes Excise in the 1970s I had earned a reputation with senior managers within the West London Region for being an intelligent, effective, modern manager and had made a good impression with the then Chairman of the Department, Paul Radford, on a visit he paid to our offices. Sometime later, I was pleased that I was selected for a high powered, six weeks residential management training course at the Civil Service College at Sunningdale. Selection was restricted to those young and middle managers who had the potential to rise to senior management levels during the course of their careers and I enjoyed the time I spent there. It broadened my outlook and provided me with an invaluable insight into how the government of the day and the Civil Service worked together. I remember one evening in the main bar, Bernard Ingham, Prime Minister Margaret Thatcher's formidable Press Secretary and general right hand man, entered the lounge area where we were relaxing after our day's exercises. He was surrounded by a jostling mob of acolytes and admirers, fawning on his every word and gesture and I realised how potent a force political power is and the lengths to which some people will go to prostrate themselves before the alter of its intoxicating influence.

In 1979, I was put forward by the regional head (Collector) for vetting for promotion to the Principal grade. David Admans, my Surveyor colleague at Hayes of whom I had always been in awe, was also put forward. We were the only two to be selected from our region. The Collector kindly arranged for us to undergo mock interviews before we both attended the official assessment, chaired by a Board member in our London Headquarters, situated then in Mark Lane, adjacent to Tower Hill. I fared disastrously at the mock interview while David apparently, and as far as I was concerned, not unexpectedly, gave a good account of himself. However, I learnt a great deal from the experience and was successful at the real thing, while, to everyone's surprise, David failed. Partly, my success stemmed from realising what qualities the selection panel were looking for and how best to present my thinking and arguments to them. I had one particularly tricky question on race relations relating to a trader who was facing strike action from a predominantly white workforce - "Were I to send a non-white officer on a control visit?" I said I would do all in my power to persuade the trader to accept the non-white officer but under severe pressure conceded that I could possibly get someone else to do the visit on this one occasion. I sensed a palpable sense of relief and agreement from the panel members when I finally suggested this solution. I guess that, given that I worked in an area with a large immigrant population, they were testing me to find out whether I harboured strong racist or anti-racist views and the extent to which I would balance my own principles and the wider issue of race relations with the more pragmatic, revenue orientated requirements of the Department. In giving my answer, I'm still not sure that I was right to suggest this concession but I have no doubt that it helped to secure my success at the interview. Throughout my adult life I have struggled with this dilemma and to some extent struggle with it still. How far should one stand by one's principles and at what personal cost? How far should one adopt the pragmatic approach and go along with the commonly held view when this conflicts with your true beliefs? I have written about this dilemma in a poem I wrote following my visit with Ros to the Nazi extermination camp at Auschwitz–Birchenau in May 2007.

While I waited for a Principal grade vacancy to come up, I transferred in October 1979 from Hayes Excise District to Southall VAT office and spent a year and a half there familiarising myself with the administration of the tax. I was elected Chairman of the Sports and Social Club and helped organise many events including a successful Christmas party to which family members were invited. Eventually in April 1981 my number came up and I was posted to Headquarters in Mark Lane where I joined Outfield Division heading up the Branch providing policy advice on Outfield manpower and finance questions. I had hoped to be appointed to a mainstream Policy Division but was nevertheless excited to be taking up my new responsibilities at the higher grade. On my first day, I was seen by Roy Lewis, the Deputy Director of the Division who greeted me with the words "You know why you've been sent here?" couched in a semi-rhetorical tone. Before I had time to answer, his phone rang. He picked it up and spoke for several minutes. When he finally put the phone down, he passed on to talk about other aspects of my appointment having obviously forgotten about the question he had posed and the fact that I had not been given the opportunity to respond. I regret that I did not interrupt him and take him back to his opening remark. Sometime later, I concluded that I had probably been specially selected to work in Outfield Division because I was considered to be an individual with the potential to become a regional head

(Collector) and this was the information he had been on the verge of giving me. Unfortunately, this message did not come across when it would have been of most value to me. Partly for this reason, I did not make the best of my opportunity in the Division. I have to say also that I was astonished by the sycophancy, indecision and self-seeking that flourished in this particular Division that was very much alien to the working environment and independent responsibility for setting policy and decision making that I had been expecting. The management style of Ron Weston, the Director of the Division who was effectively head of the whole of the operational staff of the Department was also alien to my notions of good management. He was a wooden-headed, self-important, pompous, autocrat who I made the cardinal mistake of addressing as 'Ron' in an informal meeting in his room. I should apparently have addressed him more formally and deferentially as 'Mr Weston' or 'Director' (or perhaps 'Herr Director'!). From this point on my aspirations for further career advancement levelled off. I was widely acknowledged outside the Division by other policy divisions with whom I came into contact as a fair, objective, reliable, decisive and valued Headquarters colleague who they enjoyed working with. Having said that, I was not interested in the degree to which many of my senior headquarters colleagues both inside and outside my own Division devoted their waking hours to self promotion and personal intrigue in the furtherance of their careers. I learned that the phrase 'Taking the wider view' really meant 'what's in it for me?' I was more concerned to do my job well to the best of my ability and to let my achievements speak for themselves. Unfortunately this was perhaps an over narrow outlook but at the end of the day I was not prepared to sacrifice my self esteem and my private life with my family to become a self-seeker, totally wedded to the Department. At some point just before I left Headquarters to take up an appointment as Assistant Collector London Airports Collection in October 1984, Frank Rush, an erstwhile mentor of mine who I greatly respected and who later became Director Outfield himself, told me that the consensus was that I had demonstrated that I had the brains but lacked some of the diplomatic skills necessary to get right to the top. I thought this was fair comment. Had I decided to go with the flow to further my own career, posturing and flattering those I despised and disagreed with, there were nevertheless, seriously bright ambitious people in the upper reaches of the Department serving the government of the day and British people with great integrity and efficiency who would have provided stiff competition to me. I have some regrets that I did not fare better but I achieved more than a lot of other people and was comfortable in my senior operational management role with the freedom, responsibility, status and influence I enjoyed in the remaining fifteen years or so of my chosen career.

I remained based at Custom House Heathrow for the next eight years responsible initially for the processing of freight clearance documentation, licensing and revenue raising before taking on the overall administration duties relating to operational Customs staff at all the London airports including Gatwick and Stansted as well as Northolt and Denham. In this latter role I worked directly to the Collector as his adjutant. In the last four years I became responsible for staff engaged in passenger clearance work in Terminals1 and 2 at Heathrow, Crew Clearance in the Queens Building, and VIP arrivals and departures via the VIP suite situated on the south side of the airport. I also used to cover Gatwick

Airport when the incumbent Assistant Collector went on leave and in my final year took charge of the relatively newly opened Stansted Airport freight and passenger terminals which I combined with an audit and quality assurance role covering all the UK South East Airports.

I enjoyed the buzz of working at these airports. Heathrow in particular was a mini city that worked non-stop, round the clock, 365 days a year. The throughput of passengers, baggage and freight was huge. I became Chairman of the London Airports Customs Rugby Club and fondly remember the two trips I made to Paris when we played French Customs on the weekend of the France v England International. The French were wonderful hosts. So much so that Maurice Tomkinson, Deputy Collector, who accompanied me on the second trip, failed to recover from our Friday night's alcoholic bash in time for breakfast the following morning. I had to wake him up when he didn't appear for breakfast by which time the Collector Paris had turned up and was waiting for us outside the hotel in a chauffeur driven official car for a pre-arranged private tour of the Paris sights. Maurice who was a coffee junky was gasping for a restorative cup after the previous nights indulgence but our host left immediately speeding on from sight to sight without a moment's respite. Poor Maurice was too polite to protest. When we eventually finished the tour and repaired to a pavement restaurant along the Champs Elysee selected by our French colleague, I felt so sorry for Maurice that I ordered him a coffee when the waiter came to take our order for lunch. The waiter and the Collector Paris dropped their eyes over their noses and shrugged in Gallic fashion but did not demur. However, you could see them thinking that this was yet another example of the mad

English and their lack of taste and refinement in their choice of aperitifs. Unfortunately for Maurice, the coffee when it came was not of the expected restorative proportions he was hoping for and in typical French after dinner style was contained in a tiny cup undiluted with milk. At this point we both gave up and I had to try hard not to betray too much amusement. Thankfully Maurice eventually recovered himself and we had a pleasant lunch at the Collector's expense and enjoyed a great afternoon afterwards, accompanied by Marc LeReste, the French Customs Attaché in London, in the Parc Des Princes watching France beat England with the crowd shouting "Ole!" whenever the French mounted a stylish attack on the English backline. Later back in England, I vaguely remember one hugely enjoyable, long and emotionally tiring lunch in High Holborn in London with Marc LeReste - all in the line of duty, of course! Returning to Heathrow on the tube, I nearly got involved in a fight with two Irishmen trying to help them interpret the London Undergound map, collected my car from the central area car park where I had left it and drove home. I have no recollection of driving home and fell into the living room exclaiming "F... Maggie Thatcher!" I had always strongly disliked her for her smug anti-Europeanism, for her narrow unbridled simplistic grocer's daughter approach to economics and for her disdainful and unfair treatment of loyal hardworking public sector employees like myself. Around this time she was becoming ever more self absorbed and insufferable. Imagine my delight when finally on 20 November 1990 she fell from power. I was away from home delivering a presentation on continuous improvement and quality assurance at the annual London Airports Collection Management Conference at a hotel in Ascot when the news broke. I was so pleased that we were free at last from the small minded tyranny of the wretched woman that, for the one and only time when I was away from home on business, I rang Ros from the hotel to share my joy with her.

I was also involved with French Customs when I was selected for a sponsored Exchange Visit as part of the European Union Mattheus Programme designed to promote closer co-operation and harmonisation of Customs and Internal Revenue procedures in member states. I spent two weeks in 1990 based in Lille in Northern France working alongside my French opposite number and staying with him and his family. It was a great opportunity to improve my French. We agreed that I would speak only French while I was in France and he would speak English when he paid his return visit to work and live along side me in England. By the time I flew back to England I was not only thinking in French but dreaming in French as well! It was thrilling to be taken for a flight from Rouen in a French Customs helicopter dive bombing shipping in the Channel, although quite how effective this tactic was in Customs terms seemed doubtful to me. I also had a lovely lunch with my opposite number responsible for the Boulogne coastal area. He wore silk gloves and carried a cane. He was a member of a minor branch of French aristocracy linked with Polish aristocrats. His name was Wyczeniciki. He lived in a small fortress style chateaux with views over the channel from whence, he claimed, that on a clear day you could see the English coast. He was an ardent anglophile and despite my intention to speak only in French insisted in exercising his proficiency in English. This was very good but hopelessly out of date. He sounded just like a World War II Battle of

Britain pilot, which oddly matched his attire and general air. He was married to a raven haired Basque beauty who served us with champagne, sandwiches and a whole smoked salmon born on a silver salver. She remained silent throughout while his children played on the stone floor addressing him when they wanted something as 'Sir'. This experience, coupled with the way the French Customs was structured and fulfilled its function and the hierarchical construction of French thought and the French language brought home to me the surprising realisation that, despite the French revolution in 1789, decision making was still very centralised with even minor decisions being referred to 'Paris' and there was more overt and covert social distinction operating in management cadres and among the population generally than in modern Britain. One decision that wasn't referred to 'Paris' however, was a shooting incident at the Franco-Belgian border that was casually mentioned at the after work evening gathering of senior managers in the region at a local town square cafe. Earlier in the day apparently, shots had been fired at Customs Officers as they approached a Volkswagen car in the control lane. The car sped off and the French Customs Officers who, like their French Police brethren, carried firearms as part of their standard equipment, fired back in retaliation. Nobody was hurt and the car and its occupants fled the scene un-apprehended. In England this would have caused a sensation with widespread media and political coverage. But this was France. My French colleagues behaved as though it was just part of the daily routine and quite normal.

Back in England accompanied by Patrick, my exchange colleague, an enormous flap was going on about trade statistics and long-standing procedural oversights that had led to passenger airliners not being included when first acquired by British airlines. The knives were out and I was disappointed if not wholly surprised at the behaviour of some of my senior management colleagues attempting to shift the blame away from themselves and onto other people, me included, in the ensuing witch hunt. The truth was that no one individual was to blame, certainly not me. Revised procedures were subsequently put in place to close the loophole.

Later that same year I was honoured to receive an invitation from the Lord Chamberlain to attend the Queen's Garden Party at Buckingham Palace in recognition of my contribution to the work of the Department. Ros and I attended on a blustery but sunny day in July and had an interesting time mingling with the 'Great and The Good'. We weren't actually selected to be spoken to personally by Her Majesty but were marshalled to stand in line as she passed by. Ros was thrilled as were the rest of my family. While on the subject of royalty I remember the day that Princess Diana visited Heathrow. She was a striking looking lady and caused quite a stir all round. I had of course seen a number of minor royals pass through the VIP suite at the airport which fell within my Division. Occasionally I had to attend high level planning meetings at the suite when top politicians and heads of state were due to arrive. I was present when US President Reagan emerged after a dramatic pause from Airforce One and waved to the assembled media reporters and cameramen. I was standing a good hundred yards away but his warmth and charisma came across to me straight away. He was met by Maggie Thatcher whose meticulously coiffured bouffant hairstyling was being severely buffeted in the wind. I was also present when the Russian Premier Mikhail Gorbachov accompanied by his lovely wife Raisa arrived in London some few weeks later. He had become a key figure in ending the Cold War and had struck up a good relationship with both Reagan and Margaret Thatcher. He walked from his aircraft down the red carpet side by side with Maggie each of them moving their mouths as if they were talking, for the benefit of the cameras. In the planning meetings preceding these two visits I was struck by the differences in approach and personnel fielded by the two rival superpowers. The Americans were head on, high powered, leaving nothing to chance, no nonsense and determined. Their CIA security guys were cloned clean-cut white rain-coated robots who would have killed on sight without batting an eyelid had they been ordered. The Russians by contrast were amusing, relaxed, a trifle dishevelled in dress, and one or two of them had probably been enjoying a drink or two. They were much easier to get on with and were more accommodating in outlining their requirements.

Before I left the airport, I became involved in a disciplinary case at Gatwick when I was covering for the Assistant Collector in charge at that airport while he was away on leave. One afternoon while I was there, one of the operational managers asked to see me and sought my advice on a situation that had developed in the Customs baggage hall with a young adult East Asian female. She had been stopped by a Customs officer as she was passing through the Green 'Nothing to Declare' Channel and was asked to open her bags for inspection. Young females travelling alone were regarded as high risk from a drug smuggling point of view and the officer in question had selected her for further questioning and baggage examination accordingly. The problem was that she had become hysterical when conducted to the baggage examination area. Supervising officers had been called in an attempt to calm her down to no avail and the duty operational manager had become involved. Under his influence she eventually regained her composure and told him that she had been stopped at Gatwick about two years ago in similar circumstances and was terrified that the ordeal she had undergone then was about to be repeated. She said that a uniformed Customs Officer who she accurately described had taken her down to a windowless room on the floor below which she also accurately described where she was told to strip naked and was then beaten by the officer in question with a leather belt that he removed from his trousers and told that she had been 'a naughty girl'. She had not in fact contravened any Customs requirements and following her beating was allowed by the officer to put her clothes back on again and to leave the airport. She said she told the people she was visiting that something terrible had happened to her in Customs but was too frightened, shocked and embarrassed to complain about her treatment. The operational manager said he was inclined to believe her story. I immediately authorised an approach to our Departmental internal disciplinary investigation branch who arranged to send two of their officers to Gatwick to interview the officer who fitted the description the passenger had given. He was due to come on duty that evening but never showed up. The grape vine had obviously been busy. In fact he telephoned the following day to say that he was unwell. He then obtained a doctor's certificate to cover his absence and was retired on ill health grounds some months later before he could be interviewed.

I had worked with this individual for a while in my days in the Investigation Unit in West London. He seemed normal enough then. But Customs officers do wield enormous power and in a small minority of cases, these powers can be abused. It is a pity that he was not able to be interviewed so that the matter could bc properly resolved one way or another based on the available evidence. When I was a Surveyor at Hayes Excise in the 1970s, I had myself investigated on behalf of our Headquarters Discipline Branch a similar case that had occurred at Heathrow. On this occasion we were able to interview the officer against whom the complaint had been made but he steadfastly denied any wrongdoing. The passenger, a teenage Iranian male, claimed that he had been taken by the officer to a windowless room and after he had stripped naked the officer had fondled his genitalia. The youth when we interviewed him was relatively convincing; the Customs officer less so. However at the end of the day it was the passenger's word against the officer's and nothing could be proved one way or the other. I subsequently received a letter of thanks through the Collector from the Headquarters Branch responsible for staff discipline commenting that the enquiry had been 'conducted with great diligence but with a proper regard for the need not to give unnecessary offence in any quarter' and that the report I had submitted at the end with my conclusions was 'a model of clarity and comprehensiveness' to which the Collector had added his congratulations for my 'high standard of performance in rather unusual and difficult circumstances'. I was pleased to receive this unexpected feedback.

The Department quite rightly prided itself on its integrity, a quality I unfortunately omitted to identify when asked by the recruitment interview board to specify the most important qualities a Customs Officer should possess. I must admit that when the panel member who asked the question suggested this quality to me, it had not occurred to me that this was so integral to the very traditional Department of State that I was hoping to work for, although I quickly agreed with him. Thereafter, the word always stuck in my mind and I and the vast majority of the people who worked in the Department fully subscribed throughout their careers to the trust and honourable behaviour the term implied. In my experience the service was pretty clean and there were indeed very few instances of bribery, corruption or serious staff irregularity like the aforementioned cases. This was no doubt in part due to the overwhelming time and effort customarily placed by managers on trying to catch their fellow officers out. Though justified before the invention of motor cars and modern communications when officers operated largely on their own in remote locations, the lack of trust enshrined in this one dimensional approach became counter-productive in the latter half of the twentieth century.

At London Airports and later at Maidenhead Business Centre, I was responsible, as Head of Office, for investigating all but the most serious complaints from passengers, traders, members of the public and Members of Parliament affecting the work of my Division and my staff and drafting replies up to and including Ministerial level. This was sometimes a difficult task, having to balance the interests of the staff and their morale against the need for integrity – that word again – and the opportunity to learn from our mistakes. I enjoyed a reputation for getting to the essence of the nature of the complaint and surrounding circumstances, assessing them fairly and honestly.

My draft replies for our Departmental Minister to send and draft replies to Parliamentary Correspondence in general were rarely altered. This is saying quite something when you know, as I do from first-hand experience, the way the wordsmiths and spin doctors in the upper reaches of the Civil Service and the Government work.

As a manager myself, I was always trying to shift the emphasis of the managerial focus and effort away from undiluted mistrust and hostility into more positive channels. I earned a reputation at Board and Senior Management level for being a progressive manager and was held up as an example of how the approach I adopted produced a more highly motivated and innovative workforce and better results. Belatedly the Department itself recognised the problem following a damning report by a pair of graduates from Bath University who had been charged with undertaking an independent review of management in the service. This became known as the Bath Study and led to an attempt to change the culture called the People Initiative. The initiative was well intentioned and pointed for once in the right direction as far as I was concerned but influenced by the nature of the work they do and negative management attitudes in the past, the vast majority of the staff remained deeply cynical about the whole exercise. Some aspects of the initiative like giving everyone £50 to spend on some frippery for themselves were naive and misguided, particularly when, true to form, the Department later tried to take some individuals to task for spending the money on 'inappropriate' items. Needless to say the Board had omitted to specify at the outset what would be regarded as 'appropriate' or 'inappropriate'. Numerous similarly shallow, ill-thought through, patronising management initiatives followed and are being generated to this day but judging by the letters in the Departmental magazine which, in retirement, I still receive, the underlying problems largely remain. Nevertheless, before The Department I knew and loved for all its faults merged with the Inland Revenue, I like to think that in the last ten years or so of my career when the tide from above was at last flowing in my direction, I made a small difference.

I had always sought to push out the boundaries of the Department's innately cautious and defensive culture into a more adventurous, open approach, in which people were inspired, trusted and stretched as well as disciplined when appropriate. I am sure that at times I let my frustration and irritation show with those colleagues who didn't appreciate the need to move as fast or as far as I did in this direction.

In what was to be my last move in HM Customs & Excise, I transferred in July 1992 to a Customs & Excise Business Centre, housed in a smart, modern two storey, open plan office block in Bell Street, Maidenhead, not two and a half miles from home. I have fond memories of this place and the people who worked there. As well as being Head of Office for some 150 staff employed in customer service, registration, debt collection and the auditing of 25000 small, medium and large businesses across 25 internal tax and international trade regimes raising £1.5 billion annually for the UK Exchequer, I was given the functional leadership role throughout the Thames Valley Region for the development and strategic management of specialist audit work, debt collection and the training and development of managers. I was also Chairman of the Thames Valley Sports and Social Club and organised the annual Collection

Sports Days each year. I was also chosen by my boss John Barnard, the Thames Valley Regional Director (Collector) to organise and run the National Departmental Sports Day, which our Collection successfully hosted at Oxford in August 1988 on the same running track where Roger Bannister became the first athlete in the world to run a four minute mile.

One of the reasons for moving to Maidenhead apart from the convenience of working closer to home was to enable me to accommodate more easily the fairly heavy involvement I had at that time with the running of Maidenhead Rugby Club. I had progressed from coaching in the Mini Section where I gained a coaching qualification from the Rugby Football Union to Chairmanship of the Mini and then Junior Sections of the Club. I then took over the Chairmanship of the whole of the Youth set up before taking over as Director of the Senior Playing Side of the club in the early 1990s. My involvement with the club, though demanding in terms of the time I spent and the effort I put in, nevertheless came as cathartic release from the ever increasing pressures to which I and other senior managers were being subjected in the paid employment world.

The main focus at Maidenhead was on the collection and policing of Value Added Tax (VAT). Over the eight years while I was in charge, outputs increased year on year by substantial amounts in excess of the stretching targets we had been set. I was proud of this achievement. I like to think I ran a tight ship but also a ship, to continue the analogy, where I encouraged the officers and crew to work in a friendly yet challenging atmosphere and to take responsibility and to use their initiative to improve performance. I was pleased that my success and the work of my staff were recognised when we were commended by the Cabinet Office in November 1995 for our service to the public in a competition sponsored by the Civil Service magazine *Management Matters.* We received the award for our activities designed to improve relationships with the business community. These included holding consultation meetings with representatives from local trade bodies, carrying out a trader survey, attending business exhibitions and running VAT information and education seminars. The award took the form of a certificate personally signed by Sir Robin Butler, Secretary of the Cabinet and Head of the Home Civil Service. I had the certificate framed and it now proudly adorns my cloakroom wall at home. A year later we were featured in the monthly Customs & Excise departmental magazine in an article highlighting the benefits of team working. This followed a highly complementary letter from Kinsley Lord, consultants appointed by the then Chairman, Valerie Strachan to advise her on ways of becoming a *World Class* organisation. In their field work they engaged in a workshop with my Debt Management Unit. The unit consistently produced the best results in the country and not surprisingly impressed Andrew Jackson of Kingsley Lord who subsequently wrote to my boss, Collector John Barnard, saying that-

> *In all their experience of working with teams across a whole load of different organisations, the team was quite outstanding. The team spirit and loyalty at Maidenhead was really powerful; and clearly the team leader played a very strong role in creating that. What really impressed however was how the "soft teamy stuff" really led through*

*directly to hardnosed business results. So all credit to the team, but they were also explicit that they were working in an environment which allowed them to perform in this way, so wider credit is due. I came away from the day inspired by what I had heard, and when we gave the Board feedback, they too shared that feeling.*

To which John Barnard had added in manuscript on the letter-

*Norman - Nothing I didn't know!! It's good to have such recognition for what you and your management team are doing. I heard separately how much it had cheered and inspired the Board.*

This led to the nomination of the unit for the first ever Chairman's Award introduced in the following year. The citation from the Corporate Development Group to the Chairman read-

*A major strand of the work on People and Performance, commissioned by the Board last Autumn, was a Study Programme which examined the link between business performance and the cultural style of a cross-section of operational teams judged by their respective management commands as being 'best in class' performers. The research was conducted by the Quality Development team supported by Andrew Jackson from management consultants Kingsley Lord. The main objective of the study was to identify the factors – cultural or otherwise – that contributed to the excellent performance of the teams.*

*As part of the research process, we selected for interview line managers in the same chain as the nominated team. We asked the Assistant Collector Maidenhead Value Added Tax Office (me) to tell us why the Debt Management Unit (DMU) had been chosen. He gave the following rationale for the choice:*

*"First and foremost, the team delivers results; not only in the short term but over a period of time. Long term trends demonstrate clearly the ethos of continuous improvement. On results alone this team sets the benchmark for DMUs nationally. But how the team operates is important. There is a real sense of purpose and success is based on effective team working. This has much to do with the style of the team leader who follows a philosophy of empowerment and has succeeded in creating a climate that encourages self-development."*

*These comments were born out during our work with the team. Their attitude and approach to delivering business results was based on a deep conviction that more would be achieved through working collaboratively with traders. The team talked of the need to 'listen to customer needs'. The philosophy was one of encouraging business to pre-empt enforcement action by entering into an early dialogue about possible options. To carry this philosophy through the team had to change the perception of traders so that the DMU was regarded as helping business and supporting the local economy. Evidence of their success could be found in the number of complaints received. Only one in the quarter we visited-* ***compared to eleven complimentary letters****. The team found no difficulty in finding the balance between facilitation and regulation. Their attitude was best summed up by the team leader:*

*we're not afraid to say no – we don't deal in sentiment. We deal in quality of service."*

*Under greatest achievements they listed the record lowest debt for 1995/6 – an outstanding performance. But they also described their achievements in terms of relationships they had forged with one another, their ability to cope with constant change, their total commitment to their work, and effective teamwork. These cultural factors were observable throughout our work with the team. Individuals spoke of a team characterised by 'kindness and caring', that they 'enjoyed each other's company away from work', that interactions were always 'tempered by tolerance' and 'enlivened by humour' and that there existed a genuine esprit de corps. We concluded that their style of operating embodied the principles set out in the People Framework and that it was the team leader who, through role modelling desired behaviours and putting respect for the individual at the heart of the team values, had helped to create an extraordinary team.*

*In reporting early findings to the Board's Conference in October 1996, Andrew Jackson made special reference to Maidenhead DMU. He described them as* ***the best example of effective team working he had seen in any organisation he had worked in, both public and private.*** *We agree entirely with Andrew's comments and have no hesitation in supporting this nomination for the Chairman's Award.*

I was delighted with these successes at the time. However, re-reading the correspondence in the calm of my retirement far away from the rough and tumble of everyday business life, I am even prouder. My Customer Service and Debt Management teams took the immediate glory but every one of the teams in my Division operated in the same way and were equally successful from a results and cultural perspective. I am confident that had any one of these other units been put forward for an award, they too would have won. Looking back, this represented the apogee of my contribution to the development of the HM Customs & Excise. Although in different circumstances, I could perhaps have advanced one step further in senior management, I am not stupid enough that I don't understand why this didn't happen. I regret not having achieved this ultimate advancement but I am pleased with the recognition I received for my contribution at Divisional level in my last years and the inspiration I gave to colleagues in all grades up to and including members of the Board.

My retirement from HM Customs & Excise came in March 2000 after forty years of public service. John Barnard attended my retirement 'do' held in the Bell Street Business Centre, as did Ros, Simon and Phillip and my sister Sue. In my farewell speech, thanking all my colleagues, among other things, I expressed the hope that with my departure there would be no slipping back to the inward looking, keep everything to ourselves, can't make up our minds, don't want to be criticised for making wrong decisions, macho, kneejerk, scatter gun, painting by numbers, blame game school of management. I asked that managers should continue to be bold, treating their subordinates neither as villains nor as frightened children incapable of understanding the realities of life and its attendant uncertainties. Managers should always expect great things from their staff and the latter would, I believed, surprise them. I also took the view that operational managers needed to have a greater say in the formulation of Departmental operational policy and needed to be trusted to get on with the job, not surrounded by petty, prescriptive procedures and intricate statistical systems, but held to account more directly for their individual achievements and failures.

To be frank I can't remember much of what John said in response except that it was mostly highly complementary. However, I do recall one particular, perhaps not altogether laudatory snippet. And that was when he mentioned that, when I was crossed by someone or something running counter to my strongly held principles, I could be terrifying. The thought of me terrifying someone as forceful as John left me feeling slightly surprised. But I had to take his word for it and, on reflection afterwards, I knew what he meant. He presented Ros with a beautiful bouquet of flowers and I received an inscribed tankard to which he and my fellow Thames Valley senior managers (Collectorate) had kindly subscribed. Touchingly and to general amusement, Ricky Lonmon of DMU read out one of his 'odd odes' that he had composed in my honour. I must also say that I was particularly surprised and touched by the inscribed tankard presented to me by the team leaders of the various Thames Valley DMUs when chairing my final Debt Management Policy Group meeting with them some days prior. John had written a few days earlier expressing

> *..my thanks and appreciation for the very fine contribution you have made to Thames Valley Collection since you joined Maidenhead Business Centre in 1992.*

*Our paths did not cross until I came back to our Collection at the back-end of 1993 when I immediately recognised a fellow delegation traveller. Indeed, one who had taken those principles beyond the frontiers in my own mind. No surprise then that you should have become the champion and flag-bearer of our management strategy and your role in taking that forward has had massive and beneficial impact throughout our Collection. It is an impact which will sustain through individual managers for many years to come. I cannot thank you enough for your support and your work in this area.*

*At Maidenhead you have proved the benefits of your empowered leadership style and you have created an environment which has encouraged innovation and gained strong business success. And your wider leadership has maintained and enhanced the excellence of our debt management operation across our Collection. That is a proud record and one which you can look back on with great satisfaction as you enter a new phase of your life.*

I also received, around the same time, a letter from the then Chairman of the Board, Richard Broadbent, conveying

*..my personal thanks, as well as my appreciation as Chairman on behalf of my colleagues on the Board for your 40 years service in the Department.*

*You are known as an enthusiastic and supportive leader who believes passionately in your people. A strong advocate and practitioner of the principles behind empowerment, well before the word became common currency, and you have consistently achieved strong*

*business results through your people. I believe you can look back with considerable pride on your achievements over a long and varied career and particularly your successful leadership as an Assistant Collector.*

I am happy to settle for that as my official epitaph.

As a postscript, I believe the following extracts from unsolicited letters sent to me by members of my management team at Maidenhead in the immediate aftermath of my final departure from HM Customs & Excise, reflect the values I tried to inculcate and develop in my leadership role. Chris Weeks wrote thanking me for

*..all my support and guidance over the years – if I've learnt one thing from your management, it's the importance of keeping things in perspective!*

Fiona Macanespie who had moved to Swindon and entered local government wrote saying that where she now worked, she found

*..the lack of decision making absolutely stifling. How I* yearn *for someone to say – 'just make a decision and get on with implementing it' (Sound like anyone you know?). How I dream of the good old days in Maidenhead.... I enjoyed my time in the management team at Maidenhead and that had a lot to do with your leadership style...I had great admiration of the fact that you were always keen to challenge the accepted way of things – despite the fact that it's generally more comfortable not to bother. I hope that's something I shall emulate in my own career. If you were tempted to take*

*up a new life as a management guru, you could teach local authorities a thing or two!*

And lastly Mary Gerrard, in wishing Ros and I well in the future, added

*..Maidenhead Business Centre will miss you more than they realise. You brought humanity alongside your visions of the future and endeavoured to implement the changes for the benefit of all.*

I look back fondly on those last few years in Customs. I recall the enjoyable and sometimes wet walking weekends with the Maidenhead management team, the various functions organised by the Sports and Social Committee, which I chaired, including Divali celebrations and the office-wide day of fun and competition in 2000 to inaugurate the new twenty-first century, designed to promote closer and more effective team-working and innovation. The fancy dress parade themed around '20$^{th}$ century icons' produced some amazing costumes and justificatory speeches and actions. I still miss the quarterly informal lunches hosted in my room with four intimate colleagues interested in improving our knowledge and appreciation of wine. The spur for these sessions was my discovery in conversation with Harry Turner, a stalwart member of my management team and a great wine buff, that he, like me, especially enjoyed and rated the Alsatian white wine Gewurtztraminer, At our first meeting we tasted a Gewurtztraminer he kindly provided from his extensive cellar at home and we drank another similar white wine for comparison purposes. I gave the name GWT Club to these sessions. This was short for the lovely Gewurtztraminer that we had consumed with such pleasure at our inaugural get together. The comparative tasting format continued at subsequent quarterly GWT Club meetings, although we moved away from Gewürztraminer, tasting different varieties of wines on each occasion from many different wine making regions of the world.

Although as Assistant Collector I had a personal desk top computer provided to me when I was at London Airports, computers did not become extensively available in offices until the mid-nineties when everyone finally gained access to one. The programmes that ran on these departmental computers were rudimentary to begin with and I remember one afternoon at Maidenhead losing the information I was working with as the screen went completely blank. I asked Kelvin a member of my management team at the time to see if he could help. I think he would agree that he was not one of the world's greatest people managers but had gained promotion on the strength of his technical prowess in information technology. Unfortunately the Department did not provide a career path for gifted technicians like him. In the past people were promoted on the strength of their technical ability with little regard being paid to their effectiveness as people managers and they, like Kelvin, were left uncomfortably occupying managerial positions. Anyway he came immediately and demonstrating great lateral thinking identified and resolved the problem straight away. Apparently I had somehow contrived to press buttons on the keyboard that had set the colour display on the screen to a white script on a white background! This became something of an office joke. Kelvin demonstrated his lateral thinking again on one of our annual management team walks. We came to a large cattle gate at the end of a field with a style for walkers set to one side. We all clambered over the style with differing degrees of difficulty and exhibiting differing degrees of elegance in the process. Once we were all over, Kelvin who had been bringing up the rear of our band of hikers, calmly walked up to the gate opened it and walked through.

By the time I left Maidenhead I had become reasonably proficient in working with computers, so much so that when I was asked what I would like done with the money contributed by the staff for my retirement present, I opted for a personal computer to be purchased and installed in my home. Although this has now become commonplace, without having my own computer at home, I would not be sitting here writing this history.

All in all, apart from my time in the Investigation Unit in West London, these last few years at Maidenhead Business Centre were the happiest and most rewarding of my career. I guess this was because I was virtually in sole charge of my own empire and I had the greatest opportunity and support from those above me in influencing the way forward for the Region and the Department as a whole.

I retired with no regrets – well not many anyway. Yet I was keen to find a part-time job somewhere as I didn't feel I was ready to completely give up the stimulus of working. In a way, I wanted to do something different to prove to myself that I could hold down a job and succeed outside Customs & Excise. Before I left, I applied for a position with the Office for National Statistics advertised in the Sunday press. The advert had been spotted by my Personal Assistant's husband. She recommended it to me and indeed the job seemed ideal and just the sort of position I was looking for.

It was advertised as being based on a twelve month contract, involving working from home on a part time basis to manage the 2001 National Census operation as a Census Area Manager. I felt I had the necessary managerial qualifications and the experience that they were looking for. I attended an interview in London and with the odds which I subsequently discovered were stacked at 20 to 1 against me, in terms of the numbers of people who had applied in relation to the number of vacancies, I was selected and offered the job of Census Area Manager for the County of Berkshire in May 2000.

Almost immediately after my retirement do, Ros and I went to Rome for the first ever Six Nations rugby match between England and Italy in that city. I had smoked a pipe since leaving school mostly puffing away at my favourite tobacco St Bruno. Before leaving home I was running short but thought I would be able to buy a new packet at the airport. Unfortunately there was no St Bruno available in the shops in the departure lounge and I had to make do with what I had got. When after a short while in Rome I had used it all up, I decided to make do without smoking for the remainder of the trip. As it happened, Ros had just given up cigarettes a few days earlier and I felt I could perhaps give her some moral support by not smoking my pipe either. Anyway, to cut a long story short, that was the last time I smoked my pipe apart from a ceremonial pipe which I light at Christmas each year, dusting off the lovely Meerschaum pipe that Ros had bought for me some years earlier and that I still treasure as a lovely object in its own right. I occasionally smoke a fine cigar on high days and holidays but as with my pipe, I have never inhaled, enjoying the smell and taste alone. I thought I would miss smoking which I had only ever indulged in at home, in the evenings and at weekends and on holidays, never at work: but I didn't. I instantly felt more energetic and healthy.

We spent a great weekend in Rome with many of the England fans dressed as Roman legionaries etc. On the morning of the match, sitting in the Piazza Navonna having a cup of coffee, we encountered a group of lads from Maidenhead Rugby Club, similarly attired. They were in good spirits, laughing and joking and told us they had just come from the Coliseum where they had bemused visiting American and Japanese tourists by stationing themselves at various points around the arena and shouting out one after the other "I'm Spartacus!", "No I'm Spartacus!" and so on..In the afternoon England having won the game, we met up with our friends Robbie and Margaret Stevenson who had travelled separately with some of their rugby club friends and dined with them in a typical Italian restaurant in the evening. They were staying in a different hotel from us and we agreed to meet up the following morning in St Peter's Square at 11 am with a view to visiting the Sistine Chapel in the Vatican. When we arrived at the rendezvous the following morning we found that the Sistine Chapel was closed and St Peter's Square was filled with thousands of people awaiting an appearance by the Pope. Not surprisingly, we never managed to find Robbie and Margaret in the crowds. I must say I found the air of religious hysteria and Nazi style deference exhibited by the crowds and the prelates towards this sick old man more than a little disturbing. Nevertheless it was an interesting experience. The weather was perfect for the whole of our stay and I felt the whole trip was a fitting way to bring down the curtain on my working life with Customs.

# INTIMATIONS OF MORTALITY

During the decade or so leading up to my retirement from HM Customs & Excise, the boys had grown up and left home and Ros was working on a part time basis, employing a cleaning lady to come in twice a week to help with the housekeeping. Ros had gone back to work when Phillip was six years old, temping at first and then accepting the offer of a permanent part time position from Riverlock, a company to which she had been sent by the temping agency. Originally based in Maidenhead near Boulters Lock on the River Thames – hence the name 'Riverlock' - they were situated in Holyport when Ros joined them in early 1988. They acted as agents for overseas manufacturers of automated woodworking machinery for the furniture trade. As the business expanded, they moved to High Wycombe the traditional centre of the furniture industry in this country. Ros worked mainly for Peter Hill the Riverlock Sales Director as his personal assistant, fulfilling secretarial and administrative duties both for him and the office generally. He, like the other Directors of the company, was a staunch member of the Salvation Army. Ros enjoyed working there. She remembers on one occasion talking on the phone to Alan Sugar, the self made millionaire, one time owner of Tottenham Hotspur Football Club and latter day TV star on the reality TV business show 'The Apprentice'. She says he was very pleasant to speak with and very fair. Something had gone slightly wrong on one of his contracts and he agreed without demur to split the difference with Riverlock.

In March 1989 Peter took a group of staff including Ros together with spouses to Interlaken for a skiing trip to say thank you for their hard work culminating in a successful year for the company. It was a great break and the only time I have ever been skiing. We had three days on the slopes and I managed to master the art mainly by tumbling and falling my way down the mountain to the valley below at the end of the second day. In 1993, in the same generous spirit, he donated some of his air miles to enable Ros and me to fly to New York for three days, thence to Boston in New England in the fall and whale watching in the Atlantic before flying to Orlando and Clearwater on the Gulf of Mexico for the 'Disneyworld' experience. The following year, while the company was being supported in the prevailing leaner times of the early 1990s by one of their suppliers, a company called Grenzebach from Donauworth near the river Danube in Bavaria, Southern Germany, Peter invited Ros and I to accompany him and his wife Doreen on a 'business trip' to view the Grenzebach plant and meet the personnel there. We flew to Frankfurt and took a couple of days driving south along the Romantische Strasse, or Romantic Route to our destination. It was a beautiful part of the world that I had never been aware of before with a string of vineyards, small villages and well preserved mediaeval towns like Rotenburg nestling in gently rolling hills and vales. Eating out one evening in one of these villages called Schikenhausen alongside the River Tauber, Ros got horribly bitten by flying beasties all over her legs.

On our first day in Donauworth, I remember our little posse led by Peter arriving for a welcome meeting with the German Sales Director. We were a little late. But no matter, we were greeted warmly by him although I couldn't help feeling that he was the epitome of a World War II Panzer Tank commander. As we entered his office we passed through an outer reception area occupied by a middle aged, bespectacled female secretary who also had the air of having contributed in some obscure bureaucratic way to the German war effort. Down one side of the reception area stood a silent line of earnest looking men each clasping a clip board. They were clearly waiting for a meeting with the Director after us. None of them spoke or jostled about. None of them showed any hint of annoyance that we had been keeping them waiting. I could not imagine the atmosphere being so orderly, acquiescent and deferential in similar circumstances in England

At the end of our time in Donauworth, Peter and Doreen returned to the UK while Ros and I took the opportunity to drive to Tübingen in Schwabia near the Black Forest to tour the area and if possible to delve into my maternal family history. I knew from conversations with my mother and grandmother that the German branch of my family had supposedly originated from there. This university town on the River Necker, south of Stuttgart, proved a delight. It possessed a mediaeval centre, including the magnificent town hall, or Rathaus in German, where I was able to find copies of my Great, Great, Grandmother, Katharina Friedericke Häcker's (nee Gefrörer) marriage and death certificates, recording among other things my Great Grandfather, Karl Friedrick Häcker's departure on 28 April 1876 for London where, having opened a business as a pork butcher, he married and remained for the rest of his life. I came away with photocopies that the ladies in the Rathaus kindly produced for me. I was pleased to secure this proof that my maternal family had indeed come from this part of the world where my maternal grandmother spent some of her schooldays. While I was there, I also bought a commemorative plate depicting the town which hangs above our dining room doors. When I have finished writing this story of my own life, I will return to the history of my wider family, going into greater depth about my ancestors, maternal and paternal as far as I am able and also about Ros' family.

By 1996 the good years, during which Ros had been given a company car as well as benefiting from overseas trips were over and the company was wound up. Peter was taken on by Grenzebach as an international travelling salesman and for a period became manager of their US plant and offices situated just outside Atlanta Georgia in the USA. While he was working and living there he invited us to stay with him which we did for a week taking advantage of the opportunity while we were staying there of going to the Olympic Games which were being held in the city. We were in the stadium for the 100m final which was over in a flash and I was generally amazed at how slight all the runners were; not just in the long distance events but in the sprints as well. None of them had an ounce of spare fat on them. We also attended the rowing with Peter hoping to see our British Olympic champions, Steve Redgrave and Mathew Pinsett competing in the heats but unfortunately they had rowed the day before.

On our way to Atlanta to stay with Peter, we had driven from Washington where we had spent an initial few days along the length of the Appalachian (Blue Ridge) and Great Smokey Mountain chains. It took us three days and two overnight stops on the ridge to reach Atlanta. Distances are huge in the United States and the population so spread out it takes a bit of getting used to coming from Europe where everything is so close together. On the morning of our first night on the ridge spent in a wooden lodge we breakfasted in the adjacent diner, experiencing a scary moment when a mentally sub-normal hillbilly dressed in check shirt and full length dungarees came lurching towards our table with a narrow eyed look on his face. His companion, an older man identically attired, who I concluded was his uncle, came after him and with difficulty steered him away towards the lady on the till and the exit. Apparently George, for so the uncle addressed him repeatedly in that unmistakable Southern drawl in trying to entice him away, was fascinated by the pots of home-made jam sitting on the window ledge behind our table. I watched them leave the diner and get into a pick-up truck, what else, and head off south along the ridge in the direction we were due to take. I waited for a decent interval to elapse before finishing breakfast hoping that I had given our hillbilly friends plenty of time to get well ahead of us to wherever they were going. Perched at the top of the steep sided, heavily wooded mountain chain, the road known as The Blue Ridge Parkway, a lonely winding narrow road with few intersections and a 35 mph speed limit runs the length of the 500 mile ridge. On this particular morning the road was enveloped in low cloud and mist in places. Visibility was poor and even if I had wanted to press on, as I did, it was not easy. After some twenty minutes or so with these thoughts going through my mind, we suddenly emerged into a fairly clear straight section and who should I see up ahead but the dreaded two hillbillies dawdling along in their pick-up truck, seemingly oblivious to the rest of the world. I could have overtaken them but decided to follow, at a respectful distance, for fear that if I shot past them which, in the conditions, was always going to be a tricky manoeuvre, they might alert their poor white trash brothers to hunt us down to perpetrate some inbred, mountain-men rite upon us. It was just like being in one of my favourite films 'Deliverance'. Mercifully, after about a further quarter of an hour, they pulled over into a small lay-by and I was able to glide by, accelerating gently away as they gradually disappeared from my rear view mirror. Later we stopped for late morning coffee in a lodge further down the road whose manager could have been George's twin brother they looked so alike but who was pleasant and intelligent, thank goodness! For our next overnight stop on the ridge we stayed in Gatlinburg in the Great Smokies which should and could have been a beautiful mountain resort but in typical American bad taste consisted of a single Sunset Strip style main street lined with amusement arcades, fast food joints and ugly flashing neon signs. A ride in the cable car to the neighbouring mountain peak to get away from the tatt below merely landed us in a giant skating rink surrounded by more tacky arcades fun fair rides and garish advertising signs.

In Atlanta Ros and I spent a morning visiting the home of Martin Luther King, no more than half a mile from the downtown centre of the city. The house and surrounding area had been tastefully converted into a museum and memorial and I felt much moved standing there. I was amazed at how few people seemed to be visiting – we were the only ones apart from a family on holiday of African American descent who had stopped off on their way to visiting Washington. I was staggered that Peter, a Christian man, despite having lived in the Atlanta area for a couple of years, had never visited the place himself and seemed little interested in the man or his memorial, which I must confess I found strange.

Ros joined Excel Communication in Marlow in the summer of 1996 following the collapse of Riverlock. She had got on well with Peter and the other Directors and members of the staff at Riverlock and I think she would say that this was her most fulfilling time in paid employment apart from her early days with Lummus before we were married. At the start of the following year she was head-hunted by Thakrar Coombs an accountancy firm situated in Holyport in the premises they shared with Riverlock when the latter were based there. She stayed for a couple of years leaving with the introduction of computerisation and the consequential restructuring of the firm's office administration and procedures. From there she spent a year with the Windsor & Maidenhead Sports Association for the Disabled before accepting the position of Parish Administrator at St James the Less, Stubbings along the Henley Road. She oversaw the creation of a new computerised office in the recently opened 'Soltau Centre' that replaced the old ramshackle arrangements in the vicarage study presided over by the outgoing vicar's wife. Ros retired on reaching pensionable age in August 2002 and now cleans the church and church hall once a week, arranges flowers in the church periodically and helps out with the lunches for the 'Young at Heart' and attends 'Craft Group' sessions on alternate weeks.

My father had died of emphysema on 26 November 1988 after a short illness which my mother had led us to believe was probably no more than a heavy bout of flu. Phillip told me as I was standing on the drive outside our house unloading the boot of my car after returning from a Saturday morning shopping trip. He had taken the phone call from my mother while we were out. I was suddenly overcome with sadness partly out of guilt because I had never really felt close to my father and regretted that I had not made a greater effort in his lifetime to get to know him. On the other hand I knew that it probably would have been futile given the sort of individual he was and the culture in which he had been brought up. I don't think my mother missed my father too much after he was gone. She often joked that in their retirement that she would have liked to hang him up on a peg somewhere so that he wouldn't get in the way. She was now free to pursue her own interests without restraint and we all thought that she would live to a grand old age enjoying her freedom. But, alas, some four or so years later on 27 June 1993 she died of cancer of the oesophagus despite having undergone an operation some two years previously to remove the infected section. At the time the surgeon said he would not have operated had she not been so fit for her age. Ros my sister Susan and I were present with her when she died in the early hours of the morning in her own bed. She only finally relaxed and stopped fighting for breath when I said to her that she had run a good race – she always loved athletics and other active sports such as tennis and particularly swimming in the cold English Channel which, up until her operation, she enjoyed daily with a group of hardy female friends. It was a sad yet moving experience as we sat there on her bed, Sue and I holding hands and holding her hands to form a human circle as the last breath left her body. She never complained and to the end wanted to be kept up to date with how well the British Lions rugby team were doing in South Africa as well as complaining when somebody banged a door. She was a strong lady. My son Simon says she was a Margaret

Thatcher prototype. Her neighbours and friends all remarked that she had strong views and they knew exactly where they stood with her. Good for her I say! My father's and mother's ashes were scattered in the cemetery at Weymouth after a traditional Dorset funeral procession and service in the local parish church at Bradpole. With her death I suddenly lost all the telling and amusing anecdotes about her childhood and life with which she used to regale us and I made a mental note that I would attempt to avoid the same thing happening in the event of my death; hence this story.

Ros' father died not long after my father in early 1989. His suppressed emotions bubbled out of him in his last moments; "Wonderful chap" he said with emphasis among his rambling at one point – was he talking about me? Her mother followed him in October 2004.

All our respective parents died relatively painlessly and peacefully without having to suffer debilitating long drawn out illness in their final years, for which we were thankful. The disposal of their estates meant that, for the first time in our lives, Ros and I had modest financial capital behind us and for the first time in my life, my current account at the bank was no longer overdrawn at the end of each month.

On the 2008 anniversary of Ros' mother's death, Simon and my daughter in law Theresa took their daughter N'eve to see her grave stone in St Mary's churchyard, Merton. They eventually found the stone overgrown with weeds beside the stone plaque commemorating Ros' father's death. They tidied both plaques up and paid their respects to their forebears. It was a nice gesture and preserves a sense of continuity with the past that young people today sometimes lack.

Simon and Theresa first met one evening in 1993 in the Valbonne night club at Skindles Hotel by Maidenhead Bridge over the River Thames. Simon was twenty three years old at the time and Theresa twenty. The first contact I had with Theresa was one Sunday night in the summer of that year when I received a phone call from her asking to speak to Simon. I explained that he was on holiday in Ibiza with his friends but was expected home the following day. I asked whether I could get him to ring her on his return but she declined. She did however request me to tell him that she, Theresa Boland, had called. I duly passed the message on to Simon when he got back home and the rest, as they say, is history. I saw Theresa for the first time, momentarily, some short while afterwards when Simon whisked her in through the front door and up the stairs to his bedroom. I was struck by her long black hair and statuesque physique. And a little later we were introduced and have never looked back since.

She was good for Simon giving him a sense of security and purpose at a difficult period in his life when he had not begun to carve out a career path for himself and job prospects generally were unfavourable. In September of the following year he secured a job at Mars. I am sure that his blossoming relationship with Theresa and her positive influence on him helped him to take this important step in his life. In the summer of 1997 they purchased a sweet little end of terrace house together at 10 Priors Way, Holyport. In the ensuing months I remember helping them to clear the back garden which the previous owner had allowed to become overgrown. In cutting back the tangle of vegetation, towards the end of the day, I found what looked like a wasps nest and reported this to Theresa. This was confirmed when the following day she poked it with a stick and was pursued by an angry cloud of wasps forcing her to take refuge in her conservatory. Theresa doesn't like bees and wasps at the best of times but she did see the funny side of it – eventually! I remember the Christmas day we spent in the house at Priors Way and the lovely Condrieu white wine with which we started the festive meal. Returning from a holiday cruise down the Nile which they hugely enjoyed, they were both suffering from stomach infection of the Pharaoh's Revenge variety when they came back to our house and I have never smelt anything so rank in all my life. Still their relationship gained strength and in the summer of 1999, we all four spent a holiday together touring Southern Ireland from whence Theresa's parents came. While there, we visited her mother's childhood home in Waterford and met Aunt Ann, a vigorous and delightful lady who still lives in traditional style in the family house with the exception of the mobile phone strapped to her belt.

I shall always treasure in my mind that trip to Southern Ireland. The weather was near perfect – for Ireland – and we had plenty of laughs and shared memorable experiences like the partial eclipse of the sun in Glendalough when the birds stopped singing and everything went quiet in the eerie half light. I remember the evenings spent in the Shanaghee in Kinsale where we started our tour and in various other pubs enjoying craich and Irish music over a pint or two of the 'Black Stuff'. On our last full day in Kinsale, Simon and I decided to go sea fishing while the girls relaxed without us and enjoyed some leisurely shopping. Simon and I left early with the girls in bed and joined the fishing boat for our boy's day out. As we chugged out across the large bay the wind was blowing a stiff breeze and the sea was decidedly choppy even within the shelter of the headlands on either side. The boat skippered by an early middle aged Norwegian fishing expert was bouncing about in the water and seemed to take forever to reach the open sea just beyond the Head of Kinsale. Here he anchored while he explained the procedure and plan of action for the day starting with the catching of mackerel as bait for the bigger fish we were going to seek further out in the Irish Sea. Counting Simon and I, there were about ten of us altogether lining the sides and stern of the boat as we struggled with our hired fishing tackle and dropped our hooks into the frothing water according to the skipper's instructions. Although Simon and I and most of our fellow fisherman had hired our rods and the rest of the equipment as part of the price for the trip, I had noticed when we boarded the boat an older looking gentleman who came with his own expensive looking gear. He appeared to be a seasoned expert, possibly a rich American visiting the land of his forebears and keen to demonstrate his New World prowess. Simon and I were both doing well and catching mackerel almost at will although I began to struggle. I increasingly felt my body temperature rising and not before long was feeling faint and beginning to tremble with the effort of leaning over the boat and retrieving the fish I was catching. I turned to Simon and he turned to me and we both acknowledged that we felt so bad we couldn't continue. We were obviously both suffering from sea sickness and the prospect of remaining in that state for the rest of the day's fishing on the open sea whilst not being able to participate in the planned activities filled us both with trepidation and despondency. Fortunately for us, at that precise moment, the man with the expensive equipment, casting his line, somehow contrived to embed the fishing hook in his left ear. The skipper tried to remove the hook with a special knife but other than cutting the line away, was unable to remove the hook itself. The latter had completely pierced his lower ear lobe. The skipper announced that regretfully, he was going to have to return to port so that the gentleman concerned could be given medical treatment in the local hospital. Well – Simon and I couldn't believe our luck. When we reached the quayside, still feeling groggy, we apologised to the skipper and disembarked from the boat before it headed out to sea again. So, there we were on dry land once more, with only half the morning gone. We sheepishly decided to try and find the girls and headed back to town. It wasn't long before we caught up with them in one of the local shops. Needless to say, they were surprised to see us. We tried to explain how awful we had felt on the boat and that as we were all going out for a slap up meal that evening to the Blue Harbour, the best restaurant in town to mark our last night in Kinsale, we didn't want to spoil the evening for them both by being too ill to do justice to the food and drink on offer. As we had anticipated, this explanation fell on stony ground and we had to live with the title of 'prize wimps' for the remainder of the day and whenever the story is retold.

Wherever we stayed on this trip, Ros and I were allocated the best room, and some were spectacular, until heading towards our final stop, in Dublin, we agreed that Simon and Theresa should have first choice. But all things are relative. The Talbot Hotel where we spent our last few nights was the Irish equivalent of Fawlty Towers. The bedside lamps were nailed down and the shower cubicle collapsed around Theresa while she was in it. We all laughed.

Simon and Theresa moved to their present four bedroom semi-detached house in Farmers Close, just round the corner from where we live, in June 2002 and on Christmas Eve 2005, over twelve years since they first met, I was quietly pleased when they became engaged to be married.

Meanwhile, Phillip had left Cox Green Senior School in June 1991 with three 'A' levels, in Maths, English and Economics, and had taken up a place at Bournemouth University in the following September studying for a degree in Business Administration. The first year he spent in digs on campus and I remember taking him there and leaving him with his belongings to begin his student life. He was quick to make good friends with a band of fellow students both male and female and generally had a rollicking time with the odd bit of intensive study thrown in. He became romantically involved with a female student called Rachel who was nice enough but a little lacking in self-confidence. I rather unwisely gave her my Minolta camera after I had invested in a more up to date Canon. The Minolta had a wonderful lens and I had looked after it as my pride and joy for over 30 years. When the romance ended after Phil left university, I did not feel I could ask her to return it to me, although I was tempted. However it would be no good now that digital photographic technology has replaced light sensitive photographic film. Phil had a placement year working with Rank Xerox at Uxbridge and lived back at home with us for that time before graduating with a 2.1 degree in May 1995.

It was a pleasure to attend his graduation ceremony where he wore his gown and mortar board. At least I managed to produce one son who achieved academic honours while at university. On the sporting side, he unfortunately snapped a tendon in one of his fingers playing rugby for the university which put an end to his playing days – he always had been accident prone. I was disappointed for him but not altogether surprised.

Although we helped finance his progress through university he managed his spending effectively and did not end up in debt. After leaving he got himself a temporary job with Leaseplan, a vehicle leasing company based in Slough, in order to save enough money for a gap year travelling round the world. In November 1995, having saved enough he left us for the Far East on the first leg of his journey in some trepidation and almost in tears as we said goodbye to him in the airport departure hall. However it wasn't long before he met fellow travellers and we began to get regular chirpy phone calls from him letting us know where he was and how things were going. Again, he made sterling friends on this trip, some of whom we later met in the UK and invariably liked.

He arrived back in England in May 1998 and in order to give us a pleasant surprise, had not warned us exactly when he would be returning. I was glad to see him again and to have him back home but I guess my reaction was less than ecstatically rapturous. While he was away, Ros and I had become accustomed to having the house to ourselves and watching the TV programmes and listening to the music we wanted not what our grown up children necessarily wanted. Anyway it wasn't long before Phil and one of his university pals Guy moved in together in a very nice leasehold basement flat in Upton Park on the edge of Slough – or North Windsor – as they liked to call it. By this time Phil had been head hunted by Leaseplan and was given a permanent position holding down an important role in sales/marketing which suited his personality, attributes and interests and paid good money.

One evening, in the summer of 2001, at a Leaseplan leaving do held at the Royal Oak pub in Windsor, Phil noticed Nicola Lewer who also worked for Leaseplan and when she left the pub, pursued her to the Chicago nightclub. Thus began a friendship and romantic attachment between the two which eventually led to their engagement, proposed by Phil and accepted by Nicola, in Melbourne, Australia on New Year's Eve 2002. Earlier that year, on a lovely hot day, I helped Nicola to move her stuff into the Upton Park flat after she had sold her own flat in Colnbrook. Some months later Phil and Nicola began looking for a house of their own and in an idle moment, I was fortunately able to spot a property advertised in the local paper in Brill Close about a mile away that appeared to be just what they were seeking. It was being offered at a very competitive price because the owners were emigrating to New Zealand and wanted a speedy sale. I drove round to look at it straight away and was impressed. I told Phil and he and Nicola went to view it, liked it too and immediately made an offer. Their offer was the second of four the owners' agent received. But Phil and Nicola were able to conclude immediately not having property to sell first and were successful bidders. The purchase was actually finalised after they had left for their holiday in Australia and I collected the keys while they were away. It was a four bedroom semi with a large garden in a quiet road, close to all main amenities and a really good buy. Engaged to be married to each other, they moved in on their return.

In October 2002, we celebrated Phil's 30th Birthday at the Richings Park Golf Club. It was a great evening with everyone in fancy dress. I went as Sherlock Holmes. Nicola's family were there in force and it was nice to meet them and to find out more about their background and family history.

Although I retired from full time employment in March 2000 shortly after we entered the New Millenium, I had not yet reached state pensionable age and wanted to do something different on a part time basis. While waiting to take up my appointment with the Office for National Statistics (ONS) as Census Area Manager for Berkshire, I got a temporary job for six months with CFC, a small company in White Waltham specialising in the running and administration of raffles for charitable institutions. It was to be my only incursion into the private sector as a working adult. I enjoyed being involved with ONS as a member of the senior management team in the national census operation and was able to bring all my previous managerial and administrative skills to bear on the challenges that presented themselves. I particularly enjoyed the opportunity I was given to get involved with the media and gave a number of interviews to the press and local radio including Radio Berkshire where I also took part in an hour long phone-in. At the end the presenter, Andrew Peach, complimented me on my performance, including the way I had handled some really tricky questions, and told me that he was most impressed with how professionally I had come across, given how little experience I had previously had.

Once the census was over the ONS caravan moved on and I started looking for a suitable part time job to tide me over until I reached state pensionable age of 65. I applied for and was offered a position as a Court Usher for Slough Magistrates Court and Administrative Assistant with the Royal Borough of Windsor and Maidenhead Car Parking Department. I chose the latter as it involved less travelling and the hours I wanted and I started in September 2001. The work involved dealing with the payment and accounting of parking fines and with appeals. The work was sufficiently stimulating and challenging to keep me interested while I was there without the need to worry about work issues once I left the building. This suited me fine. I liked the people I worked with and effectively retired on my 65th birthday with a small monthly pension, although my last day with accumulated leave taken into account was actually in March 2006. On my last day, Ros joined me and the team for a lovely send off lunch, paid for by the Council, at the Riverside Thames restaurant.

More or less immediately, I embarked on a twice weekly, month long course of radio therapy at the Royal Berks Hospital for prostate cancer. The cancer had been confirmed in the summer of 2002 and I underwent an operation at Wexham Park Hospital in August of that year to remove the prostate surgically. The radio therapy was recommended because although periodic blood tests after the operation showed a very low level of the relevant indicator (PSA), the concentration was increasing steadily over time. The radio therapy treatment was successful in again reducing my PSA to a fraction above zero where it has more or less remained ever since. I continue to have blood tests from time to time and reviews with the consultant.

Looking back I must say that I was lucky in that I was able to benefit from the system of annual medical checks introduced at work during the latter stages of my time in Customs. The doctor who examined me then found some hardening of the prostate gland and suggested I approach my local doctor so that he could monitor the situation. Under my local doctor I went for periodic blood tests supplemented as my PSA count steadily increased by biopsies. The first biopsy showed no actively aggressive cells but the second over a year later disclosed abnormal cells in one of the five samples. I was deemed young enough and fit enough to undergo surgery and have nothing but praise for the quality of clinical treatment I received at both Wexham Park and also the Royal Berks, and also the care and attention I received from the nursing staff at each of these hospitals in aiding my recuperation. 'Praise be!' for the much maligned National Health Service, say I.

I was also lucky to have the opportunity while still working in Customs to volunteer as a guinea pig in an extensive medical research project being undertaken by University College London. The aim of the project known as the 'Whitehall Study' was to investigate the causes of heart disease embracing serving officers in the home Civil Service. Over the years the nature of the research has broadened, albeit retaining the main focus on heart disease, and retired civil servants are encouraged to continue participating. Every two years or so I attend University College London for a thorough medical examination for which I am paid my travelling expenses and receive feedback on any incipient or actual conditions which I can then follow up with my local doctor. The examination is better than anything I could get privately and I am grateful to have my general well being kept under review in this way as well as being able to contribute to the research, which has received wide acclaim in international medical circles.

While on the subject of health and mortality, I must mention how proud I am of my sister Sue for the calm, unruffled way in which she coped with the twelve months and more of chemo and radio therapy when undergoing treatment for a life threatening attack of Non Hodgkin's Lymphoma. Her hair fell out although it has now grown back again. Thankfully, the cancer was sent packing. She remained her usual delightful self throughout, showing no fear or bitterness. We compare notes on our current state of health when we meet having been fellow travellers on the potentially lethal cancer road.

Phillip and Nicola's Wedding 10 July 2004

25

We Laughed......! Cottee family holiday in the Argave

26

Simon and Theresa's Wedding 19 August 2006

27

At Simon and Theresa's Wedding with old school pals Terry French and Robbie Stevenson (part obscured) sister Sue and Robbie's wife Margaret

28

With Robbie and Margaret in Peru 2006

29

Visiting the Good Soldier Svejk's hostelry in Prague, New Year 2008; brother-in-law Ken in Background

30

My new grandson Austin

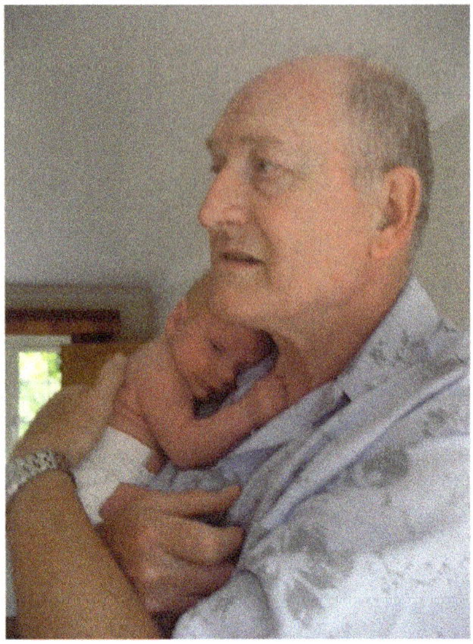

31

Holiday in Spain with Simon, Theresa and grandaughter Neve

32

Last Night in Spain with Simon, Theresa and Neve celebrating with Ros our 43rd Wedding Anniversary

33

Phillip, Nicola and grandsons celebrating Christmas 2009

34

Grandsons Oliver and Austin at play, summer 2010

35

Watching the changing of the guard at Buckingham Palace with Neve and Ros

36

# OLD MEN SHOULD BE EXPLORERS

As my favourite poet, T S Eliot, remarks in 'Four Quartets', *'Old men should be explorers, here and there does not matter.'* Bearing in mind that old age is creeping up on me and that, to all intents and purposes, I am now fully retired, being an explorer sounds fine

It is true that I have taken on the role and responsibilities of The Verger and Sidesman at our local church, St James the Less at Stubbings in the Parish of Burchetts Green. It is a lovely little church which Ros and I have attended since we moved to Maidenhead. I enjoy meeting and greeting people and helping them to get the most from their personal experience of the marriage, funeral and other religious services that are held there. Despite my personal lack of religious conviction, I nevertheless feel that, without succumbing to its more existential and questionable doctrines of supernatural divinity, I am nevertheless contributing to the life of an important institution and helping to preserve its place in our English cultural and moral history. I am also on the church locking and unlocking rota and a member of the team who erect and dismantle the marquees owned by the church when required for church or private functions. Apart therefore from this small formal commitment, my time is essentially my own to do with as I wish.

Consequently, I shall continue to enjoy my hobbies which include travelling abroad, playing badminton, golf, watching live and televised sport, especially rugby union (I am still a member and Vice President of Maidenhead Rugby Club), writing poetry, going on walks in the country, visiting historic houses and sites (Ros and I are members of The National Trust), going to classical music concerts and the theatre (I am a member of The Royal Shakespeare Company based in Stratford on Avon and of Shakespeare's Globe Theatre in London), cooking, entertaining and socialising with friends and family and researching my family history. In particular I shall enjoy helping my sons and daughters-in-law and supporting my treasured grandchildren who I hope may one day read this story and find it interesting.

I am proud of my two sons who have both turned out well in their different ways. They are both successful in their respective careers and have a wide circle of strong friends. I am glad that Ros and I didn't make too great a mess of bringing them up. There is no ready-made script for being a parent. I remember when I was undergoing my training for the Census being asked what my most difficult decision at work or in my personal life had been and I replied along the lines that at a certain point in the process of bringing my children up, I had concluded that I had to accept my sons, particularly my eldest son, on his own terms and that I should stop trying to mould him into becoming a replica of Ros and myself with all our own faults, virtues aspirations and values. Making this change in approach was difficult at the time but having chosen this path, I am glad that, as a result, my relationship with both my sons has strengthened and deepened over the succeeding years.

I was especially touched to be invited to their respective stag dos. First up was Phillip. We went to Edinburgh for the weekend in June 2004, not I may say without my entertaining some considerable degree of apprehension as to whether I would last the pace as far as the marathon drinking stakes were concerned. I must also say that I was amazed by the number of hen parties that were celebrating in the city and found that their antics were amusing but at the same time slightly unsettling bearing in mind how brazen and forward they were (in more senses than one), – not like the young females in my day. Anyway, I was quietly pleased that I survived relatively unscathed, apart from a few paint ball bruises. It was during one of the evening drinking sessions that I overheard Phillips saying to his mates 'My old man's quality', which made me feel that despite my age and limitations, I could still hack it with the younger generation. This included being woken by the hotel fire alarm at 3.30 am in the morning after I had just fallen into a heavy alcohol induced sleep. We all had to evacuate the hotel and wait in various states of undress for the fire service to arrive and investigate. We were eventually given the all clear to go back to bed after finding out through the whispering grapevine that the fire alarm had been triggered by Simon and his roommate smoking in their bedroom. To save them a lynching, we thought it wise not to pass this information on to the firemen or to the other hotel guests.

Life with Simon had always been eventful and his stag do in May 2006, held at the internationally famous golfing centre, The Belfry, near Birmingham, was no exception. On the Saturday evening, after my worst round of golf ever, we ate in the restaurant and had a few drinks in the bar before transferring later to the nightclub which was all part of the complex. As midnight approached, a minor altercation broke out involving one of the members of our party and a couple of men who had apparently travelled up from London. I must say that the taller of the two looked distinctly spaced out and was probably on drugs. Anyway everything was smoothed over and the night wore on with everyone drinking, discoing and dancing amicably enough, until suddenly out of the blue, in what was by now the early hours of the morning, a fight erupted between the spaced out ogre and one of our party. Quick as a flash Simon got involved and instinctively, I suppose to protect him, I too dived on the pile of bodies writhing around on the floor and attempted to get an arm lock on the ogre's neck. He was a big powerful man but I was congratulating myself on beginning to get the arm lock to tighten when I was hauled clear by a muscle-bound bouncer. The whole incident had been captured on closed circuit TV and the security guards knew that we were not to blame. The Police were summoned and the ogre and his chum were expelled. However, I did wonder if I might make the headlines in that morning's Sunday papers, along the lines of - '*PENSIONER ARRESTED IN NIGHT CLUB BRAWL!*'

Phil and Nicola were married on Saturday 10 July 2004 at Savill Court, Egham, Surrey, where the reception was also held. It was a lovely occasion and the venue was perfect although the bedrooms for those staying overnight were generally a little cramped. The room that Ros and I were allocated seemed large enough however, only to discover the following morning at breakfast that due to a mix up, we had been given the bridal suite! At the reception, which had a rugby football theme, I delivered a speech which went down well, especially as the sun miraculously came out bang on cue, and I am including the text in the Appendix to this narrative. A framed copy also now hangs in Phil and Nicola's downstairs toilet. Phil and Nicola arranged for an excellent video recording of the whole event. I have a copy in my audio-photo-video disc library. Ros and I take it out and watch it from time to time and it never fails to bring a lump to my throat. We also have the usual photos to remind us of a special day.

Similarly with Simon & Theresa who got married in our little church at Stubbings on Saturday 19 August 2006. It was a lovely service followed by a splendid reception held at Stoke Park, a luxury hotel in South Buckinghamshire, featured in the Bond movie Goldfinger. Again I gave a speech which went down well and the whole day was filmed by one of Simon's friends. I will always cherish the moment in the evening at the disco when Simon, who is not the most tactile of persons, gave me a heartfelt hug and thanked us for all that Ros and I had done for them. This time we didn't secure the bridal suite, although our room was opulent enough.

Over the years we have celebrated many family occasions including my 25$^{th}$ wedding anniversary and my mother's 80$^{th}$ birthday, both of which were held at Maidenhead Rugby Club. I also enjoyed and recall with pleasure my retirement party held in my HM Customs & Excise office building in Bell Street, Maidenhead and Ros 65$^{th}$ birthday celebration at 'The Waterside', the Michel Roux, Michelin Star restaurant in Bray. The evening at 'The Waterside' cost me an arm and a leg because I paid for Simon and Theresa and Phil and Nicola as well as Ros and me. But it was worth it.

As part of her 60th birthday celebration I took Ros to Moscow and St Petersbug hoping to see the Bolshoi Ballet.

Unfortunately the world famous company were abroad trying to earn some hard currency in the aftermath of the fall of Communism a couple of years earlier. However, we did attend a performance of Tchaikovsky's 'Swan Lake' in one of the other Moscow theatres and afterwards visited a stretch of open water just outside the city centre which had allegedly provided Tchaikovsky with his inspiration for the ballet only to find that it resembled a dirty stagnant pond more than a romantic lake. The Russian rouble was worth almost nothing and in any case there was hardly anything upon which to spend any local currency. I remember sitting on my hotel bed one night feeling like a king counting my respective piles of US Dollars, German Deutschmarks, UK Pounds and largely worthless Rouble notes wondering how I could contrive to actually spend some of them. There were virtually no privately owned shops or cafes and restaurants as we know them, only the Intourist controlled tourist venues, for which read KGB. However, MacDonalds had just opened their first hamburger restaurant along the main drag which proved so popular with the Muscovites, the queue outside was regularly around 100 yards long and you had to wait in zigzag lines before you could even get inside the building. We took my sister-in-law Ann with us and we had loads of laughs. It really was an interesting time to visit. We were able to witness at first hand, the sterility of the old Communist system and the emerging entrepreneurs taking the opportunity to offer tours at less than half the Intourist rate, provided you could pay in hard currency like US Dollars. The Intourist people hated these interlopers in what had been until recently their exclusive monopoly and tried to stop them making contact with us but we persisted and went on a memorable trip organised privately by a group of young Russian university graduates to the wonderful monastery at Jaroslav, 50 miles north of Moscow, with its wonderful icons and gold encrusted cupolas. While in Moscow we stayed in a massive, concrete, square shaped Soviet era hotel, since demolished, just off Red Square, complete with worn carpets, blown light bulbs, hideous, brown 1970s wallpaper, resident cockroaches, a complete absence of bathplugs and magnificent candelabra in the public rooms. The conglomerate boasted four huge restaurants at each corner and a superfluous swimming pool on the roof. We never knew from one day to next which of the four restaurants, if any, would be open for breakfast and evening meals, still less what would be available on the menu. Sometimes we could get wine, sometimes not and the main dish was invariably a choice between Chicken Kiev and Chicken Kiev followed if you were really fortunate by ice cream. However the starters were magnificent consisting of a pyramid of dishes with several types of caviar, various fish dishes, pates, tomatoes and cucumbers etc. One night we found a special tourist restaurant at the top of a tower overlooking the Kremlin and Moscow River. There was the usual live band and, looking to the west over the city, the pink tinted sunset was truly memorable. It was probably the most prestigious restaurant in Moscow at that time. The meal cost us six US dollars each with a twenty percent discount because we hadn't drunk enough champagne and vodka! The chaos and arguments among the Russians with whom we came into contact had us in stitches of laughter. One sensed that despite the new opportunities and freedoms, the powerful and palsied hand of the former Soviet bureaucracy and the habits of thought and behaviour that stemmed from it remained largely intact, lurking malevolently just below the surface. That said, I found a surprisingly strong degree of continuity with pre-revolutionary Russia. Many of the churches, monasteries and palaces had been left in place during the Soviet years, not demolished as I thought they had been, and many had been lovingly maintained and restored to their former glory. This was particularly true of Petroverts a palace on the Gulf of Finland built originally by Peter the Great that had been virtually raised to the ground by the advancing Nazis in their siege of Leningrad in the Second World War. There is no doubt that the people for all their surliness and intransigence bore a wildly generous, exuberant and artistic streak. Musicians playing all sorts of music from jazz to folk to classical music were to be found everywhere; on street corners, subways and squares and in that monumental work of art itself – the Moscow Metro. Most of the bands and instrumentalists were playing from memory or from music sheets copied by hand in pencil. Although complete strangers, we were invited out of the blue one night to join a wedding party and a lad who I stopped on the street to ask the way went out of his way metaphorically and literally to escort us via the Metro to where we wanted to go.

In St Petersburg, formerly Leningrad, we visited the huge cemetery opposite our hotel, another Soviet era monolith at the top of the main avenue Nevsky Prospect. The cemetery contained the tombs of many famous Russian poets, writers and composers. As we approached the Tchaikovsky memorial we noticed several bunches of fresh flowers laid on the stonework and a Russian woman wearing a typical brightly coloured and patterned peasant headscarf standing before it praying. As she turned away I saw tears streaming from her eyes. I am sure she was not a relative but an ordinary Russian lady. I could not conceive of a similar outpouring of emotion being shown in my country or anywhere else in the world come to that for a long dead artist. It was a touching moment for her and me too. I had always loved Russian music. My favourite and my first vinyl recording given to me in my youth by a friend of my parents who lived opposite had been Rachmaninov's 2nd Piano Concerto played by Julius Katchen. In conversation with Tony Jacobs and his partner Mary, another English couple in our party, I learned that my esteem for this recording was shared by Tony who was a professional singer. He had a tremendous sense of humour and we became friendly and spent most subsequent evenings together including a marvellous evening watching a performance by the Red Army, Red Star singers and dancers. Despite the usual incompetence, lack of marketing awareness and meaningless bureaucracy, we eventually managed to surmount all these obstacles and to get our tickets and take up our wooden seats in the theatre. In the West the performance would have been sold out three times over but the theatre was barely half full. The troop, like the Bolshoi Ballet was suffering financially after the withdrawal of state funding. Such a pity! When we got back to the hotel where we had reserved with one of the waiters a table for the three of us plus Tony and Mary, we were shown to our table, groaning under a cascade of plates holding the usual delicacies for the starter course. We enjoyed the meal and the music and cabaret style dancing provided as entertainment. Time wore on and I did begin to wonder who was going to be eating at the table next to ours which had been laid in similar extravagant fashion for the same number of people. To cut a long story short we realised when a loud argument broke out between our waiter and another waiter who had been hovering anxiously around the other table that between them they had somehow contrived to double up our booking. We could barely contain our amusement, so typical an example was this of the prevailing chaos. Anyway we kept our heads down: we were not bothered; it was their problem not ours. Funnily enough the word *problem,* pronounced with heavy inflexion and stress on the last syllable by the Russians, was a word we heard quite often. Our Russian hosts used it to cover any situation where they were unable to fulfil a request which occurred pretty frequently. On our last full day in St Petersburg for instance we and several of our fellow tourists booked and had paid in advance for a boat trip on the canals that criss-cross the city. It was an experience we were looking forward to and a fitting end to the holiday. We boarded the coach with our Intourist guide and drove to the boarding point only for the guide to announce on our arrival that because of the strong wind blowing up the Gulf of Finland, the water level in the canals had risen to such an extent that the canal boat could not achieve clearance under the bridges that lay along our intended route. We were disappointed but understood that there was nothing that could be done in the circumstances other than to abandon the trip and have our money refunded. *"Ah problem!"* said our guide. *"So instead we will take you to the Maritime Museum." "Well we don't want to go to the Maritime Museum – we would prefer to have our money back thank you." "Ah problem, we will take you to the Maritime Museum, it is wonderful." "No you don't understand; we are not interested in going to the Maritime Museum no matter how wonderful it is. We want our money returned." "Ah problem - the money has been sent away and we can't get it back." "Well that's your problem; you'll have to get it back."* Surprise, surprise, the following morning in the transfer coach to the airport we were finally, somewhat grudgingly given our money back. To end on a positive note, Ann, two days earlier had left her purse on the counter of a US Dollar shop in a busy tourist arcade along the Nevsky Prospect where we had gone to buy souvenirs. She didn't realise she had left it behind for several minutes afterwards by which time we had left the arcade and had walked some distance away down the street. We rushed back expecting with all the poverty around that her purse containing all the US dollars she had and her bank cards would have disappeared but no; her purse was in plain view on the counter where she had left it and despite the crowds nobody had made off with it. We all felt that we would not have experienced the same fortunate outcome in London.

I felt privileged that we had visited Russia at an important time in world history and experienced similar feelings when Ros and I went the following year 1993, with her mother on a coach trip to the newly formed Czech Republic and Slovakia, formerly Czechoslovakia.

It was only after my mother's death a few weeks earlier that same year in 1993 and with the consequential sale of her bungalow in Bradpole that for the first time in my adult life I felt financially secure. I no longer had to worry about servicing an overdraft at the bank at the end of each month and was able to put by some modest savings. This allowed me to indulge my love of travelling and exploring more extensively, venturing beyond Europe for subsequent holidays and going on our first Safari in Africa when we visited Zimbabwe in 1994 staying near the majestic Victoria Falls. Zimbabwe, formerly Southern Rhodesia is a lovely country and full of potential. The people were poor but laid back and happy which made me wonder if we in our sophisticated, but pressurised Western world were really that much better off. However they desire the goodies and opportunities like foreign travel that we have. The young lad who paddled us in a canoe down the Zambezi skilfully avoiding the extremely dangerous submerged hippos told us that economically things were getting worse with Mr Mugabe in power and most locals yearned for the return of Mr Smith, the last white prime minister of the country leading up to the granting of independence from colonial rule by the British government a few years previously.

Visiting South Africa with Robbie and Margaret for the 1995 Rugby World Cup also came at an interesting time with the hated racialist Apartheid system having ended only the year before with the accession of Nelson Mandela as head of state. There was no doubting his widespread popularity even among many whites, although we experienced at first hand a couple of instances where white individuals spoke to non- whites in a way that we would not speak to a dog. Old habits and prejudices die hard. Again we had lots of laughs. I particularly remember the quarterfinal in Cape Town between England and Australia which England won with a Rob Andrew drop goal in the dying minutes. It's always a pleasure to beat our old rivals. When we arrived at the ground about an hour before kickoff we decided to go for a drink before settling in to our seats to watch the match. The nearest bar was at the top of the stand, quite a demanding climb up steeply inclined steps. At the top we entered the bar which had three areas, a bar selling alcoholic drinks in a room to the right and a soft drinks bar in a room to the left with a circulating area in the middle as you entered. We decided that the girls would go into the left hand bar as they wanted soft drinks and Robbie volunteered to go into the right hand bar which was heaving with people to get a beer for him and me, while I stayed in the central area which was less crowded where we could meet up again to enjoy our drinks. Left alone, I looked around and observed a large, corpulent middle aged Boer sitting by himself on a curved wooden slatted seat by the left hand wall with a glass of beer in his hand. I thought to myself that he was probably sitting quietly there to recover from the exertion of climbing all the way up to the bar as we had. Shortly afterwards he again caught my attention as his whole body slid almost gracefully down the seat, spilling his beer as he glided to rest face up on the floor just to my left. I could tell, straight away that something was seriously wrong with him and called out – I couldn't believe I was doing this in real life – "Is there a doctor in the house?" The girls and Robbie recognised my voice and seemingly within seconds a doctor emerged from the beer bar and started examining the prostrate Boer but I knew instinctively that he was already dead. In what seemed like just a few seconds later, paramedics arrived and started giving him stun gun treatment to get his heart going again but alas to no avail. His face was deathly white. The wags said - 'what a way to go – with a beer in your hand and a game of international rugby in prospect.' One wag went further – 'has he got any spare tickets in his pockets' which was greeted by respectful laughter. What a way to go indeed. I can't think of a better way.

On the flight from Cape Town to Johannesburg for the semi final which England lost to New Zealand having been overrun literally by the giant Maori winger Jonah Lomu, the air stewards on the South African Airlines flight tried to give the usual pre flight safety drill complete with the normal arm gestures when everyone on the plane rose to their feet (the plane was full of rugby supporters) and imitated the air stewards until they gave up convulsed in laughter shared by we passengers. It was a great moment encapsulating the fun and enjoyment shared by rugby fans around the world. I was present at the final which South Africa won and watched the historic moment when Mandela dressed in a Springbok Rugby shirt bearing the same number as the winning team captain to whom he presented the Webb Ellis Cup brought the whole crowd to their feet. It was a clever and inspiring gesture which helped soften the attitude of the largely white supporters of the national game in South Africa and moved the process of racial reconciliation forward.

While name dropping, I should mention that on a beach outside Cape Town I met the British inventor of the clockwork radio Trevor Bayliss when his aide and minder, a BBC lady asked me to take a photograph of them both. Trevor and I fell into conversation and found that we had grown up in the same area of South London and had gone in our youth to the same jazz clubs. He was in South Africa to receive from Mandela in person an award for his invention. At that time he was little known in the UK but he became quite famous subsequently through BBC programmes and media interest generally taking on the mantle of the archetypal, eccentric, amateur British inventor coming up with a world beating original invention in his garden shed. He was all of those things and a humble, modest, interesting and friendly man.

Other famous people I have met and talked to in the rugby world are Nigel Melville, England Scrum Half and broadcaster, Phillipe Sella, French Centre Threequarter, in my opinion, one of the best ever in the game in what was my old playing position. This meeting occurred during a visit to the Rugby Bar in Agen after France had beaten Canada during the 1991 Rugby World Cup. Robbie, his friend John Welsh and I were on a boy's tour that I had organised for the World Cup, travelling to the South West of France for the Romania versus Fiji game at Beziers and the Agen game. English people like to hate the French but I have found them delightful and generous companions whenever I have been in their country and our trip to Agen was no exception. Although the French people we met casually over the couple of days we were there had never met us before and didn't know us from Adam, as strangers and foreigners we were nevertheless treated as honoured guests and weren't allowed once to buy a drink or anything to eat but had food and drink bought for us and to cap it all were given free entry to the local night club.

I have also met and spoken briefly to a number of well known personalities from the sporting world who attended the Maidenhead Rugby Club Annual Dinner as guest speakers while I was involved in the coaching and management of the club. These included Frank Bough the later disgraced BBC TV sports presenter whose sons played at the club, David Duckham, the former classy England Centre and Wing, Willie John Mc Bride, the granite Irish Lock Forward and Lions captain and the footballers Dennis Law and Jack Charlton. They were all lovely, modest, amusing men. However for sheer exuberance, joie de vivre and entertainment value, breaking out into impromptu song and dance and chasing a buxom barmaid round the outside of the marquee at 4 o'clock in the morning, the giant footed Scottish Lock Forward and British Lion, Gordon Brown, Broon of Troon as he was known, takes the prize. Sadly he died a comparatively young man sometime after his two guest appearances at the club but I don't suppose that as he lay on his death bed, he harboured any regrets. I also got to know Dick Best the former England and Harlequins rugby coach when he led our tour to South Africa for the 1995 World Cup and Gareth Chilcott the former England and Bath Hooker who led our trip in 2007 to the International Rugby Board Seven a Side Tournament in Dubai. On the second day of the tournament Gareth was lucky to remain alive when, driving in a hire car to the stadium, which had recently been constructed in the middle of the desert, his car was blown off the road by a sudden sand storm and turned somersault. We were already in the stadium at the time, having travelled to the venue an hour earlier in the tour bus with the assistant tour guide. We thought it was going to pour with rain when the sky went dark and looming black clouds began hurtling towards us but instead of the wet stuff we were bombarded with high wind and stinging sand, mercifully for only about a quarter of an hour, after which the sun again appeared in a cloudless blue sky.

Other famous people not mentioned elsewhere in this story who I have seen at close hand but not personally spoken to are the conductor Sir Colin Davis, years ago at a party I attended in a tennis club friend's house on Wimbledon Hill, Prince Charles when he visited White Waltham Airfield locally for a big flying display a few years back, the film actress Elizabeth Taylor – she had violet coloured eyes but wasn't really my cup of tea, and Michael Jackson the spectral pop star who passed through the arrivals hall at Heathrow Airport within my Division when I was in charge there.

My only other claim to be associated with fame was the night we were invited to dinner by my old friend from Maidenhead Rugby Club days, Sandy Stratton, who was managing Director of Taplow Paper Mills at the time. At the table, I sat next to Sheila Ferguson, the middle one of The Three Degrees singing group who had also been invited with her husband. I told one of my best risqué jokes and she laughed so much she asked me whether I would like to become part of her warm up act. She was living by the river at Bray at the time as do the TV interviewer Michael Parkinson, the entertainer and artist Rolf Harris and singer Marion Montgomery all of whom one sees in Maidenhead town centre from time to time.

Over the last several years, in addition to the places I have already mentioned, my love of foreign travel has taken Ros and me to Sorrento and Salerno, where we stayed with her half-cousin Pam who married an Italian millionaire and sailed while staying with them by sea to Capri for the day in his boat, travelling subsequently to Frascati, twinned with Maidenhead and to the eternal city of Rome for a few days. This was in 1990. The following year I went with Phillip and the Maidenhead Colts rugby team to Paris where I led the Dambusters' March, in the wee small hours down the Rive Gauche, in the middle of the city, arms outstretched to act as improvised wings, banking and slewing from side to side of the road in imitation of Lancaster Bombers approaching their target. The boys on the way home on the cross channel ferry managed to steal the flag from the mast at the stern: quite a feat in the circumstances. Apart from one broken bed in the hotel in which we had stayed, it was a relatively bloodless excursion which I much enjoyed, recalling the exuberance of my own youth. To the boys' amusement, I was the only individual who got stopped in Customs at Dover on the way back. I was wearing a particularly unusual and expensive looking sheepskin coat which Ros had bought me in Petticoat Lane in London some years previously and I am sure this was the reason I got picked out. It was late at night and we were all anxious to rejoin the coach and be on our way. However when I asked the young officer if he could spare me the routine questions which I had heard so many times before and explained that I was an Assistant Collector of Customs & Excise at Heathrow Airport in charge of passenger terminals but that he could nevertheless search my bags and my person as much as he wanted. He apologised and waved me through. Later that same year Ros and I went to Corfu and subsequently to Amsterdam, Brussels, The Waterloo Battlefield, The Ardennes, The Loire Valley where for once the local French population were not particularly hospitable, and Bruges where the Belgians certainly were. In 1998 after a trip to Spain when we toured Andalucia by car, visiting Ronda, Arcos de la Frontera, Jerez, Seville, Cordoba and the Alhambra in Granada, we returned to South Africa spending a week in Durban and a week in the Drakensburg Mountains visiting Isandlwana, Rorke's Drift, Spion Kop and Lladysmith of Boer War fame. Holidays followed in 1999 to Gocek in Turkey taking the opportunity while we were in the country of visiting the ancient Greek city of Ephesus and with Simon and Theresa to Southern Ireland.

In the new century we have visited the cities of Vienna, Lisbon, Cairo, Krakow including a particularly moving trip to the Nazi slave labour and extermination camp at Auscwitz-Birkenau, Prague, Barcelona, Sienna, Verona and Berlin. We have enjoyed relaxing holidays in Ibiza with my sister Sue and her husband Ken and in The Gambia in West Africa, Taormina in Sicily and in the Red Sea near Sharm El Sheik and Taba Heights. We have also been to Dubai, Singapore, Australia, Bali, Peru including the lost Inca city of Macchu Picchu, Bolivia on the shores of Lake Titicaca, and Rio de Janeiro, Brazil. We have also visited Washington and the Southern States of the USA following a historical trail taking in the colonial period, The American War of Independence and the American Civil War. In the spring of 2010 we went on a cruise up the Nile seeing the ancient temples. The week cruise turned into a two week cruise when towards the end of the first week, all European flights were suspended due to the effect of a volcanic ash cloud from Iceland drifting over the UK and the Continent.

With members of our family we have enjoyed holidays together in the Algarve in Portugal where we hired a lovely villa on the outskirts of Carvoeiro; also in a converted farm building near Totnes in Devon where, true to English conditions, it rained most of the time and most recently with Simon, Theresa and my granddaughter N'eve to Guadalmina in Southern Spain. While I can afford it and am healthy enough to get about, I will endeavour to travel to other parts of the world for interest and relaxation, at least a couple of times each year.

When not holidaying, I enjoy socialising with family and friends and will continue to do so for the remainder of my days. Since the early ninety's, we have seen the New Year in with our longstanding friends John and Irene Rees, Jean and Tony Harris, Rick and Wynn Smith, although sadly for Rick, Wynn died in 2006, and assorted other friends. In 1997 we hired a converted barn for a week over the New Year period in Uploders in Dorset, near where my mother used to live and enjoyed a great, extended house party, playing games such as charades in which we became highly expert by the end of the week, a murder mystery evening where we all dressed up and dining in the local pub. While heavily involved with the running of Maidenhead Rugby Club, I became particularly friendly with the aforementioned Sandy Stratton who is now divorced and remarried and living in Portugal. We stayed with him and his new wife for a few days in 2002 in their splendid villa in the hills above Luz on the Algarve. Ros and I also enjoyed the company of Dai Walters and his partner Gabrielle and travelled with them to many of the Maidenhead away games some of which, in Devon and Cornwall, involved an overnight stay. We had some good times together and I remember particularly one weekend trip to St Ives in the far south western tip of Cornwall where our boys were playing the town side. We stayed in a hotel overlooking the spectacular bay and rose for breakfast on the Sunday morning after some fairly heavy drinking the night before. Gabrielle was a lovely Irish girl of a somewhat sensitive and nervous disposition but she was prone to the demon drink and had been imbibing heavily the previous evening so I was not surprised when she failed to appear in the hotel breakfast room on the Sunday morning. However just as Ros and I and Dai were finishing, she appeared asking us if we had felt the room shaking. We laughed and joked about the effects of alcohol having strange manifestations but she insisted that she had felt the walls and floor of her bedroom moving. She became quite despondent and complained subsequently of not feeling well as we drove back home stopping at the famous Jamaica Inn of Daphne Du Maurier and Rebecca fame on Bodmin Moor for lunch. Gabrielle felt too unwell to get out of the car and lay there looking uneasy while Ros, Dai and I went into the Inn. We found a table and I went into the bar to order some drinks. While I was waiting, I overheard a conversation at the bar, the jist of which was the severity of the earthquake that had shaken western Cornwall earlier that morning. Earthquakes are rare in Britain but not altogether unknown. Apparently this one had measured 4.7 on the Richter scale, not drastic by world standards but enough for the effects to be felt. I asked what time it had struck and was told around 8 am; exactly the time that Gabrielle had felt her first floor bedroom shake. I went and told Dai and we all trooped out to the car and roused Gabrielle with the news that she had been right all along. She immediately recovered, extremely relieved in her own mind that she wasn't suffering from alcohol induced delirium tremens.

Some lifelong friends have died along the way. Ros' friend Chicky Bond died in 2003. She and Martyn had failed to appear as promised for Ros' 60th birthday party bash held here at home in August 2002. Strangely they never contacted us afterwards to tell us why they had not turned up. The next contact we had with them was a telephone call about a year later from Martyn to tell us that Chicky had just died of a brain tumour. And more recently, I learned through his ex-wife Jenny in 2009 that my old school chum Martin Biddiscombe who had a longstanding drink problem had passed away.

With the notable exception of my favourite Aunt Dorothy who celebrated her 90th birthday in October 2009, members of the previous generation of the Cottee and Arber families with whom I grew up are also, no longer with us. Recently my Aunt Hilda and Uncle George, always known as AG, died within a month of one another. AG had been a navigator in the Fleet Air Arm flying torpedo carrying Swordfish biplanes, known affectionately as 'Stringbags', during the Second World War. He was lucky to survive when his aircraft ditched in the sea, unable to land on the deck of the parent aircraft carrier in the heavy swelling sea. His fellow crewmen were not so lucky. Some years later he invited me, my mother and father, brother Roger and sister Susan to look over HMS Hermes, one of the Royal Navy's aircraft carriers in Portsmouth Dockyard. During our tour below decks, I was surprised and amused to find, in a distant echo of the days of Empire, Chinese personnel still employed in the ship's laundry. The Cottees were generally a rum lot, tall in stature, highly intelligent, occasionally sensitive but generally lacking in empathy and social skills, with an uncanny ability to stand too precariously on their own dignity to the extent that they were invariably not talking to one another as a result of some imagined and unexplained trifle or other. I never knew my paternal grandparents but of the seven of my father's siblings, I liked my Uncle Bob the best. He seemed more even tempered and considerate than the rest. And I say this, not entirely because he always gave us pocket money whenever he visited us in Wolsey Crescent or we travelled over in Dad's car to his terribly boring, semi-detached, suburban house in Erith near the aptly named Gravesend. However, even he became engaged in a furious row with his son, known to me as Cousin Brian when the latter, who was considerably older than me and by now in his thirties, discovered during the course of their argument that his mother, my Aunt Mary was not his real mother and that he had in fact been adopted by her and uncle Bob as a baby. Brian never spoke to my Uncle Bob and Aunt Mary again. They both and she in particular were staunch Catholics and in those days the fact that a child had been born outside wedlock and adopted was regarded as a deeply sinful embarrassment which they had contrived for years to conceal. Aunty Noll, the eldest of the Cottee siblings, and the least prickly, herself a dedicated Catholic had become a nun in her early adult life and entered a Convent situated in beautiful grounds in Grayshott, Surrey where she remained for the rest of her days. Convent life at Grayshott was governed by an austere introspective regime with little verbal or other communication permitted and virtually none with the outside world. She was a gentle, quietly spoken, physically fragile soul and we used to visit her in the Convent from time to time for a strictly limited hour on a Sunday afternoon. We always met in the Mother Superior's drawing room overlooking the garden. We never saw her own accommodation in the Convent or where she worked - in the laundry apparently. I once asked her why the Christian liturgy required us to 'Fear God' but the explanation she gave me was not in the least illuminating or convincing. My mother, coming from the far more down to earth, striving and hardworking Arber family, never hid her view that Aunty Noll was wasting her life in the Convent and like many of the Cottees (my father, by implication, included) they shied away from challenging alternatives, preferring a quiet life, uneasy in the company of people with differing opinions. I have to agree.

My surviving cousins, all now drawn from the Arber side, share with me an appreciation of the family traits we have inherited. The Arbers generally look at life positively, prefer action to inaction and are not afraid to exhort others to follow their precepts and leadership. Some would say they can be bossy at times but I couldn't possibly comment! Certainly I feel more affinity with the Arber side of the family than I do the Cottees. Of the cousins, I am the oldest, surpassed only by two or three weeks by Richard (Dick) Bergman whose father Stan died when Dick was but eleven years old and had the added pressure of my mother telling him, unfairly I thought at the time, that he was now the head of his family and was responsible for looking after his mother and brother and sister. To those unused to their ways, the Arbers' urge to organise and to exhort others to follow can sometimes come across as a trifle overpowering and lacking in sensitivity. However, we are what we are. But when eventually the family headship descends to my generation, the iconic Arber sayings, drawn from the late Victorian, early 20$^{th}$ Century era, such as silence at meal times - leaving clean plates - waste not want not - always try your best - and children should be seen and not heard, will be invoked no longer.

With the death of friends and family, chunks of my past fall away. Life meanwhile thrusts up new shoots. I now have three grandchildren. My first grandson, Oliver George Cottee, was born on 1 November 2006 to Phillip and Nicola. Oliver gained a younger brother, Austin Harry Cottee, my second grandson, on 3 June 2009. My granddaughter N'eve Frances Cottee was born to Simon and Theresa on 22 January 2007. Phillip and Nicola have already added a substantial two storey extension to their house in Brill Close and Simon and Theresa have extended their property in Farmers Close. I am proud of the success they have already achieved in establishing their financial independence and stability and their care for and involvement in their growing families. It helps that both Simon and Phillip have each married attractive partners, my daughters-in-law, who, following my mother's example, are strong-willed, feisty individuals, ambitious to provide the best opportunities and stable, loving, support for their children in a changing and challenging world. The future of my genes is safe in their hands. Nicola's maiden name is Lewer, her father Howard's family coming from the Langley area of Middlesex and her mother Marion's paternal MaCinnes line, coming from Eriskay in the Outer Hebrides. Theresa's father, Patrick Boland, was born and grew up in County Cork in the Republic of Ireland and moved to the Slough area in England to find work where he met Theresa's mother Cathy, who had similarly been born and raised in the Republic of Ireland, in County Waterford. They married over here and lived in Maidenhead until they divorced some years later when Theresa was in her teens. Theresa's Mum retains her distinctly Southern Irish brogue and usually spends Christmas Day with us. She amused us once when we took her out for a meal to The Walnut Tree restaurant near Henley one night when she ordered smoked salmon for her starter not appreciating that it would be served cold. When the dish was put in front of her she looked at it and exclaimed in a shocked, Irish voice "It's not cooked!" We had to explain that was how smoked salmon was usually served in this country. Luckily she has a good sense of humour. She unknowingly amused Theresa a few months ago when telling her that Council workmen had turned up at her house the previous day "for the annual trim of my bush". Theresa struggling to keep a straight face, knowing that Cathy was talking about the hedge in the front garden, not 'other more sensitive personal matters' and fearing that her suppressed giggles would get the better of her, managed only with considerable self-control and difficulty to let the moment pass thereby avoiding the potential embarrassment of having to explain to her somewhat naive mother exactly what she, Theresa, found so funny. It is sad that because of the circumstances in which her parents' marriage ended that her father has never seen his beautiful Granddaughter, N'eve. He has missed such a lot.

Because the boys as I still call them live relatively close by - Simon less than half a mile and Phil about a mile away - Ros and I pursue our own lives but meet them regularly for barbeques and meals either pre-arranged or impromptu. We also see a lot of our lovely grandchildren and help out by looking after them in emergencies and when Mum and Dad have other commitments. Now that my erstwhile Friday night squash, soft ball and more latterly, badminton partner, Rick Smith has developed other commitments; I have started playing badminton with Phil. He, Simon and I also enjoy the occasional round of golf, a game which I began to play in 2003, having inherited a set of clubs from Simon when he purchased a new set. Ros has also taken up the game and she and I try to play three or four times a month on local Pay and Play courses, usually the local one at Bird Hills. I have since replaced the set of clubs Simon gave me with a set more suited to my ageing physique and dynamics. I am gradually improving and was pleased when I breached the average for most golfers, which according to the Daily Mail, whose every written word I always believe, is 105 strokes for 18 holes. In 2009 my target was to get below 100 and I am pleased that I am now consistently scoring just under this benchmark when I go round. I feel I could genuinely justify an official handicap of 28, if not slightly less. My target for 2010 was to consistently score around 95 supporting a consequential handicap of 23/24. I have recently achieved this goal but problems with my right hip joint mean that I am unlikely to get any lower: so be it.

I am fortunate to have spent the majority of my time on this earth living in what, with hindsight, may well be regarded in the future as a golden age. I am lucky that I enjoy a generous final salary, inflation-proofed, government pension and the prospect of several years in which to benefit from not having to work for a living. Personal wealth, technology, health care and life expectancy have increased enormously over my lifetime without any downside costs intruding. Despite the anxieties engendered by the Cold War, I have lived through a largely peaceful era. I have not been called upon to serve my country at war as my father and his contemporaries were. When I was growing up there were no such things as computers, mobile phones, washing machines, dishwashers, cheap air travel and foreign holidays. We were one of the first families to have a television in the early 1950s. The screen was only nine inches square and of course the picture was in a grainy black and white. I remember neighbours and friends crowding into our small living room with the furniture re-arranged to watch the Coronation of Queen Elizabeth II. I also recall similar flickering pictures being transmitted of Winston Churchill's funeral. Breaks in transmission were commonplace and our set was hardly reliable, powered by rudimentary electronics with bulb sized valves that took time to warm up and glowed when the current was switched on.

Through the medium of newsreels shown at the cinema, radio and later television, I became aware of international developments in the second half of the twentieth century although none of them really touched or affected me directly. Certainly along with most other people I was shocked and saddened when President Kennedy was assassinated in Dallas having promised so much in leading the world away from the old rigidities and prejudices. And, earlier in his presidency, we had all spent a couple of days wondering if we would all be blown to smithereens as a result of the Cuban Missile crises which Kennedy handled with such aplomb. It was odd. We all knew that there was a real threat that we would die in a nuclear holocaust but nobody panicked and we just carried on with our daily routine hoping that it wouldn't happen but resigned and unflustered because we knew there was nothing we could do individually to affect the outcome.

I also remember the tension created during the early part of the Cold War by the Russian closure of land links between Berlin and the West and the subsequent successful Berlin Airlift organised and operated by the NATO allies, principally the Americans. While I admired the American commitment to the defence of freedom and democracy in Europe and elsewhere in the world it was painfully apparent to me then that Great Britain much as she wished to retain her pre-eminence in world affairs was simply incapable financially, economically and militarily of matching the American effort. Memories of past glories evidenced by the exploits of the

'Glorious Gloucesters' fighting the Communist insurgents in Korea and the subjugation of the Communist threat in Malaysia by British forces left one feeling proud yet aware that the country was still on an irreversible slide and that loyalty, courage and justice alone were insufficient to prevent the decay of our once great empire. Although we did subsequently quit our empire in a largely civilised and honourable way, following the last embarrassing hurrah of Suez, I felt then and have felt ever since that we did not adapt quickly enough to the new world order. I guess that most British people are still innately pro empire or Commonwealth as it is now called and by the same token are anti European Union. I am not one of them! The only time I voted for the Conservative Party was when Edward Heath took the country into membership of the European Community. Before that, my mother and I had voted for the Labour Party led by Harold Wilson after the Tory old guard had shot themselves in the foot demonstrating their ineptitude and condescension in the Profumo Affair. We had to keep this a secret from my father who was a lifelong, died in the wool Tory supporter, although goodness knows what the Tory party had ever done for him. My mother and I exchanged knowing glances when the general Election results came through and it was difficult to keep from smiling and shouting for joy while watching the TV in the same room with my father. Politically, I am a moderate progressive. I think that we are quite capable of managing our affairs without the assistance of a hereditary monarchy. I like to assess issues on their intrinsic merits rather than fixed political principles. I am naturally prejudiced against those who blindly extol the virtues of the Conservative party and its often narrow, self interested beliefs and principles whilst condemning out of hand in vitriolic terms policies of the centre left and its leaders. I also believe more in change and progress rather than falling back on tradition and the status quo, with the exception of retaining the use in pubs of beer glasses with handles and reading from the King James Version of the Bible and Book of Common Prayer in church services

Suddenly at the start of the 21st century, I find the glitter of the Golden Age beginning to lose a little of its former lustre as I contemplate the unexpected growth of new and dangerous religious, cultural and racial dissensions, whilst global issues such as climate change and the distribution and depletion of finite fossil energy resources become more problematical. Clearly effective solutions will not be easy to find or implement. Conventional military, diplomatic, political and economic policies will need to change radically to meet the new difficulties we in this country and elsewhere in the free world are facing. We must not shrink from the challenges. If this means standing up to and removing tyrants and mass murderers like Hitler, Stalin, Mao Tse Tung in the last century, Slobodan Milosevic, Saddam Hussein, The Taliban and Al Qaeda in this century, then so be it. I support the military action taken by the Western allies in the Balkans, in Iraq and Afghanistan. Equally I support the various formal and informal international groupings such as the United Nations, NATO, the European Union, the G20 countries, the International Monetary Fund etc who seek to bring about concerted action in a peaceful, constructive and forward looking way. Also I believe that democratic parliamentary government of the kind we in this country have been instrumental in developing throughout large areas of the world is by far the least bad form of government. This cause deserves more objective and sympathetic support than our sensationalist media give it. I propound these views because I would like my grandchildren to grow up in a safer better world. To do this, good must prevail over evil. We should never forget this basic truth and must fight, taking positive measures if necessary to ensure that freedom and good prevail over tyranny and evil.

For me, the defining moment when the old certainties and the inexorable forward march of social, economic and political progress took on a different hue, came in the middle of one afternoon – the 11th September 2002 to be precise - when I was working for the Royal Borough of Windsor & Maidenhead Car Parking Team. Our General Manager suddenly appeared on our floor to tell us that two passenger planes had crashed into the twin Towers in New York. I knew the landmark building well, in the sense that I had photographed it on a visit to the city in 1993. When I got home, I saw the TV broadcasts of the attacks and realised that the world was entering a new phase; one that would not be so cosy, so clear cut and as progressive as I had been used to. This murderous act starkly highlighted the growing virulence of religious intolerance, particularly of the Islamic strain, emerging mainly from the Middle East, where a small minority of zealots, appear intent on stopping at nothing in order to achieve their misguided and inhuman objectives.

# AND ANOTHER THING!

As Benjamin Franklyn once observed, *'There are only two certainties in life – death and taxes.'* In my working life I have been heavily involved in collecting taxes and will one day become acquainted with death. I don't know precisely when or from what immediate cause. No doubt a few surprises, joys and tribulations yet lie ahead of me. In the meantime as Hamlet remarked (my favourite play by the way) *'we defy augury: there's special providence in the fall of a sparrow. If it be now, 'tis not to come; if it be not to come, it will be now; if it be not now, yet it will come: the readiness is all.'*

My house paid for, financially secure, reasonably healthy for my age, my children independent and settled with young families, I have little baggage to weigh me down while fumbling forward into my twilight years.

And so it just remains for me to invite you to browse through the Appendix to this narrative. I felt it was worthwhile including additional material in this form in order to give a more rounded rendition of my story which, I hope, my treasured grandchildren, or their children, or children's children or their friends may one day read and find of interest. At any rate, I hope the contents provide further perspectives in relation to the interests and influences that have informed and embellished my life on this lonely and beautiful planet. And, finally, for the sake of completeness, I must add that I have a great love of poetry and have written several poems of my own over the years which I have published separately.

# APPENDIX

This Appendix was initiated by me in 2018 at the age of 77as it became gradually ever more likely that the grim reaper was getting ever closer. Some aspects therefore relate to a period of my life beyond that with which I concluded in 2011 the narrative section of My Story.

I have included a list of the terms and titles in common use in HM Customs & Excise during my time in the Department; an index of the strange but true incidents and people I encountered during my forty years service, referencing the relevant section in the narrative; my curriculum vitae; copies of speeches I gave at my retirement from HM Customs & Excise, at my sons' weddings, my mother-in-law's funeral service and my 70$^{th}$ birthday celebration; a compilation of my favourite books, films, quotes etc. and a brief description of the artefacts that have come into my possession over the years which I prize, not for any intrinsic value they may have, which in most cases is slight, but for their value to me as pleasant objects and for the association they have with certain aspects of my life. I like to think that, as in pre-Christian times when people were buried with grave goods, these items might metaphorically be buried with me.

## HM CUSTOMS & EXCISE TERMS AND TITLES

When I worked in HM Customs & Excise we almost had a language of our own, much of it made up of abbreviations to the extent that whenever a few of us got together and inevitably started talking shop, the un-initiated could barely understand what we were saying. This even happened to me when I transferred from an Excise to a VAT office. This apart and because most of the abbreviations since I retired from the Department have no doubt been overtaken by newer ones, this jargon has largely evaporated from my memory. Nevertheless, I do recall with some fondness some of the technical terms and titles that formed part of my working life, particularly in the earlier part of my career.

Before listing and explaining these terms I should mention that unlike the rest of the Civil Service we enjoyed our own Departmental titles and grades and our own pay scales too for the first few years after I joined. The last of the Departmental titles finally disappeared only after I retired when the Department merged with the Inland Revenue. The strange thing was how mundane these titles were. For example the lowest caste was designated **'Watcher'**. Watchers were recruited largely from the military and police forces, wore uniform and literally watched activities in Customs controlled areas and warehouses. This included tallying cargo being unloaded or loaded onto ships and into or out of bonded warehouses and in some case extended to 'cart following' that is accompanying commercial vehicles carrying goods under bond to and from wharves and inland warehouses to ensure that the goods in transit were not diverted onto the home market without duty payment. There were also a few strange characters designated **'DCOs' or 'Departmental Clerical Officers'** who did some of the more repetitive clerical work in Customs stations. They were un-uniformed as were all the grades above them. Officers of the Outdoor Service as it was called were responsible for making value judgements and executive decisions in relation to import and export customs transactions. They were referred to as **'Officers of Customs & Excise'**, a career grade that was later subdivided into **'Officer' and 'Senior Officer of Customs & Excise'**. Above them was the **'Surveyor'**, the first management grade: the title came from the French word 'Surveilleur' for one who supervises. Above them and responsible to **'The Board of HM Customs & Excise'** appointed by The Crown and made up of the **'Chairman'** and half a dozen or so **'Honourable Commissioners of H M Customs & Excise'** was the grade of **'Collector'**. The latter were responsible for the discipline and effectiveness of all operational activity and staff under their command and were in charge as the name implies of physically collecting the money due from the taxes and duties we enforced. Although recruited as an Officer of Customs & Excise, before I was appointed to my own fixed area or **Fixed Station** as it was known, I was referred to in the department as an **Unattached Officer** or **UO**, denoting the fact that my conditions of employment dictated that I and my carefree band of fellow UO brothers could be moved anywhere in the country at the Commissioners behest at a moment's notice to assist or supplement the endeavours of the fixed staff.

The technical terms listed below are ones I probably would not have come across had I not worked in Customs & Excise. They may sound odd, even in some cases faintly suggestive, but were all genuine technical terms used by us and the people we worked with in the relevant industries and trades.

**Promiscuous Visits** Visits made to various traders without warning to check that they were complying with revenue regulations and licensing requirements.

**Blue Book** A soft, blue coloured covered note book in which calculations were recorded in order to assess the specific duty chargeable on revenue goods such as wine, spirits and tobacco.

**Baggage Prime** A Customs declaration form used by shipping agents to clear privately owned unaccompanied baggage.

**Adulteration** The term given to the practice adopted by unscrupulous public house landlords and off-licenses of diluting duty paid beer and spirits with water prior to sale to members of the public thereby diminishing overall revenue yield.

**Cautionary** The name given to work involving mainly promiscuous visits to traders handling revenue goods such as public houses, off –licenses, tobacconists, laboratories using distillation equipment, and hardware stores selling methylated spirits to check that they were complying with revenue regulations and licensing requirements.

**Surveys** Prescribed visits to registered traders such as manufacturers, brewers and distillers whose activities led to the production of goods on which tax or duty was payable. The physical checks and audits performed on these visits to guard against illicit diversion and fraud were recorded in Survey Books and Survey Folders.

**Guaging** The term used for the method of determining by physical measurement and calculation the content of casks and other containers of beer, wine and spirits in order to assess the specific revenue duty due.

**Landing Station** The name given to designated offices within Customs approved ports and airports and the officers (Landing Officers) based therein who dealt with the duties levied on the import, export and transhipment of cargo.

**Rummaging** The practice of searching ships and aircraft for concealed revenue and unlicensed goods and prohibited substances.

**Presumptive Charge** A calculation made by Excise Officers in breweries and distilleries using an empirical formula to determine, from known quantities of basic ingredients the strength and volume of likely finished dutiable product; used as a check on the illicit diversion by brewers and distillers of fermenting liquor prior to the duty point.

**Tares** The term for the average discrete weights of packaging such as cigar bands and boxes known as 'Inners' and the external case or carton in which they were packed known as 'Outers'. These discrete standardised weights were then deducted from the overall gross weight of the packages in the consignment in order to arrive at the total net weight of product liable to duty, thereby avoiding the need to unpack and repack every individual package.

**Cocking Up** The term given to the requirement when recording observations on the pre-printed 'Line of Survey' in the 'Survey Book' in breweries and distilleries for acknowledging a clerical error by inclining the entry immediately following at an angle of 45 degrees showing that the error was recognised and corrected at the time thereby guarding against collusion with the trader and subsequent falsification of the record. This may be the derivation of the common expression 'cock up' to denote a mess or muddle created by a mistake or series of mistakes.

**Entry** The official form used by importers and exporters to declare the description and quantity of goods for Customs purposes and the duty payable either on the basis of physical characteristics mainly in the case of revenue goods such as beer, wine, spirits and tobacco known as a Specific Entry or in the case of general cargo on the value of the consignment known as Ad Valorem Entry from the Latin 'according to value'. When I was working in the London Docks these Entry forms were known as 'Sale' forms because importers, exporters and shipping agents had to buy the forms from us as well as completing them correctly and paying the appropriate duty and taxes. The main import entry form was known as a '107 Sale'.

**Dip** This was the measurement of the gap between the top of the barrel, cask or other container holding beer, wine or spirit using a calibrated wooden 'dip stick' or weighted steel measuring tape which taken, with other measurements, enabled the liquid content to be ascertained.

**Drawback** A term used both for the entitlement and also the process of receiving a repayment of Excise Duty when revenue duty goods such as beer, wine, spirits and tobacco were exported or deposited in bonded warehouse.

**Jerquing** The audit function performed by members of the Surveyor grade based in the 'Collector's Office' who were known, unsurprisingly, as 'Jerquers'. Their role was to review and question, where relevant, the accuracy, effectiveness and probity of the scrutiny, physical examination and Customs clearance of import and export goods performed by Landing Officers as recorded on the official Entry documents. The term derives from the French verb 'jerquer' to throw over.

**Spiralling** The illegal practice perpetrated by distillery employees of drilling small holes into pipes containing spirit on which duty has not been paid and extracting the contents for personal consumption or disposal to friends and acquaintances.

**Stuffing** The term for the method of concealment on the person employed for smuggling illegal drugs into the country by packing drugs in condoms and stuffing them via the anus into the bowel area.

**Swallowing** As above for stuffing, except that drug packages were ingested through the mouth and concealed in the stomach area.

**Mules** The name given to individuals employed to smuggle drugs on the person using the stuffing or swallowing method.

**Bung** A circular segment of cork used to seal the liquid content of barrels and casks of beer, wine and spirits.

**Bung Rod** A wooden dip stick calibrated in inches with a sliding brass haft giving the appearance of a long wooden sword with hand guard, inserted vertically through the bung of a cask or barrel used to measure the depth of the wet contents and the internal girth of the cask or barrel.

**Flogger** A mallet shaped wooden hammer used by coopers to release bungs from barrels etc by hammering in the area immediately surrounding the bung hole or, conversely by sealing the bung in the bung hole by hammering directly on the bung.

**Valinche** A suction tube approximately two feet in length and made from light metal used manually to extract samples from barrels and casks in order to ascertain the nature of the liquid content and the alcoholic strength.

**Ullage** The term given to the difference in volume between the overall capacity of a barrel, cask or other holding vessel and the actual content. Ullages could be treated as acceptable if they fell within certain calculated limits that were designed to allow for natural evaporation and seepage. Above these empirical and somewhat generously prescribed limits, ullages were required to be investigated to determine whether they arose from unavoidable damage or from illicit abstraction. The term was also used for shortages discovered in dry goods consignments although in such cases, for obvious reasons, no allowances for natural loss were granted.

**Liquor** The name given to water in the brewing trade.

**Mashing** The process adopted in the brewing and distilling trades for soaking basic ingredients such as malt and barley in hot liquor (water) in a large vessel known as the 'Mash Tun' in order to extract enzymes and sugars in solution for fermentation and distillation.

**Sparging** The process at the end of the mashing cycle when hot water is sprayed on the mash to assist in extracting the maximum amount of fermentable or potable ingredients in the resulting solution.

**Wort** The term used in brewing beer to refer to the liquid solution resulting from the mashing process after boiling with hops in a 'Copper' and collecting in a 'Collecting Vessel' to which yeast has been added before removing to a 'Fermenting Vessel' for fermentation. The term is also used for the resulting fermenting liquid.

**Wash** The equivalent term used in the distillery trade for the resulting liquid solution derived from initial ingredients such as malted barley, ready for extraction of alcohol by distillation.

**Cleansing** The name given to describe the thick head of foam that builds up on fermenting wort in the initial stages of fermentation.

**Skimming** The removal after a suitable period of the cleansing head using a large wooden spatula.

**Fining** The name given to the thin crusted head that forms on top of the wort after the cleansing head has been skimmed off. Also refers to substances (Finings) that are added to gravity filter and clarify the finished product.

**Racking** The term referring to the process of drawing beer, wine and spirits from production vessels into barrels, casks and tanks for maturing and ageing.

**Coursing** The term referring to the practice of shift working by Excise Officers in large breweries and distilleries that operated round the clock.

**Float Rod** A long wooden dip stick with a cork float affixed to the bottom used for measuring the 'Dip' in 'Collecting Vessels'.

**Immature Spirits** Spirits that have not been aged.

**Certificate of Non Plunder** A certificate that could be given by Landing Officers where they were satisfied that there was no evidence that unacceptable ullages in imported consignments of wet or dry goods had resulted from illicit extraction i.e. 'plunder' in this country.

**Scrutiny** The examination by landing Officers of Entry documentation with a view to determining whether goods would be cleared with or without physical examination.

**CWE** The widely used term referring to consignments declared to Customs which were 'Cleared Without Examination'.

**Examined, Verified, Satisfied** The widely used certificate given by Landing Officers and Excise Officers after checking entries and official declarations such as Purchase Tax Returns and finding no error or evidence of fraud.

**Bill of Sight** A Customs Entry Form used where the importer, unaware of the precise nature, quantity or value of imported goods, needed to examine the consignment before rendering a full and accurate declaration.

**Perfect Entry** The official declaration to Customs which replaced a Bill of Sight once the full facts were ascertained by the importer or shipping agent.

**Feints** The lowest fraction of distillate containing various impurities sent to waste in the distilling process.

**Peeko Fannings** The name given to a type of tea imported from India on which a low grade specific duty of the same provenance that provoked the 'Boston Tea Party' in colonial America was payable.

**Tinctures** Spirits mixed with other ingredients used for flavouring culinary products.

**Prolate Spheroid (Middle Frustrum)** The mathematical term for the shape of a barrel or cask used as the theoretical and practical model for gauging and calculating capacity and liquid content.

**Port Pipes** Elegant wooden casks with long sloping shoulders used for importing and storing port wine from Portugal.

**Manifest** A comprehensive line by line statement carried on every ship and aircraft providing information about each consignment carried on board, a copy of which was lodged with Customs at the Custom House and against which Customs Entries lodged by importers, exporters and their agents were checked to ensure that all consignments were entered with Customs.

**Bonded Warehouses** These were commercial privately owned and operated warehouses that were approved to store and perform limited operations such as bottling in a duty free environment subject to official restrictions and conditions imposed to secure the revenue for which a financial instrument known as a 'Bond' had to be lodged. In the event of any infraction or irregularity in the running of the warehouse, the terms of the bond allowed financial restitution to Customs & Excise to be affected for any revenue loss arising.

**Crown Locks** These were large official padlocks used to secure buildings and plant in which high duty revenue goods such as spirits were produced or stored. Both the locks and keys were retained in official charge which meant that distillers and bonded warehouse keepers were unable to use plant or open their buildings other than in the presence of the designated Excise Officer. As well as the usual key mechanism, additional security was provided by covering the keyhole internally with an official paper label before closing the lock. This ensured that the label would puncture providing evidence of interference if any unauthorised person attempted to insert a key in the padlock without the Excise Officer in attendance.

**Wet Warehouses** These were bonded warehouse secured under crown locks where wines and spirits were held without payment of duty for eventual release onto the domestic market as demand required, allowing for ageing and bottling where appropriate in a duty free environment.

**Dry Goods Warehouses** These were bonded warehouses where dry, that is other than wet, goods on which revenue duties were levied were held without payment of duty, such as tobacco, tea, coffee, matches, sugar, molasses, saccharin, hops, oriental carpets and controlled drugs for medical use such as opium.

**Hydrometer** An officially calibrated and approved brass float to which various tapered weights could be added by pushing into a loop protruding from the base containing a receiving aperture. The instrument was used to measure specific gravity of wort and thus the potential alcoholic strength of beer for duty purposes.

**Original Gravity** The specific gravity of wort prior to fermentation as measured by a hydrometer which taken together with the volume of wort was used to calculate beer duty payable; the higher the original gravity or 'OG' as it was known, the stronger the concentration of alcohol in the finished brew.

**Gyle Number** The unique reference number given by a brewer to identify each individual batch of beer brewed.

**Sikes Saccarometer** An officially calibrated and approved brass float with calibrated stem in a range of sizes-weights used for determining the alcoholic strength of distilled spirits in degrees of proof.

**Proof** An empirical measure of the alcoholic strength of distilled spirits expressed in percentage terms. Under-proof meant any concentration less than 100% (whisky was normally bottled at 70% proof) and over-proof over 100%. Absolute alcohol registered around 175% proof. The term originated in the 18$^{th}$ century when payments to British sailors included rations of rum. To ensure that the rum had not been watered down, it was proofed by dousing in gunpowder, then testing to see if the gunpowder would ignite. It was found that gunpowder would not burn in rum containing below 57% alcohol by volume. This concentration was therefore deemed to be 100% proof and became the benchmark for assessing spirit strengths until 1980.

**Head Rod** This was the name given to a five foot long wooden slide rule used by Landing and Warehouse Officers in calculating the liquid content of casks containing wines and spirits which also doubled as the name implies as a measuring instrument to determine the diameter of the ends of each cask known as the front and back head respectively.

**Endometer** This was a metal measuring instrument shaped somewhat like a hook used in gauging casks for determining the thickness of the front and back heads.

**Calipers** A set of metal instruments similar to the endometer used to determine variously the thickness of staves and the length of casks.

**Cavendish Tobacco** This is the name given to a sweetened form of tobacco originated by Sir Thomas Cavendish who commanded a ship on an expedition to Virginia in 1585 and discovered that dipping tobacco leaves in sugar produced a milder and mellower smoke.

**Probate** Excise Officers were empowered to grant probate without charging a fee where the value of a deceased's estate fell below a certain value.

**Purchase Tax** This was a high yielding indirect tax introduced to help finance the Second World War which intelligent people in the media and in politics who should know better nowadays foolishly refer to as a stealth tax. It was imposed mainly on manufacturer's and wholesaler's sales of luxury goods such as cars, jewellery and televisions and was superseded in 1972 by Value Added Tax.

**Green Dragon** This was the nickname universally applied by Excise Officers to the loose leafed Station Register in which details of licenses and licence holders and other matter of revenue interest were entered. It was around two feet in length by one foot in depth and bound with thick green metal reinforced covers – hence the soubriquet.

**Excess Units** Excise work was not based on time attendance but on what was known as the Units Scheme. Every item of work such as surveys to purchase tax traders would be evaluated and given an agreed time negotiated centrally between the Official Side and the Staff Side (Trade Union). The make-up and geographical shape of Excise Stations was periodically adjusted, known as rescheming, in order to provide sufficient timed units to produce a fair year's work but individual Excise Officer were left to themselves to decide how and when individual elements of work were performed. Over time some stations gained work and in such cases Officers could claim financial compensation in the form of Excess Units Allowance pending future rescheming.

**Mp 10/pn, Ep2/4** For evidential and accountability reasons, Excise Officers recorded the start and finishing times of their visits to and surveys of traders. However they did so in an antiquated abbreviated, albeit convenient notation dating back to the time when Officers rode around their stations on horseback and took their time not from the commonplace wristwatch of today but from the chiming of the local church clock. The notation took the form of 'mp', standing for morning past with the addition of the relevant hour for example mp/10 stood for morning past 10 o'clock and mp/n morning past noon: similarly 'ep/2' meant evening past 2 o'clock, that is to say 2 o'clock in the afternoon. Thus a visit could be recorded as mp10/11 meaning that it lasted from 59 minutes past 10 in the morning to 1 minute after 11 – that is for two minutes in total or at the other extreme from 1 minute after 10 am to 59 minutes after 11 am totalling 1 hour 58 minutes in all.

**Surveyors Diary** This was the much feared official book required to be kept by Surveyors recording the supervisory and disciplinary checks they performed on Officers of Customs & Excise whose Stations fell within their administrative District.

## HM CUSTOMS & EXCISE RECOLLECTIONS

The headlines which follow were drawn up by me in the last few days before I retired from HM Customs & Excise in March 2000. They were intended to jog my memory in retirement of some of the strange but true incidents and people that I encountered during my forty years service in the Department.

I have incorporated these anecdotes into the narrative of My Story and quote below the relevant page number where each anecdote is elaborated.

- Who's Afraid Of The CIA (VIP Suite, Heathrow Airport)
  196
- The Order Of The Belt (Gatwick Airport)
  196
- Twentieth Century Icons (Maidenhead VAT-Excise Division)
  206
- The GWT Club (Maidenhead VAT-Excise Division)
  206
- White On White (Maidenhead VAT-Excise Division)
  207

# MY CURRICULUM VITAE

These comprise my GENERIC CV, a summary of KEY COMPETENCIES submitted with my job application for the position of Census Area Manager with the Office for National Statistics for the 2001 UK Census operation and a similar tailored COMPETENCY SUBMISSION forwarded with my application for my part-time job with the Royal Borough of Windsor and Maidenhead collecting parking fines and deciding appeals.

## GENERIC CV

| | |
|---|---|
| ***Name CV*** | **NORMAN COTTEE** |
| ***Address*** | 18 Barn Drive, Maidenhead, Berks, SL6 3PR |
| ***Date of Birth*** | 3 May 1941 |

***Profile***

I retired from full time employment after 40 years service in HM Customs & Excise, (now HM Revenue & Customs) in 2000, having worked in ports, airports and internal tax offices, eventually becoming a successful fraud investigator and spending the second half of my career in middle and senior operational, management positions. Subsequently, I acted as the Census Manager for the county of Berkshire during the National 2001 Census operation on a 12 months part time contract with the Office for National Statistics. Following the conclusion of the Census in 2001, I worked part time as an Administration Officer in the Royal Borough of Windsor & Maidenhead for 5 years dealing with the payment of parking fines and appeals. Now that I have passed state pension age, I hold the position of Verger and Sidesman at St James the Less Church, Stubbings, presiding over weddings, funerals and other services. I also engage actively in my hobbies. I am computer literate, and have extensive experience of using 'Word', 'E-mail', 'Excel', 'PowerPoint', 'Internet' and bespoke commercial databases.

### *Career History*

| | |
|---|---|
| 2007 - | Verger and Sidesman, St James the Less Church, Stubbings |
| 2001 - 2006 | Administration Officer, Royal Borough of Windsor & Maidenhead |
| 2000 - 2001 | Census Area Manager for Berkshire, Office for National Statistics |
| 1992 - 2000 | Business Area Manager, HM Customs & Excise, Maidenhead |
| 1984 - 1992 | Divisional Manager, London Airports (Heathrow, Gatwick, Stansted) |
| 1981 - 1984 | Principal, Headquarters Policy Division |
| 1979 - 1981 | District Manager, Southall VAT Office |
| 1972 - 1979 | District Manager, Hayes Excise Office |
| 1968 - 1972 | Senior Investigation Officer, West London |
| 1966 - 1968 | Fixed Officer, Notting Hill/Bayswater Excise District |
| 1960 - 1966 | Unattached Officer, London Docks and South West London Excise Districts |
| *Jobs while at school* | Waiter, Stagehand, Grocer's Assistant, and Newspaper Delivery Boy |

***Duties/responsibilities in previous positions held***

- Presiding as Verger and Sidesman over weddings, funerals and other services
- Collecting parking fines issued in the Royal Borough and deciding appeals
- Recruiting, training and managing 800 Census field staff in Berkshire during 2001 UK Census
- Managing 150 professional field staff in HM Customs & Excise employed in customer service, registration, debt collection and auditing of 25,000 businesses across 25 internal tax and international trade regimes, raising £1.5 billion annually for the UK Exchequer
- Leading at regional level in HM Customs & Excise the development and strategic management of debt collection, specialist audit and the training and development of managers

***Training***

Equality & Diversity, Strategic Leadership, Presentation & Media Skills, Time Management, Stress Awareness, Recruitment, Selection & Interviewing, Computer Skills, Business Systems Analysis & Consultancy, Investigation Techniques & Procedures, Rugby Football Coaching.

***Hobbies***

Vice President Maidenhead Rugby Football Club, Associate Member of Royal Shakespeare & Globe Theatres, Member of Wine Society and National Trust - Golf, Squash, Walking, Family History, Travel, Languages, Music, Theatre, Science, History, Literature, Wine, Cooking, Socializing with Family and Friends. (Charities supported: Maidenhead Rugby Club-England Rugby-Wooden Spoon Rugby-Royal

Shakespeare Company-Globe Theatre-National Trust-Church of England-Church Urban Fund)

**LEADERSHIP POSITIONS HELD**

Morden Boy Scouts 1951 - 1957

- Patrol Leader

Raynes Park Grammar School 1953 - 1959

- Prefect
- House Rugby Captain

HM Customs & Excise 1960 – 2000

- Manager Hayes Excise & Southall VAT Offices
- Chairman Southall VAT Office, Sports & Social Committee
- Principal Headquarters Outfield Division
- Divisional Manager London Airports
- Chairman London Airports Rugby Club
- Divisional Manager Thames Valley Region, Maidenhead Business Centre
- Chairman Thames Valley Region, Management Strategy & Development Group
- Chairman Thames Valley Region, Debt Management Group
- Chairman National Sports Day 1998 Organizing Group
- Chairman Thames Valley Region & Maidenhead Business Centre Sports & Social Committees

Maidenhead Rugby Club 1977 – 2002

- Chairman Mini Section
- Chairman Junior Section
- Director Playing, Senior Section
- Director Playing Administration

Office for National Statistics 2000 - 2001

- Manager in County of Berkshire for National 2001 Census

Church of England, Burchett's Green Parish 2007 -

- Verger, Sidesman and Lay Reader

**KEY COMPETENCIES FOR CENSUS ROLE**

***Managing a large and diverse operation***

18 years experience as senior manager in HM Customs & Excise, heading HQ manpower/budget policy and frontline operations Divisions at London airports, and Maidenhead tax office. In last 7 years, managed 150 diverse staff at Maidenhead employed in customer service, registration, debt collection and auditing of 23000 small, medium and large businesses across 25 internal tax and international trade regimes; producing better qualified and more effective people and substantial improvements in business outputs and relations with business.

***Recruitment and Selection***

HM C&E trained and approved chairman and panel member of recruitment and selection interview/sift panels. Served on many local, regional and national panels successfully recruiting and selecting executive, managerial and specialist staff against defined job specifications and competencies. Received complimentary feedback from observers and moderators on objectivity and fairness.

***Staff Management***

Led small team which developed middle and senior managers across a region, receiving high praise from regional director, Chairman of Customs & Excise and colleagues for the lasting improvements made in management culture and practice. Functional responsibility at regional level for debt management taken forward by instigating and successfully leading network group of 7 independent unit managers, practicing and encouraging corporacy, team working, the sharing of best practice and open, inspiring, effective communication which consistently produced the best results in the United Kingdom by any region.

***Staff Training***

Trained as an occasional trainer when frontline officer and specialist fraud investigator, helping to design and successfully deliver technical training to fellow officers; for example, in tax law and fraud identification.

As senior manager, helped regional management trainer to design and deliver effective training to managers and staff in process improvement, staff development and empowerment. Occasionally acted as senior management resource on introductory training courses run for junior grades. Complimentary feedback received in all instances.

***Public Relations***

Initiated, helped to design and run open days for professional advisers and representatives of small and medium businesses. Also promoted off-site seminars targeted at certain types of new businesses, and a business survey all of which achieved improved understanding, better mutual relations, greater compliance with revenue law and reductions in costs. Responded as head of office to local press enquiry about investigation of complaint case for which I was complimented by regional public relations officer. Achieved recognition by Cabinet Office in government-wide competition to improve customer service.

***Using a PC and software packages***
Comfortable with personal computer used daily with 'Word', 'E-mail', 'Excel', 'Intranet/Internet' applications and various in-house data bases.

***Why Suitable for Post***
Long experience at operational unit and strategic levels planning business outcomes and financial and human resource requirements, flexibly and effectively, monitoring and reporting progress, reprioritizing and complying with deadlines successfully. Personally well organized, mature in outlook and reliable, combined full time and demanding job over many years with family interests and commitments, socializing with friends and pursuing personal hobbies. Qualified as rugby union coach and elected Chairman of Mini and Junior sections of Maidenhead Rugby Club. Playing Director on the main Management Board of the club for the last 7 years. Chaired Customs & Excise Sports & Social committees at local and regional levels for last 5 years and chaired steering group which successfully organized and ran the national Departmental annual sports day at Oxford in 1998. In conclusion, I consider I have all the qualities and skills required and am able to meet the specific requirements of the job. I have the time enthusiasm and dedication to fulfill the role effectively and extensive experience of directing, influencing and managing people and organizations of many different sizes and types in both public and private sectors.

## COMPETENCY SUBMISSION FOR ADMIN POSITION WITH ROYAL BOROUGH

Having retired on full pension from Customs & Excise in March 2000, after 40 years government service, I want to remain active by working part time, locally. My fixed term employment with the census office has now finished and I am seeking an interesting, worthwhile and stimulating part time job to make use of the skills and experience I have acquired over the years, whilst supplementing my income.

This position is attractive because it is locally based, part time and involves working with colleagues and members of the public as well as operating and developing administrative systems in support of local government policy.

In both my previous roles, I have had extensive experience of communicating orally and in writing with people, including dealing responsibly, effectively and calmly with antagonistic individuals and replying to complaints, at all levels up to ministerial level, for which I was complimented by regional public relations officers and senior managers. In Customs & Excise, I initiated and helped to design and run open days for professional advisers and representatives of small and medium businesses. I inaugurated seminars targeted at new businesses and conducted a business survey which achieved improved understanding, better mutual relations, greater compliance with revenue law and reductions in costs. I achieved recognition by Cabinet Office in a government wide competition to improve customer service. During the census, I successfully liaised with local community representatives, giving reassurance and information about the census and responded through local television, radio and press to wider concerns and specific complaints from members of the public.

I am familiar with the assessment and verification of applications from businesses and members of the public, including customs and VAT declarations, invoices and other supporting documentation. My skill in spotting anomalies in such paperwork led me to become a successful tax fraud investigator during the early part of my career with Customs & Excise. I have also had extensive experience as a manager in recruiting and selecting staff from written job applications. I have served on many local, regional and national panels successfully recruiting and selecting executive, managerial and specialist staff against defined job specifications and competencies for which I received complimentary feedback from observers and moderators on my objectivity and fairness.

In my previous roles, I effectively organized my own time, managing heavy workloads without sacrificing professionalism and accuracy, invariably meeting reporting deadlines and improving business outputs and relations with business. I introduced quality improvement processes and identified and implemented many specific procedural improvements. I have developed and written clear procedural guidance covering complex issues such as payroll and management audit for a 'paperless' office that was welcomed by the managers who worked for me.

I am proficient in 'Word', 'E-mail', 'Excel', 'Power Point', 'Internet' applications and various national, in-house databases. I have a personal computer at home and, in my previous employment, I used business computers daily for communicating, producing presentations and contributing to the collection, collation, monitoring and analysis of management and financial information systems.

I am personally well organized, mature in outlook, enthusiastic and reliable. I am a qualified rugby union coach and have served as chairman of the mini and junior sections and Director of the senior playing section of Maidenhead Rugby Club. I am currently Director responsible for senior playing administration.

In conclusion, I consider I have all the qualities and skills required and am able to meet the specific requirements of the job. I have the time, enthusiasm and dedication to fulfil the role effectively and extensive experience of administration in public and voluntary sectors.

# SPEECHES

## MY RETIREMENT FROM HM CUSTOMS & EXCISE

Five weeks ago last Tuesday I completed 40 years service in this Department, a longer sentence than most murderers receive; so I hope you will forgive me if I take a few moments of your time to dip into my past before bringing the threads together in the present. I will try to keep my reminiscences short and I promise not to keep you too long from your lunch.

My 40 years in Customs began in the long hot summer of 1959. I was a carefree youth of 18, armed with a thick head of hair, believe it or not, and A levels in maths and physics. I could have gone to University but the prospects for graduate scientists seemed unpromising, so I returned to school in the Autumn leaving my Mum to look for a job form me; not that she needed much encouragement – a bit of Margaret Thatcher type my mother. Anyway, I did stipulate that I didn't want a boring nine to five office job and was looking for something more varied, preferably involving travel and foreign languages. She got hold of some literature on the Outdoor Service in HM Customs & Excise which sounded interesting and a scheme for recruiting and training airline pilots for BOAC ( British Overseas Airways Corporation). I promptly completed both sets of application forms and sent them off. Now this is where fate comes in. Customs were first to reply. They offered me an interview and I passed, narrowly. BOAC then offered me an interview but encouraged by my mother, I accepted the Customs job. She felt that the Civil Service offered security – which was all important to her, remembering, as she did, the great stock market crash and depression of the Thirties.

In many ways the job has lived up to my expectations; in some ways it hasn't. I haven't travelled much, for example. I've spent most of my working life in and around London, although as Assistant Collector, Heathrow, I spent two enjoyable weeks based in Lille in Northern France with a member of the French Collectorate on a Matthaeus exchange when I was able to use my language skills. Nevertheless, it has proved a varied and at times exciting job.

I joined as an Unattached Officer, or UO, as we were generally called and signed on in London South Collection, one of five London Collections in those days. Sobering to reflect that from 1 April under the Modernising Government changes, this number will drop to a single Collection for the whole of the London area excluding the Airports. After basic training I was appointed to London Port Collection spending most of my time in the upper docks at Free Trade Wharf in Wapping which is now a yuppie block of flats. While there, I heard about the UO grand tour. Tis was a well paid opportunity to travel round the country at the Board's expense starting with the Channel Ports in the summer season, moving to east Anglia in the autumn for the sugar beet harvest, on which there was an Excise Duty and travelling up to Scotland in the winter for the whisky distillery season. The subsistence was legendry and with the proceeds you could afford to buy an open-topped sports car with which to beguile a string of landladies' daughters round the country. This was the life for me I thought and in July 1961 I applied for a 'crown' transfer to Dover Collection. A few months later with my application on file, two things happened which determined the future course of my career and indeed, my whole life.

The first was that I received a phone call from the Appointer telling me that I was the senior man on the list for a vacancy that had just come up in Dover Collection – 'senior' because seniority ruled everything and 'man' because the Outdoor Service comprised men only. However, he wondered whether I would allow the next most senior UO in line for the vacancy to go in my place. This officer apparently had a wife and children living in Dover whereas to all intents and purposes I was unencumbered on the domestic front. I agreed. I was disappointed but calculated that another vacancy would soon come along.

The second thing that happened, arising from the first, meant that I continued living at home with my parents, socialising with my rugby playing ex school friends, one of whom, quite by chance, introduced me to a junior school friend of his called Ros. We went to her house after he and I had failed to gatecrash a party round the corner. After I had impressed Ros by taking her out on our first date to a wedding reception for which she bought a new dress wearing my favourite drinking sweater and pair of jeans with a hole in the crutch, I withdrew my transfer application for Dover and secured a move instead in October 1963 to London South Collection. Working there as a UO, I acquired a fair amount of expertise in the brewery, distillery and wet warehousing regimes and found myself not just assisting the fixed officers but officiating for them and covering unfilled vacancies. Mortlake Brewery, Wandsworth Distillery and Merton Abbey Bonded Warehouse became fixed stars in my UO firmament.

In 1965, the 'Parker Reorganisation' finally rung down the curtain on the old style Department, full of independently minded and eccentric characters and, by today's standards, laughable inefficiencies. It also meant that as a UO, I at last had the chance to apply for my own fixed station. Because of my juniority, I only managed to secure my 75th choice out of 77 and was appointed from 1 January 1966 to Notting Hill Excise District. By then, Ros and I were engaged and saving to get married. We started house hunting, looking for easy commuting via Paddington. This led to Berkshire and our first house at Arborfield Cross, south of Reading, which we moved into after we got married in September 1966.

I really enjoyed my time at Notting Hill, during which Betting Duty was successfully introduced. I remember the quirky characters I worked with and am proud that I was the first officer in London West Collection to identify Betting Duty and Purchase tax frauds and to investigate them successfully. Later, as an Unattached Surveyor in Reading Collection, I instigated and helped to successfully conclude the first ever Purchase Tax fraud in that Collection, of which I am also proud. In January 1968 I joined the newly formed London West Investigation Unit. This was the highlight of my career from a personal point of view. I found the challenge of the work enervating. And the path finding success we achieved in the field of fiscal fraud was extremely satisfying.

With the onset of VAT, I was promoted to Surveyor in 1972 and, after a spell as Unattached Surveyor, moved house to Maidenhead and took charge off Hayes Excise District situated within sniffing distance of Nestlé's instant coffee factory. My fondest claim to fame during the seven years I spent at Hayes was to have the air raid shelter which guarded the entrance to the building demolished. I fully expected World War II skeletons in the rubble and was slightly disappointed when none were found. Two years followed as a VAT Control Surveyor at Southall before I went to Headquarters on promotion in 1981. Cash limits had just been introduced for the first time in the public service and that's where I learned that 'taking the wider view' means 'what's in it for me'. I escaped back to the Outfield in 1984 as Assistant Collector Heathrow Airport from the rarefied policy making atmosphere of Headquarters. The London Airports are mini cities that work round the clock 365 days a year and the next eight years, forgive the pun, flew by. I headed up cargo and passenger Divisions, officiating for the Assistant collector Gatwick and taking charge of Stansted Airport before moving here to Maidenhead VAT and Excise Division in July 1992. While in London Airports Collection, I became Chairman of the Heathrow Customs Rugby Club and fondly remember the two trips I made to Paris when we played French Customs on the weekend of the France v England international. The French were wonderful hosts. And later, just before I left the Airport, I vaguely remember on hugely enjoyable, long and emotionally tiring lunch with the French Customs Attaché in London – all in the line of duty, of course.

It was T S Eliot in his poem The Four quartets, a great favourite of mine, who says that 'Old men should be explorers. Here and now cease to matter'. I don't know about old. I certainly don't feel old....but explorer......yes. I guess I've always been a bit of an explorer, particularly once I took up the management role – seeking to push out the boundaries of the Department's innately cautious approach into a more adventurous, open stance, where people are inspired, trusted and stretched rather than suspected and used as scapegoats for failures of leadership. This led to frustration and irritation on my part which may occasionally have shown. However I have tried to be understanding of colleagues who don't see the need to move as fast or as far as I do and to hone my powers of persuasion accordingly. The last ten years have been particularly encouraging; the tide at last seems to have been flowing in my direction. The introduction of the 'People Initiative' and the 'Management Strategy' have meant that apart from my time as an investigator in London West, this has been the most exciting, enjoyable and rewarding phase of my career. I would like to thank John (Thames Valley Regional Director) for the freedom he has given me to pursue his ideas and my own beliefs about management.

Through my lead role on the Management Strategy Group, I think I have helped to create a more modern, forward looking management in the Collection. In that respect, I should like to pay tribute to Ina Elliott for the unstinting support she has given me and to thank Jim Treherne and others in the Management Strategy and Debt management Groups for their support. The battle is not yet won, of course. Outfield managers should have a stronger voice in policy making and the Headquarters army of theorists needs to be streamlined. Managers should be trusted to get on with the job, not surrounded by petty, prescriptive procedures and over-detailed statistical returns. Conversely, they need to be held more directly to account for their achievements and failures. However, it is now for others to take these concerns forward.

As to 'Here and now ceasing to matter', the here and now of results and achievements have concerned me very much. I believe that I leave an office which is on the leading edge culturally and which consistently produces operational results in the top drawer and improves on them year by year. I have to thank my management team here at Maidenhead for all the help and support they have given me over the last seven years in achieving such success. Success which has been recognised, for example, when our Debt Management Unit won the first ever 'Chairman's Award, proving conclusively that the management approach I believe in, which some call 'pink and fluffy' actually works and produces better results and better qualified people. This year will prove no exception with all the indicators suggesting that Maidenhead Division will, once again, meet or exceed key revenue targets and I have to thank everyone for the effort they have put in, the commitment they have shown and the experience and expertise they have applied. I am most grateful to you all.

I am also grateful to those outside this office, including my Senior Manager colleagues on the Collection Management Board, who have helped in their own way, have listened and gone along with many if not all of the ideas and arguments I have put forward and have kindly laughed at my sporadic attempts to lighten the tone with the occasional humorous remark. Work should not always be serious and I should like to say how much I have enjoyed the company and repartee of my colleagues in this office. Indeed, I think I may have learned more about the wines of the world in my time here than I have about the more arcane technicalities of VAT. I have also enjoyed chairing the Maidenhead and the Thames Valley Sports & Social Clubs and was proud to chair the Steering Group that successfully organised the Departmental Sports Day at Oxford in 1998.

Many memories will remain with me. I have tried to recall some of them in the past few weeks and have compiled a list to chuckle over in my dotage. The list which I have called 'Strange But True' gets longer the more I think about it and if I find the time in my retirement, I may expand it into some kind of autobiographical work so that my past and the Department's past are not altogether lost. I plan to be active in my retirement and with the money you have kindly raised am getting a home computer so that I can continue to use email and access the worldwide web. I shall carry on with my involvement on the Maidenhead Rugby Club Board and will be looking for a part time job of some description for two to three days a week. I shall continue to travel the world and want to explore as much of it as I can before I pop my clogs, as well as pursuing my other hobbies and interests.

Those of you who took part in our team event last September will remember that Lawrence of Arabia who forged a set of wild and individualistic people together into an effective and victorious fighting force was one of our 'Twentieth Century Icons'. Lawrence concludes his autobiography 'The Seven Pillars of Wisdom' with the words – 'I made to Allenby the last request I ever made to him; leave to go away. For a while he would not have it. In the end he agreed and then at once I knew how much I was sorry'. Having surrendered my commission to John, standing before you on the threshold of retirement these words very much reflect my own feelings. It only remains for me to thank you all for your retirement gifts and for being here today to ease me over that threshold to the world of adventure beyond Customs and Excise. I greatly appreciate the support and help you have all given me. And I must not forget to thank Chris, Christine, Irenka, Linda, Sylvia, Mark and Gordon for organising today's event, thank you.

I have only this left to say. I am confident that you will fare forward with enthusiasm and resolution in the new Collection, that you will face up to the challenges that lie ahead and will overcome them. I wish you all well

## PHILLIP & NICOLA"S WEDDING

Ladies and gentlemen, my son Phillip and his lovely bride, Nicola, have asked me to give a short address on this special occasion and I am pleased and proud to be able to do so.

Some 18 months ago, Phillip and Nicola flew away for a month and a day to Australia, where one Melbourne night, that wise owl Phil, gazed up at the moon above and sang to a lager tinny "O lovely Nicky, O Nicky my love, what a beautiful creature you are, you are, what a beautiful creature you are." Said Nic to this owl "You eminent fowl, how charmingly tuneless you sing. O let us be married, too long we have tarried, but what shall we do for a ring?" "Dear Nic are you willing to take for one shilling" (and some), "this ring." Said young Nic, "I will." So they beavered away and are married today in this elegant house called Savill.

Just over a mile from here, lies a meadow called Runnymede, where on the 15 June, a four thousand word document was drawn up and signed. Not, I hasten to add, a pre-nuptial contract but a great charter, or Magna Carta as it was called. Those who drew the charter up in the year 1215, sought to bring about a marriage, in the everyday sense of that word, between all the contending parties and interests in the land. However, King John repudiated the Charter shortly afterwards and only a handful of copies remained. But the will to honour the fundamental theme of this universal marriage document survived and has shaped our people and our institutions over the centuries

In the long run, the will to honour an agreement counts as much as the words contained within it. And as Phil and Nicola reflect upon their wedding vows, may they embark on married life together with a will to honour the lifelong commitment of this day, knowing only that they venture forth, sharing aspirations and visions, successes and failures, supporting strengths and frailties-recognized and redrawn, exchanging opinions and priorities-respected and built upon; hard not easy, rewarding not stale, mates and lovers, bound but free; 'sic transit gloria mundi.'

The slow and silent river of time will surely 'Make Its Utter Changes', bringing trials and tribulations, sadness and celebrations. But as Phil and Nicola progress through life together, allergic to onions and strawberries but not to each other, passionate about rugby football and retail therapy but not blindly so, may they rejoice with Ulysses in Tennyson's epic poem of the same name 'That which we are, we are; one equal temper of heroic hearts, made weak by time and fate, but strong in will, to strive, to seek, to find, and not to yield.'

And so we wish Phillip and Nicola well; to be strong in will and not to yield but to prosper and to endure, to bring sunshine and laughter to those around them, to family, friends and colleagues, now and always. Two hearts in union (whistle), the game's begun. Enjoy today and your life to come.

## SIMON & THERESA"S WEDDING

Ladies and gentlemen, some while ago, Simon & Theresa asked me to give a speech here today. Something amusing, you're so amusing they said; a trifle, a tall tale maybe of star crossed lovers and how Simon met his CheesyB. But it's difficult to know where to begin.

Suffice to say that life with Simon has never been straightforward. At his birth, the midwife had to force a potion down his throat before uttering his first sound 'Chelsea' he looked around as if to say "Well nobody told me to breathe". Or as a teenager, losing his front tooth by falling on a plank of wood (allegedly) to find out later that it was knocked from his mouth while he was fighting for his friends. Edging into manhood, however, we did begin to see the light. Friends of ours started telling us they had met Simon in the pub, where else, and what a charming lad he was.

Then one evening at the Valbonne nightclub, he met his nemesis. The raven haired, the milk white skinned, the top bomber of the bombers, the lovely Theresa from old Ireland sprung, whom the Dublin born poet Yeats, must have had in mind, when he wrote, '*You need but lift a pearl-pale hand, And bind up your long hair and sigh, For all men's hearts must burn and beat, And live to light your passing feet.*' Inspired by Yeats or not, Chelsea Boy Blue was smitten and romance blossomed free after Simon's vetting by the Boland Brothers three.

Partners now for several years, Simon & Theresa differ yet strangely complement one another. For instance, Theresa saves money and Simon spends it. Theresa loves animals, moving frogs in her garden to a more suitable habitat, while Simon would still like to strangle that peacock that, with a single well aimed peck, made off with his ice cream cornet, at a local wildlife park. Theresa adores TV soaps and Big Brother. Simon hates celebrity TV but loves sport, especially football, although secretly, he is terrified that Jose Mourinho is really a breed of sheep and the Chelsea glory story is nothing but a dream.

Talking of sheep, Simon & Theresa share Aries the Ram as their birth sign. They also share a love of luxury and good taste, witness our surroundings today. On holiday, they always stay in the best hotel rooms, except that is when touring Southern Ireland with Ros and me. Wherever we stayed, Ros and I were allocated the best room, and some were spectacular, until heading towards our last stop in Dublin, we agreed that Simon & Theresa should have first choice. But all things are relative. The Talbot Hotel where we spent our last few nights was the Irish equivalent of Fawlty Towers. The bedside lamps were nailed down, and the shower cubicle collapsed around Theresa while she was in it. Earlier in this same trip, I remember that eerie moment in the Wicklow Mountains when the birds stopped singing, the sky drained and everything went still, in a partial eclipse of the sun. That was a magical moment; one we shared and one I shall never forget.

But history is now and England and this too is a magical moment. So I should like to raise a glass to you both and to wish you fun, friendship and fantastic fortune for the future, remembering only that an Irish schoolgirl, in answering a test on religious education wrote, 'Jesus preached holy acrimony - which is another word for marriage'. I think she meant 'holy matrimony' but she could be right first time, for every great sauce needs a dash of vinegar; but only a dash mind you. I hope therefore that this modest appetiser before we embark on the main celebration has been to your taste. Have a great day and a rewarding and vibrant married life together. And as the Irish zoo keeper, who named his pet zebra Spot declared *"Live long - And may you get to heaven before the devil realises you're there"*.

## MY 70th BIRTHDAY

When I look back over the 70 years I have spent on this beautiful and lonely planet, I can't help thinking that I have been extremely fortunate.

Fortunate to have had good friends and family to share in my joys and pleasures and to help me through the difficult times.

Fortunate to have grown up during a period, which later generations may come to regard as a golden age, when the standard of living continually improved and nobody worried about health & safety, dwindling natural resources or global warming.

Fortunate also to have gone to a wonderful school, Raynes Park Grammar, whose principles of challenging received wisdom and thinking for one's self have remained with me throughout my adult life.

My old school friends Robbie and Terry are here today and we have decided, by way of entertainment, to treat you to a brief rendition of the school song, the words of which were composed by the poet W H Auden a friend of the first headmaster.

The song means a lot to us but we are going to spare you the full six verses with choruses by singing just three, for which we will be accompanied on the piano by Robbie's wife Margaret. I should warn you that all exits have now been blocked and any resemblance to a trio of screeching cats is entirely coincidental.

SCHOOL SONG
Time will make its utter changes,
Circumstance will scatter us;
But the memories of our schooldays
Are a living part of us.

*CHORUS*
So remember then, when you are men
With important things to do,
That once you were young and this song have sung
For you were at school here, too.

Man has mind but body also;
So we learn to tackle low,
Bowl the off-breaks, hit the sixes,
Bend the diver's brilliant bow.

Boys and cities, schools and natures,
Though they change like you and me,
Do not simply grow and happen,
They are what they choose to be.

In conclusion, I should just like to say that, I count myself lucky to have won first prize in the lottery of life, as my son Simon puts it, by being born English. Despite this Fairest Isle's changeable climate, there are many worse places in the world to live and I am happy to have whittled away my days in this tolerant, green and pleasant land.

I am fortunate too that I still love my wife and want to take this opportunity to thank her for all the work she has put into our marriage over the years and more specifically into making this gathering a success.

I am proud of my sons and the way their lives are evolving - and love them too in a manly way – so long as they let me win the odd hole at golf, that is.

I couldn't have chosen more alluring and feisty daughters-in-law, who put me in my place whenever I get out of my tree - a rare occurrence, I hope they will agree!

And I of course adore, absolutely and unreservedly, my grandchildren.

Family, friends, including the two Lyndas and Mary who have provided the catering this afternoon - Cousins, one and all, not forgetting Dorothy and Graham, the oldest members of the family, who unfortunately cannot be with us today,

Thank you for your support and friendship over the years and for helping to celebrate this milestone in my life.

70 not out in cricket is passing fair.
70-Nil at rugby, I'll take that – whey hey hey!
So, please eat, drink and be merry for, as the saying goes, tomorrow is another day.

## FAVOURITE QUOTES, FILMS, POEMS, BOOKS ETC

The following, in no particular order, are quotes, sayings, extracts from poems and writings that I particularly like and that chime with my take on life. I also include, again in no particular order, titles and authors of my favourite poems, books and films.

### T E LAWRENCE (LAWRENCE OF ARABIA)

*EXTRACTS FROM HIS AUTOBIOGRAPHY 'SEVEN PILLARS OF WISDOM'*

However high handed I appeared, I had a reserve of confidence to carry the whole thing, if need be, on my shoulders. They used to think me boastful when I said so: but my confidence was not so much ability to do a thing perfectly, as a preference for botching it somehow rather than letting it go altogether by default.

We slept there that chilly night, happy with bully beef and tea and biscuit, with English talk and laughter round the fire, golden with its shower of sparks from the fierce brushwood.

When Faisal had gone, I made to Allenby the last (and also I think the first) request I ever made for myself – leave to go away. For a while he would not have it; but I reasoned, reminding him of his year old promise, and pointing out how much easier the New Law would be if my spur were absent from the people. In the end he agreed; and then at once I knew how much I was sorry.

All men dream: but not equally. Those who dream by night in the dusty recesses of their minds wake in the day to find that it was vanity: but the dreamers of the day are dangerous men, for they may act their dream with open eyes, to make it possible.

**CAPTAIN JAMES COOK**

*BIOGRAPHY BY RICHARD HOUGH*

Sailing from North East tip of Australia heading for Jakarta in Dutch East Indies

Cook attempted to ply along the shore but the wind turned foul and the Endeavour's 'croakers' (the inveterate pessimists to be found in every ship) expressed their ill informed view that the westerly monsoon had caught them. But two days later 'The wind became fair' reported Banks, adding caustically, 'and left our melancholy ones to search for some new occasion of sorrow'.

**OLIVER CROMWELL**

*GOD'S ENGLISHMAN BY CHRISTOPHER HILL*

The Earl of Manchester after the battle of Naseby in the English Civil War, warned Cromwell - 'If we beat the King ninety nine times, yet he is still King but if the King beat us once, we shall all be hanged.' Cromwell replied with irrefutable logic 'My Lord, if this be so, why did we take up arms at first? This is against fighting ever hereafter.'

Cromwell offered this advice when addressing the Parliamentary Army before the Battle of Preston.
'Trust in God..... And keep your powder dry!'

**ABRAHAM LINCOLN**

*FROM 'MY LIFE' BY BILL CLINTON*

Whenever anyone made a snide remark about Yeltsin's drinking, I was reminded of what Lincoln allegedly said of General Grant, by far his most aggressive and successful commander in the Civil War: "Find out what he drinks, and give it to the other generals."

**ANONYMOUS**

*PLAQUE ON WALL OF 'THE BELL' PUBLIC HOUSE, ALDWORTH, BERKS*

Everyone needs to believe in something,
I believe I will have another beer.

**ALAN TURING**

*POSTSCRIPT TO BIOGRAPHY BY ANDREW HODGES – TAKEN FROM POEM REFLECTING ON AMERICAN CIVIL WAR BY WALT WHITMAN*

As I lay with my head in your lap camarado,
The confession I made I resume,
I know I am restless and make others so,
I know my words are weapons full of danger, full of death,
For I confront peace, security, and all the settled laws, to unsettle them,
I am more resolute because all have denied me
Than I could ever have been had all accepted me,
I heed not and have never heeded either experience, cautions, majorities, nor ridicule,

And the threat of what is called heaven is little or nothing to me,
And the lure of what is called heaven is little or nothing to me,
Dear camerado, I confess I have urged you onward with me, and still urge you,
Without the least idea what is our destination,
Or whether we shall be victorious, or utterly quelled and defeated.

**THOMAS PAINE**
*FROM THE AGE OF REASON*
My mind is my own church

**ANONYMOUS**
*REVELATIONS 21 (KING JAMES VERSION OF THE BIBLE)*
I saw a new heaven and a new earth,
For the first earth had passed away
And the sea was no more.
And I saw the holy city, the new Jerusalem,
Coming down out of heaven from God,
Prepared as a bride adorned for her husband.

And I heard a loud voice from the throne saying
*'See the home of God is among mortals.*
*He will dwell with them; they will be his peoples*
*And God himself will be with them;*
*He will wipe every tear from their eyes.*
*Death will be no more;*
*Mourning and crying and pain will be no more,*
*For the first things have passed away.'*

And the one who was seated on the throne said
*'See, I am making all things new.'*

Also he said

> *'Write this, for these words are trustworthy and true.'*

Then he said to me,

> *'It is done! I am the Alpha and Omega, the beginning and the end.*
> *To the thirsty I will give water*
> *As a gift from the spring of the water of life.*
> *Those who overcome shall inherit all these things*
> *And I will be their God and they will be my children.'*

**WILLIAM SHAKESPEARE**

*HAMLET*

(Hamlet) There are more things in heaven and earth, Horatio, than are dreamt of in your philosophy.

*Also –*

(Horatio) I will forestall their repair hither and say you are not fit.

(Hamlet) Not a whit, we defy augury: there's a special providence in the fall of a sparrow. If it be now, 'tis not to come; if it be not to come, it will be now; if it be not now, yet it will come: the readiness is all: since no man has aught of what he leaves, what is't to leave betimes

*TWELFTH NIGHT*

(Sir Toby Belch to Malvolio) Dost thou think because thou art virtuous there should be no more cakes and ale?

**ANONYMOUS**

*12th DYNASTY ANCIENT EGYPTIAN TEXT*

Death is before me today, like a sick man's recovery, like going outside after confinement.

Death is before me today, like the scent of myrrh, like sitting under a sail on a windy day.
Death is before me today, like the scent of lotuses, like sitting on the shore of drunkenness.
Death is before me today, like a well trodden path, like a man's coming home from war.
Death is before me today, like the opening of the sky, like a man's grasping what he did not know.
Death is before me today, like a man's longing to see home, having spent many years abroad.

**WALT WHITMAN**

*EXTRACT FROM POEMS OF THE FUTURE*

I will make the true poem of riches, and I will show
That there is no imperfection in the present
And can be none in the future,
And I will show that whatever happens to anybody
It may be turned to beautiful results,
And I will show that nothing can happen
More beautiful than death,
And I will thread a thread through my poems
That time and events are compact,
And that all the things of the universe
Are perfect miracles,
Each as profound as any.

I will not make poems with reference to parts,
But I will make poems, songs, thoughts,
With reference to ensemble,
And I will not sing with reference to a day,
But with reference to all days,
And I will not make a poem, nor the least part of a poem,
But has reference to the soul,

Because, having looked at the objects of the universe,
I find there is no one, nor any particle of one,
But has reference to the soul.

*EXTRACTS FROM LEAVES OF GRASS & PASSAGE TO INDIA*

Behold, the sea itself,
And on its limitless heaving breast, the ships:
See, where their white sails, bellying in the wind, speckle the green and blue,
See, the steamers coming and going, steaming in and out of port,
See, dusky and undulating, the long pennants of smoke
And after the sea-ship, after the whistling winds,
After the white-gray sails taut to their spars and ropes,
Below, a myriad, myriad waves hastening, lifting up their necks,
Tending in ceaseless flow toward the track of the ship,
Waves of the ocean bubbling and gurgling, blithely prying,
Waves, undulating waves, liquid, uneven, emulous waves,
Toward that whirling current, laughing and buoyant with curves,
Where the great vessel sailing and tacking displaced the surface.

O we can wait no longer,
We too take ship,
Joyous O soul,
We too launch out on trackless seas,
Fearless, for unknown shores on waves of ecstasy to sail
Amid the wafting winds.

Away! Hoist instantly the anchor!
Cut the hawsers, haul out, shake out every sail!

Have we stood here like trees in the ground long enough?
Have we not grovelled here long enough, eating and drinking like mere brutes?
Have we not darkened and dazed ourselves with books long enough?
Sail forth – steer for the deep waters only,
For we are bound where mariner has not yet dared to go,
And we will risk the ship, ourselves and all.
O my brave soul!
O farther, farther sail!
O darling joy, but safe!
Are they not all the seas of God?
O farther, farther, father sail.

**T S ELIOT**
*EXTRACTS FROM 'FOUR QUARTETS'*

Footfalls echo in the memory,
Time and the bell have buried the day.
*(BURNT NORTON)*
The black cloud carries the sun away.
Will the sunflower turn to us?
Will the clematis stray down, bend to us;
Tendril and spray, clutch and cling,
Chill fingers of yew be curled down on us?

In my beginning is my end.
*(EAST COKER)*
As we grow older the world becomes stranger,
The pattern more complicated of dead and living.
Not the intense moment isolated, with no before and after,
But a lifetime burning in every moment.

And what the dead had no speech for, when living,
*(LITTLE GIDDING)*
They can tell you, being dead.
The communication of the dead is tongued with fire
Beyond the language of the living.

We die with the dying:
See, they depart, and we go with them.
We are born with the dead:
See, they return and bring us with them.

Footfalls echo in the memory,
*(BURNT NORTON)*
Down the passage which we did not take,
Towards the door we never opened, into the rose garden.

And the end of all our exploring
*(LITTLE GIDDING)*
Will be to arrive where we started
And know the place for the first time
Through the unknown remembered gate
When the last of the earth left to discover
Is that which was the beginning.

And all shall be well
And all manner of things shall be well,
When the tongues of flame are in-folded
Into the crowned knot of fire
And the fire and the rose are one.

**WILLIAM TECUMSEH SHERMAN**

On hearing of South Carolina's secession from the United States, Sherman observed to a close friend, Professor David

F Boyd of Virginia, an enthusiastic secessionist, almost perfectly describing the four years of civil war to come:

'You people of the South don't know what you are doing. This country will be drenched in blood, and God only knows how it will end. It is all folly, madness, a crime against civilisation! You people speak so lightly of war; you don't know what you're talking about. War is a terrible thing! You mistake, too, the people of the North. They are peaceable people but an earnest people, and they will fight too. They are not going to let this country be destroyed without a mighty effort to save it....Besides, where are your men and appliances of war to contend against them? The North can make a steam engine, locomotive, or railway car; hardly a yard of cloth or pair of shoes can you make. You are rushing into war with one of the most powerful, ingeniously mechanical, and determined people on Earth-right at your doors. You are bound to fail. Only in your spirit and determination are you prepared for war. In all else you are totally unprepared, with a bad cause to start with. At first you will make headway, but as your limited resources begin to fail, shut out from the markets of Europe as you will be, your cause will begin to wane. If your people will but stop and think, they must see in the end that you will surely fail.'

**DOC HOLLIDAY**

As depicted in the 1993 film 'Tombstone', the dissolute yet gifted Doc Holliday, played by Val Kilmer, when handing back to his friend Wyatt Earp, played by Kurt Russell, the Marshall's badge he had borrowed to legitimise his gun duel with the outlaw Ringo, explains that -

'My hypocrisy has its limits!'

Later, in the sanatorium where he lies dying from Tuberculosis, having just received the last rights from a Catholic priest, Doc confesses to his friend Wyatt by way of explanation in reference to the departing priest that -

'My hypocrisy knows no bounds!'

**WH AUDEN**
*WORDS OF RAYNES PARK GRAMMAR SCHOOL SONGCOMPOSED BY THE POET AN INTIMATE FRIEND OF THE SCHOOLS FOUNDING HEADMASTER JOHN GARRATT*
Time will make its utter changes,
Circumstance will scatter us;
But the memories of our schooldays
Are a living part of us.

*(Chorus)*
*So remember then, when you are men*
*With important things to do,*
*That once you were young and this song have sung*
*For you were at school her too.*

Daily we sit down in form-rooms,
Inky hand to puzzled head;
Reason's light and knowledge power:
Man must study till he's dead.
*(Chorus)*

Man has mind but body also;
So we learn to tackle low,
Bowl the off-breaks, hit the sixes
Bend the diver's brilliant bow.
*(Chorus)*

Man must live among his neighbours
For he cannot live alone;
Friendships, failures and successes
Here we learn to make our own.
*(Chorus)*

Tractors grunt where oceans wandered
Factories stand where green grass grew;
Voices break and features alter
We shall soon be different too.
*(Chorus)*

Boys and cities, schools and natures,
Though they change like you and me,
Do not simply grow and happen
They are what they choose to be.
*(Chorus)*

**OZYMANDIAS OF EGYPT** by Percy Bysshe Shelley
I met a traveller from an antique land
Who said: Two vast and trunkless legs of stone
Stand in the desert. Near them on the sand,
Half sunk, a shattered visage lies, whose frown
And wrinkled lip and sneer of cold command
Tell that its sculptor well those passions read
Which yet survive, stamped on these lifeless things,
The hand that mocked them and the heart that fed;
And on the pedestal these words appear:
'My name is Ozymandias, king of kings:
Look on my works, ye Mighty, and despair!'
Nothing beside remains. Round the decay
Of that colossal wreck, boundless and bare,
The lone and level sands stretch far away.

## TITLES & AUTHORS OF FAVOURITE POEMS

DULCE ET DECORUM EST by Wilfred Owen

ELEGY IN A COUNTRY CHURCHARD by Thomas Gray

IF by Rudyard Kipling

UPON WESTMINSTER BRIDGE by William Wordsworth

THE DAFFODILS by William Wordsworth

TO HIS COY MISTRESS by Andrew Marvell

THE TYGER by William Blake

SEA FEVER by John Masefield

CARGOES by John Masefield

SONNET XLII FROM THE POTUGUESE by Elizabeth Barratt Browning

FOUR QUARTETS by TS Eliot

LOVE SONG OF J ALFRED PRUFROCK by T S Eliot

JOURNEY OF THE MAGI by T S Eliot

MACAVITY THE MYSTERY CAT by T S Eliot

JABBERWOCKY by Lewis Carroll

KUBLA KHAN by Samuel Taylor Coleridge

OZYMANDIAS OF EGYPT by Percy Bysshe Shelley

HOME THOUGHTS FROM ABROAD by Robert Browning

SONNETS 18, 29, 33, 60, 64, 97, 98, 106, 116 by William Shakespeare

O MISTRESS MINE by William Shakespeare (Twelfth Night Act II Scene IV)

THE OWL AND THE PUSSY CAT by Edward Lear

LOVELIEST OF TREES THE CHERRY NOW by A E Houseman

ULYSSES by Alfred Lord Tennyson

BREAK, BREAK, BREAK by Alfred Lord Tennyson

THE SONG OF HIAWATHA by H W Longfellow

GAHTER YE ROSEBUDS WHILE YE MAY by Robert Herrick

PSALM 23 by Anonymous (King James Bible)

LEAVES OF GRASS by Walt Whitman

AS I LAY WITH MY HEAD IN YOUR LAP CAMARADO by Walt Whitman

INVICTUS by William Ernest Henley

## BOOKS

**SEVEN PILLARS OF WISDOM** by T E Lawrence
A literary triumph in its own right, this is a finely written semi-autobiographical description of Lawrence's part in the Arab Revolt during World War I.

**ALICE IN WONDERLAND** by Lewis Carroll
Speaks to children and adults alike. A marvellous feat of the imagination that used to scare the shit out of me when I was a child.

**THE GOOD SOLDIER SWEJK** by Jaroslav Hasek
This is an unfinished meandering, frustrating, humorous, annoying, piquant, irreverent saga of the small man's (and small nation's) inventive attempts to avoid and ignore the unrelenting blandishments, stupidities, hypocrisies, inefficiencies and retributions of bureaucratic and military authorities.

**THE PICKWICK PAPERS (AND ALL HIS OTHER NOVELS)** by Charles Dickens
Incomparable stories that carry you along with fantastic characters and atmospherics – don't worry too much about the intricacies of the plots – they are largely incidental – just enjoy the rich panoply of life that teams from the pages and the irony of his social observation and commentary.

**TREASURE ISLAND** by Robert Louis Stevenson
One of the best opening chapters of any adventure story; immortal, atmospheric story-telling, bringing to iconic life flawed, ambivalent, colourful, individualistic characters, each out for their own ends, whose destinies and aspirations overlap, subtly concealing an underlying moral concerning

the appreciation of intrinsic rather than worldly value and leaving little settled or gained by the characters themselves as a result of their adventure except the marvellous and exciting experience itself. The film starring Robert Newton as Long John Silver is superb and one of my favourite films.

**DON QUIXOTE** by Miguel Cervantes
A poignant, lengthy, rambling, gently humorous epic tale of the 'quixotic' exploits of the aging Spanish Knight of the Sad Countenance and his younger, practically minded, down to earth, loyal servant, Sancho Panza; their evolving companionship and deep humanity though drawn from wholly different social and intellectual backgrounds.

**THE BOOK THIEF** by Marcus Zusak
This is a wonderfully touching story told by the author and based upon his German mother Lisle's childhood in the country of her birth during the Second World War. He etches her quest for survival, knowledge and intellectual liberation despite the difficulty she faced in a fresh, idiosyncratic yet engaging language that brings tears to the reader's eyes. Sad yet hopeful at the same time, the nastiness of war, the degradation of life, limb and moral compass is redeemed by her curiosity and humanity. I gave my copy of this book to my then 10 year old granddaughter with a dedication I wrote inside the front cover because I thought she resembled Lisle so much in character.

**ALL QUIET ON THE WESTERN FRONT** by Erich Maria Ramarque
An iconic novel: one of the world's greatest anti-war, humanist novels set mainly in the trenches of the First World War and written from the German foot soldiers point of view. Ramarque creates a striking perspective, calmly

distilled in an unforced, temperate and lastingly persuasive way about the inhumanity of mass violence triggered by unbridled nationalism and the shared suffering and comradeship of the ordinary young men on both sides, so many of whom were to lose their lives so indiscriminately in the conflict. The shared experiences they endured, the identical consequential priorities and values they both evolved became more overidingly important to them than any of the war aims for which they were supposedly expected to be killing each other.

**THE VISIBLE WORLD** by Mark Slouka
The Second World War again but at heart a despairing and deeply felt love story providing the central theme: a love between the author's mother when she was a young woman living in Prague and a Czech resistance fighter executed by firing squad after hiding in Prague Cathedral, after assassinating the hated Nazi Gauleiter, Heinrich.

**THE GOD OF SMALL THINGS** by Arundhati Roy
A compelling story which somehow marries the smallest personal emotions with a panoramic vision. The poetry of certain phrases and passages remain in the mind as the author deftly and sinuously incorporates poignant kaleidoscopic details into an impressive overarching thematic structure in which the hauntingly final tragic consequences surprise, shock and empties the soul. And from which we are unable to escape.

**THE COMPLETE WORKS OF SHAKESPEARE AND CHARLES DICKENS**
From a literary and dramatic point of view these two writers have no equals. Plug in anywhere and you will come away

with a sublime jewel. The human condition and life in its manifold complexity and variety have never been plumbed so masterfully and the characters that people these tales are unforgettable because they are us.

## FILMS

**VIVA MARIA** directed by Louis Malle
Quirky sweet irreverence, great visual gags, two sparkling, sexy, intelligent female leads in Jeanne Moreau and Bridgette Bardot who combine brilliantly (for female leading ladies!) and a wonderfully apt and moving musical score: the theme of warm and distracted humanity being drawn in to rebelling against tyrannical established order appeals to me.

**THE GRAND BUDAPEST HOTEL** Directed by Wes Anderson
My kind of film; similar to Viva Maria; quirky, irreverent, inventive: humorous in the characters portrayed, situation and script, not to mention flawless performances by all the actors, both leading and supporting; great unique music on the soundtrack, the film touches on profound and important strands of human life and our values in a gentle self-mocking but significant and brave manner. Great entertainment and I loved the geometric byzantine style in which it was shot that held good throughout and added real verve and concentration to the unfolding of events which always led in an a new and unexpected direction.

**LA GRANDE ILLUSION** directed by Jean Renoir
Beautifully filmed in black and white with images that could be framed individually and that stick in the mind. The film is a touching portrait of combatants and ordinary people

holding on to their innate goodness and caring for their fellow men against the upheaval of the Great War.

**PATHER PANCHALI (SONG OF THE LITTLE ROAD)** by Satyajit Ray
This beautiful, graceful black and white film set in rural India in 1955 is a low key yet universal story of humble family life seen through the eyes of a young boy. It touches the souls and minds of viewers transcending cultural and linguistic barriers. Full of tenderness and humour it brought a new vision of India to the screen with the inestimable bonus of a musical score by the ravishing Ravi Shankar.

**ON THE WATERFRONT** by Elia Kazan
Set in the New York docks area this apocryphal production was justifiably showered with Oscars portraying the stark reality of the small man's fight against organisational coercion and endemic corruption and crowned with iconic performances by Marlon Brando, Rod Steiger and Yves Marie-Saint.

**THE LAST VALLEY** directed by James Clavell
A still, quiet, beautiful, secret place sheltered from the ravages of the Thirty Years War in Europe. A place to which in my imagination I could escape from the stress of modern living. Off-beat subject magically and unpretentiously filmed with a heart aching musical score; plus Michael Cain and Omar Sharif in good 1970s form. In my heart of hearts I very much identify with 'The Captain', the character portrayed by Michael Cain in this film.

**DELIVERANCE** directed by John Boorman
Why do I like 'Deliverance' so much? Because it doesn't pan out in the end; something is lost along the way, never

to be recovered; no happy ending; at best a reappraisal; disturbed thoughts remain; a compelling, evocative musical score and a convincing performance from John Voight who emerges as leader when terror strikes and the chips are down. Don't mess with nature!

**SHAWSHANK REDEMPTION** directed by Frank Darabont
No matter how many times I watch this film it flies by and yet I end up feeling that I have literally spent years with the protagonists in the prison; great economy of dialogue, acting, editing and the surprise at the end remains a surprise.

**CARRY ON UP THE KHYBER** directed by Gerald Thomas
What can I say? This is a marvellous romp – by far the best of the 'Carry On' films. I love the scene at the end where the governor's residence is under siege and stiff upper lips and true British decorum are maintained hilariously in spite of surrounding havoc and imminent disaster.

**ZULU** directed by Cy Endfield
Michael Cain playing an officer extremely well despite his working class background. All the ingredients – historical events well told – the thin red line – bravery against overwhelming odds – what made the Empire Great!

**PARIS TEXAS** directed by Wim Wenders
This is a bleak yet moving diminuendo of dying love and hope that evokes a poignant sense of place and space.

**THE WIZARD OF OZ** directed by Victor Fleming
A delightful reinforcement on life's journey of the value of friends and family and the vulnerability of childhood and

adulthood come to that; catchy unique tunes, incomparable Judy Garland – she would never better her role as the young farm girl in atmospheric Kansas – and good triumphing over bad.

**GONE WITH THE WIND** directed by Victor Fleming
A masterly and epic adaptation fully justifying the quality, scope and minutiae of Margaret Mitchell's literary masterpiece on the American Civil War told from a Southern perspective. Offers iconic performances by Vivien Leigh as Southern Belle, Scarlett O'Hara 'I'll think of that tomorrow' and Clark Gable as the Northern opportunist charmer Rhett Butler 'My dear I just don't give a damn!' Works on a number of levels; great set pieces; real events – real people – real issues and although over four hours long rushes past with the speed of the wind.

**LIFE OF BRIAN** directed by Terry Jones
Always look on the brightside....! Archetypal British schoolboy humour strung together in pearl like pantomime set pieces on a Biblical canvas, taking the piss while displaying strains of decency, modesty and sensibility. Many of the lines from the film script have passed into the English language and many of the scenes absorbed into the English cultural psyche.

**FITZCARRALDO** directed by Verner Herzog and starring Klaus Kinsky
A beautifully filmed story set in the upper Peruvian reaches of the Amazon River and two of its tributaries. The story revolves around the quixotic odyssey of the central character Fitzcarraldo to build a grand opera house in his home town of Quito where the two tributaries flow into the Amazon and

to invite his favourite tenor, the world renowned Enrico Caruso, to sing there on the opening night. Full of well paced tension, social observation, joy, humility, eccentric ambition and determined endeavour, the eponymous hero triumphs in the end, yet not in the way he intended but he doesn't care and nor do we .

**BEYOND THE HILLS** by Cristian Mungui
This is a wonderfully off-beat tale of two troubled and insecure friends who seek in different ways to escape from their impoverished and uncertain background in post-communist Romania. The film is shot in black and white and grips from the start when one of the girls arrives at the local train station to visit her friend who has joined a convent situated in an isolated, bleak wintry landscape 'beyond the hills'. Against the deprivations and rigour of convent life in this setting, they each battle to resolve in increasingly different ways their love for and loyalty towards each other. External pressures and circumstance which they are unable to cope with gradually overwhelm them leading to a shocking and tragic outcome mirroring the trial and execution of Jesus Christ by his peers.

## QUOTES

**EXTRACT FROM THE GREAT GATSBY** by F Scott Fitzgerald
For a while these reveries provided an outlet for his imagination; they were a satisfactory hint of the unreality of reality, a promise that the rock of the world was founded securely on a fairy's wing.

**THE TEMPEST** by William Shakespeare
This thing of darkness I acknowledge mine.

**KING ALFRED THE GREAT**
What I set out to do was to virtuously and justly administer the authority given to me and to do it with wisdom, for without wisdom nothing is worthwhile; it's always been my desire to live honourably and to leave my descendants my memory in good works; for each man, according to the measure of his intelligence, must speak what he can speak and do what he can do.

**ARL BARTH (Swiss Protestant Theologian)**
It may be that when the angels go about their task praising God, they play only Bach. I'm sure however that when they are together 'en famille', they play Mozart; and God evesdrops.

**BBC NEWSNIGHT- REVIEW**
Memory is something we create; it's an invention; it's never the truth.

**NATIONAL THEATRE PRODUCTION - MY FAIR LADY**
Professor Higgins to Eliza Doolittle – "I know you're tired.... But think what you're trying to accomplish. Think what you're dealing with – the majesty and grandeur of the English language. It's the greatest possession we have. The noblest sentiments that have ever flowed in the hearts of men are contained in its extraordinary imaginative and musical mixture of sounds. That's what you've set yourself to conquer Eliza. And conqueror it you will."

**MATHEMATICS** by Norman Co*ttee*
Whilst it is important for everyday living; anyone with enough practice can master the mechanical stuff

(arithmetic); but it's the inherent beauty of numbers, orchestrated by the art of mathematics, that is so magical and exciting, enabling us to develop our thoughts and ideas about the world we live in and to make discoveries about phenomena, universal laws and truths. If there is a God it is certain he is a mathematician.

**WORDS** by Norman Cottee
Words are the harbingers of imagination and thought.

**DEATH OF RICHIE BENAUD** by Justin Langer former Australian batsman
Wise men often don't inundate you with words but when they speak you listen to everything they say.

**SNOBBERY** by Norman Cottee
It's not where you live that matters but how you live.

**OVID**
Laudamus veteres sed nostris utimur annis
We praise the good old times but live today

**DEMOCRACY** by Justin Webb, Presenter BBC Radio 4
We need to grow up. One of the great features of modern democracy is the disconnect between the instant gratification we demand from out gadgets and the slow endlessly disappointing business of governing and being governed. We need to understand that government is not a smartphone. Clashes and inefficiencies and slow processes are part of what gives democracy its strength and legitimacy. So let's give our politics a chance to breathe and, imperfectly but inexorably, to deliver.

**BBC DOCUMENTARY – FULL STEAM AHEAD - Old Sheep Breeders and Drovers' Mantra dating back to the pre Steam Age**
Hurry Up and Go Along Steady.

**A MID-SUMMERNIGHT'S DREAM** by William Shakespeare
I have had a most rare vision. I have had a dream, past the wit of man to say what dream it was. Man is but an ass if he go about to expound this dream. Methought I was... there is no man can tell what. Methought I was and methought I had... but man is but a patched fool if he will offer to say what methought I had. The eye of man hath not heard, the ear of man hath not seen; man's hand is not able to taste, his tongue to conceive, nor his heart to report what my dream was. I will get Peter Quince to write a ballad of this dream: it shall be called Bottom's Dream, because it hath no bottom.

**SHAKESPEARE'S GLOBE MAGAZINE ARTICLE - 'LOVE' AS PORTRAYED IN SHAKESPEARE'S PLAYS**
It is a complete world because no-one goes to the plays to find out about life or love in Elizabethan England; we go there to find out how we live and love now. The stage lets us eavesdrop on other lives, except that those lives turn out to be our own.

**BBC 2 NEWSNIGHT**
The old political alignment of left versus right, that is to say the rich versus poor, is being replaced by tribalism versus humanism and wall builders versus bridge builders.

**THE GOD OF SMALL THINGS** by Arundhati Roy
It didn't matter that the story had begun, because Kathkali discovered long ago that the secret of the Great Stories is

that they have no secrets. The Great Stories are the ones you have heard again. The ones you can enter anywhere and inhabit comfortably. They don't deceive you with thrills and trick endings.

**BBC DRAMA PRODUCTION OF 'LITTLE WOMAN' BY LOUISA MAY ALCOTT**
Professor Bhaer advised Jo March, an aspiring writer, when handing her a copy of The Complete Works of Shakespeare; 'There's a universe of literature between these covers. Shakespeare earned his living by his pen. He wrote spectaculars and he entertained the people but he also created works of such beauty that the world is still sustained by them.'

**THIS THING OF DARKNESS** by Harry Thompson
Harry Thompson's first novel masterfully embroils the reader in a carefully researched, illuminating, sensitive and convincing tale of the parallel yet interacting worlds of Captain Robert Fitzroy and Charles Darwin, his companion on the historic 1831-1835 voyage of HMS Beagle to Tierra del Fuego and the Galapagos Islands. The shattering consequences of this exploratory voyage for the two men and for the native Fuegans concluding fatally poles apart are deeply etched, tenderly portrayed and enlightening. We are left saddened yet heartened by their respective legacies, blessed with a better understanding and a more profound appreciation of the questing nature of our universal humanity.

**THE TRANSYLVANIAN TRILOGY** by Miklós Bánnfy
This majestic panoramic three part historical novel is full of arresting detail beautifully describing the privileged way of

life pursued by his own and other Transylvanian noble families and the fatally flawed society that supported them that was to vanish forever in the unforeseen carnage of the First World War in Central Europe. The author rivals Tolstoy for sweep, Pasternak for yearning romance and Hardy for his evocation of place and the nostalgic, heart rending portrayal of the beauty of his Transylvanian homeland. The three books use apt titles from 'Belshazzar's Feast - The Writing On The Wall' in the Bible which neatly encapsulate the essence of the progressive developments in each book about which he writes so fluently and intelligently.

The first is 'They Were Counted' - the second "They Were Found Wanting' and the concluding one 'They Were Divided' viz:-

"And the first word that was written in letters of fire on the wall of the King's palace was **MENE** - the Lord hath numbered thy kingdom. But none could see the writing because they were drunken with much wine and they called out in their drunkenness to bring out the vessels of gold and silver that their ancestors had laid up in the temple of the house of God, and they brought forth the vessels and drank wine from them and increased in their drunkenness and madness. And the Lord's vessels were wasted among them as they abused each other and quarrelled over their own gods , each man praising his gods of gold and silver, of brass, of iron, of wood and clay".

"And as they drank and quarrelled among themselves the fiery hand wrote on in flaming letters upon the plaster of the wall of the King's palace. And the second word was **TEKEL** - Thou art weighed in the balance and art found wanting."

"And the finger went on writing in letters of fire upon the plaster of the wall of the King's palace. And the third word was **UPHARSIN** - thy kingdom shall be divided. But none could read the writing so drunk were they with much drinking of wine and they wasted the Lord's vessels of gold and silver which their ancestors had laid up in the house of the Lord and they argued with each other praising their false gods made of gold and of silver of brass, of iron, of wood and of clay until there was no strength left in them. And the armies of the Medes and Persians stood ready before the wall of the city and in the same night everyone within it was slain."

It seems to me that Bánffy's three part Transylvanian masterpiece and Belshazzar's Feast are still worrying relevant today!

**INSCRIPTION ON T SHIRT DISPALYED IN KYRENIA SHOP WINDOW**
Common sense is not very common.

**BBC NEWSNIGHT**
Boris Johnson claims that the Brexit Dream is dying. The Brexit Dream was never a living organism in the first place: it was dying under its own internal contradictions.

**ST PAUL"S LETTER TO THE CORINTHIANS**
When I was at Raynes Park Grammar School, before lessons began each morning, the boys and masters would assemble in the wood panelled school hall. We would sing a hymn and listen to a reading from the King James Bible read by the Deputy Headmaster, followed by notices. On the last day of term, assembly would be held after morning

lessons had finished and we would then be dismissed for the school holidays. The masters always wore their teaching cloaks, university degree sashes and mortar boards to this final assembly. It was treated by everyone as a special valedictory occasion and one I personally treasured. The Bible reading was always the same - and what a masterpiece of prose and philosophy it is. I give it here in the original King James version which uses the term 'charity' instead of the modernised overworked word 'love'. Charity stands for a deeper wider concept of devotion and attachment and fits the rhythm, alliteration of St Paul's letter far better; particularly when read out loud.

'Though I speak with the tongues of men and of angels and have not charity, I am become as sounding brass or a tinkling cymbal.

And though I have the gift of prophesy and understand all mysteries and all knowledge; and though I have all faith so that I could remove mountains and have not charity, I am nothing.

And though I bestow all my goods to feed the poor, and though I give my body to be burned and have no charity, it profiteth me nothing.

Charity suffereth long and is kind; charity envieth not; charity vaunteth not itself; is not puffed up; doth not behave unseemly; seeketh not her own; is not easily provoked; thinketh no evil; rejoiceth not in iniquity but rejoiceth in the truth; beareth all things, believeth all things, endureth all things.

Charity never faileth; but whether there be prophecies, they shall fail; whether there be tongues, they shall cease, whether there be knowledge, it shall vanish away.

For we know in part and we prophesy in part but when that which is perfect is come, then that which is in part shall be done away.

When I was a child, I spake as a child, understood as a child, but when I became a man, I put away childish things.

For now we see through a glass darkly; but then face to face: now I know in part; but then shall I know even as I am known.

And now abideth faith, hope and charity, these three; but the greatest of these is charity.'

**RAYNES PARK GRAMMAR SCHOOL GRACE**
Benedict nobis
Domine Deus
Et his donis,
Quae ex liberalitate tuas
Et tui summus:
Per Jiesum Christum
Dominum nostrum
Amen

*Bless us Lord God*
*And what we are about to receive*
*Which of thy great goodness*
*Thou hast provided for us:*
*Through Jesus Christ our Lord*
*Amen*

**ALBERT CAMUS**
The purpose of a writer is to keep civilisation from destroying itself.

**BBC DOCUMENTARY ABOUT V S NAIPUL**

In literature we look to see the world: we look to see our place in the world and understand that place.

**EDMUND BURKE**

The only thing necessary for the triumph of evil is for good men to do nothing

**ST THOMAS AQUINAS - RELIGION**

God is not the answer. He is the question.

**WILLIAM HUGHES MEARNS**

Yesterday upon the stair
I met a man who wasn't there.
He wasn't there again today
Oh how I wish he'd go away

**JOHN DONNE**

No man is an island,
Entire of itself.
Each is a piece of the continent,
A part of the main.
If a clod be washed away by the sea,
Europe is the less,
As well as if a promontory were,
As well as if a manor of thine own
Or of thy friend's were.
Each man's death diminishes me,
For I am involved in mankind.
Therefore, send not to know
For whom the bell tolls,
It tolls for thee.

## HEROES

In a naughty world, though not as illustrious as my heroes, I have tried to make a positive contribution to the progress of mankind, in my own small way. I am proud to have lived my life as an Englishman and my heroes are individuals who I look up to because they to some degree or another displayed in their lives, the qualities I admire and to which I aspire. They tended to be people who mainly, though not exclusively, emanated from modest backgrounds, achieving success and justified fame on merit; who were determined and enduring, not swayed by pessimists nor defeatists, nor the general clamour nor conventional wisdom but were inspiring and innovative leaders in their field who made a lasting and beneficial difference both to this country and to Western Democracy in general. In no particular order they are –

Horatio Nelson
Wolfgang Amadeus Mozart
Captain James Cook
William Shakespeare
T E Lawrence (of Arabia)
Abraham Lincoln
Alan Turing
Charles Darwin
Charles Dickens
Elizabeth Tudor
Jesus of Nazareth
Alfred the Great
Albert Einstein
Oliver Cromwell
Simon de Montfort
Ludwig Van Beethoven

George Washington
Florence Nightingale
Pablo Picasso
Galileo Galilee
Ulysses S Grant
Werner Herzog

**GUY BROWNING - BRITISH HUMOURIST - 1964**
Men love women because women are the loveliest things on God's earth. Women love men because chocolate can't mow the lawn.

**PREFACE TO JOSEPH CONRAD'S NOVEL 'NOSTROMO'**
So foul a sky clears not without a storm (William Shakespeare)

**NORMAN COTTEE**
Intelligence without wisdom is a poor thing.

**WILLIAM SHAKESPEARE - MIDSUMMER NIGHT'S DREAM**
Though she be but little, she is fierce.

**KOHIMA EPITAPH**
When you go home
Tell them of us and say
For your tomorrow
We gave our today

**THE DISABLED EYE - BBC TV CHANNEL 4 PROGRAMME**
Their paintings are like all great paintings; a question; a moment in a narrative with the viewer providing the rest of the story.

**ACTING by Norman Cottee**

Anyone can play the hero: it takes real talent to play the fool.

Or, as Shakespeare has it in the words of Feste the Clown in 12th Night - "This fellow is wise enough to play the fool and to do that well ***craves a kind of wit*** (in modern parlance ***"requires particular talent")***.

**ROSE - ONE WOMAN PLAY by Martin Sherman**

A restless people produce restless minds.

On the other hand.... maybe God is just a question; like everything else.

**ULYSSES S GRANT by Ron Chernow**

As always he studiously avoided jockeying for position. Ethical and honourable, he wanted to receive jobs based squarely on his merits. Refusing to grovel, he considered it unseemly to profit from favouritism. It irked him to watch others manoeuvre for position and was sickened at the political wire pulling for commissions and would not engage in it.

**ELIZABETH I**

I seek not to pry too deeply into men's souls. (sound advice during the religious turmoil of the Reformation: and dare one say it - now)

## MY GRAVE GOODS

**TRAVEL SOUVENIRS**

I guess I must like figurines because they tend to catch my eye when I am travelling are generally inexpensive to purchase and back home, speak to me of the places I have been and the experiences I have enjoyed. The serene, modest humanity represented by their carving appeals to me too. On top of my drinks cabinet I have a charming little piece that I believe represents a supplicant **'Hindu Goddess'** of some kind, of whose precise identity I am unfortunately ignorant. It was given to me by a pleasant young Asian girl, who worked for me as my office clerk when I was the Divisional Manager based in the Central Area at Heathrow Airport responsible for the Customs personnel operating in Terminals 1 and 2, the Queens Building at Heathrow Airport and the South Side VIP Suite. I was touched by her kindness and support in giving me this unsolicited and delightful little object reflecting her own background. The other figurine with religious and Far East connotations is the **'Black Buddha'** I bought this Buddha, not particularly cheaply I may say, in the tourist hotel shop in Bali during a stopover on our way back from a trip to Australia with our friends Robbie and Margaret. The iron-wood head of an **'African Chief'** previously sat on my desk at work when I was in charge of the regional VAT and Excise office in Bell Street, Maidenhead. I sometimes looked to it for solace and ran my hand over it to calm my senses in trying moments. I bought it on our way back from the Falls in the shop in the prestigious Victoria Falls Hotel where Ros and I went for afternoon tea one day having run the gamut of swarms of local Africans trying to sell me similar wood and stone souvenir carvings and wanting to buy my baseball cap. If they had only left us alone to browse, I probably would have bought a wood carving of a chief's head smoking a curly pipe at half the price I paid in the hotel shop but Ros and I and almost all English people I have spoken to abroad do not like being pestered in this way. Anyway, I am more than pleased with *'My Man'* as

I call him. Although not normally interested in speculative shopping, for some reason I felt a strange compulsion to wander round an impromptu open air market on the outskirts of Leominster as we were returning from a morning walk to the spot where we had left the car. We were visiting my favourite Aunt Dorothy with my sister Sue and her husband Ken on what has become an annual pilgrimage following the death of my mother. Lo and behold I spotted my **'Leominster Maid'** to which I took an immediate fancy. I enquired the price and was told 50p. Slightly embarrassed at having to wait while the man on the stall fumbled to find change for the £1 coin I had tendered, I almost succumbed by telling him to keep the change – but a bargain is a bargain – and before altruism and shame got the better of me, he duly handed me a 50p piece to close the deal. I walked off pleased as punch to show the others. I was the only one to buy anything in the market that day, a reversal of the normal outcome of a speculative foray to the shops in the company of others. Later acquisitions of this nature are **'Three Inca Ladies'** in South American Indian garb which I bought inexpensively in Arequipa a former Spanish colonial town in Peru in 2006 and my **'Pilgrim Wife'** that I bought in 2009 in Jamestown, Virginia, USA, the site of the first permanent English settlement in North America. More valuably from Zimbabwe and purchased jointly by Ros and I at an outdoor exhibition of sculpture in the extensive and fascinating walled Tudor Garden at Loseley Park in the Surrey Hills comes the 'S**tone Head'** echoing Picasso, Henry Moore and indigenous African art which I absolutely adore. It cost a bob or two but it's worth it. I am equally fond of the **'Statuette of Don Quixote** purchased far less expensively from a shop in Malaga opposite the city's picture gallery devoted to the works of its most famous son

Picasso. The delicacy of the carving of the head and the expression on the face capture exactly my vision of the blessed Knight of the Sad Countenance as described in Cervantes rambling yet glorious tragi-comic tale. In the same vein I have carved heads of **'Socrates** purchased after diligent searching when on holiday in Athens and of a beautiful **'Greek Youth'** purchased on a visit to the Roman villa site in Fishbourne, West Sussex. The statuette of the **Greek Goddess Hera** was purchased on the same trip to Athens.

Also from Zimbabwe came the **'Wooden Rhino'**. I can't remember exactly where we bought it but we must have braved the street traders at some point or acquired it at a lodge when we were on safari. Anyway, it and the **'Small Elephant'** purchased for Ros in Maidenhead remind me of the animals in the 'wild' we saw on our Southern African safaris. The **'Silver Llama'** was given to me by Robbie and Margaret for organising our trip to Peru and Brazil in 2006. The **'Brass Bull'** represents my star-sign Taurus. Neither Ros nor I can remember where we got it from. In the bathroom sitting on the edge of the bath is a miniature replica of the **'Gaudi Tiled Lizard'** from the Parc Gaudi in the city of Barcelona where Ros and I went for a short break in 2008. The **'Wooden Camel'** is a memento of our 'two for the price of one' trip up the Nile brought about by the passage over the UK and Europe of an ash cloud from an Icelandic volcano. Lastly, I was given the brown china horse when I was a child. I christened it **'Starlight'** because of the white patch on its head. I still think this is a good name and I still treasure this piece; not that I particularly like horses, although it fed into my dreams at the time of fleet footed stallions, ridden by dashing cowboys.

Concerning holiday mementos, I also have a penchant for miniature replicas of buildings that remind me of places I have enjoyed visiting. My first purchase was on a school trip to Lugano, Switzerland in 1959 and was a gift for my mother, who among other things, had found my passport and sent it to me through the post after I discovered on the outward trip that I had left it at home. What I bought her was a **'Swiss Chalet Music Box'**. I think she was mildly disappointed when she discovered that the tune it played was not some cow-bell-tinkling Swiss folk song but Colonel Bogey. When she died I took it into my possession and it now sits on the living room window sill with a small one inch square photograph of my mother in her younger days in the cavity under the hinged roof. The next purchase I made in this category was on a trip the following summer with school friends to the Continent when we ended up in the Pisa region of Northern Italy having hitch-hiked from Paris in pursuit of some young English girls who were spending their holiday in Livorno. We of course climbed the famous tower while we were in the town and I bought the little metal facsimile of the **'Leaning Tower of Pisa'** from a local souvenir stall. The **'Peachtree Tower Pottery Cocktail Drinking Receptacle'** is an example of the American interest in size as against quality. It was given away as a freebie when we dined at the top of the Westin Hotel in the centre of Atlanta Georgia with Ros' former boss, Peter Hill who was working in the city at the time. It is cast in the same shape as the hotel itself which claims 'To Be the Tallest in America'. Whether this is true or not, I must say that although the cocktail drink it contained and that I drunk was undistinguished, the 360 degree panoramic view over the city and beyond was stunning. In the kitchen cupboard where we keep cups and glasses is the equivalent that Ros had her cocktail in. It is equally crass in taste and is shaped and coloured like a peach: practically everything in Atlanta and the State of Georgia has Peach or Peachtree in the name which is particularly confusing when it comes to navigating roads and finding your way around. Two miniature pottery **'Amsterdam Canal Houses'** come from a city break in Amsterdam; the **'Dublin Front Door'** from Dublin, where else from Taormina in Sicily, the **'Ayumento'**. Each is typical of the local architecture. My trip to Berlin in September 2010 yielded a glass hologram of the **'Brandeburg Gate-Fernsehenturm (TV Tower)'**.I also brought back from Berlin a tiny **'Fragment of the Berlin Wall'**. I hasten to add that I didn't chip it from the wall itself but picked it up off the ground where it was lying loose at the foot of the wall. While in Berlin I bought a small but charming blue and black figurine of the city mascot, the **'Berlin Bear'** to remind me that the citizens of that surprisingly attractive, one might almost say, beautiful city, have redoubtably kept to a markedly idiosyncratic and independent outlook on life contrary to the conformist minded tendencies encountered elsewhere in the German lands.

My friend Robbie and I admire and empathise with the eponymous character created by Jaroslav Hasek, the non-conformist Czech novelist in his rambling, annoying, funny, unfinished masterpiece 'The Good Soldier Svejk'. The illustrations in the book match the ribaldry and irreverence of the narrative perfectly. When I went to Prague in 1993 with Ros and her mother, I managed to find the pub where the author and Svejk in the novel drank. The pub is called 'The Chalice' (in English) and has been re-created as a pub-restaurant trading heavily on the Svejk theme; I went there again in 2008 when we were in the city with Robbie and Margaret and my sister Sue and husband Ken for the fantastic Prague Winter Festival. On the first pilgrimage I made to this notorious establishment I bought a **'Svejk Plate'** which bears our hero's wonderful insouciant likeness. On the second occasion I treated myself to a replica of **'Svejk's Czech Infantry Cap'**. From an ancestral point of view I am glad that I acquired a decorative **'Tubingen Plate'** which I bought in the South Western German university town of the same name where my maternal great grandfather came from. The three **'Oval Serving Plates'** we keep for special occasions were probably a wedding gift to my mother. I kind of like them as they are designed in an unpretentious simple clean 1930s style which oddly appeals to me. I also like the heavy **'Alabaster Egyptian Vase'** brought back by Theresa and Simon following a cruise up the Nile before they got married and the little cut glass **'Waterford Crystal Vase'** they bought us when we holidayed together in Southern Ireland. Alas the Waterford Company whose reputation for quality glassware had existed for over two centuries ceased trading recently under the impact of the Credit Crunch and changing tastes. This little piece is relevant for me also because Theresa's mother was born and grew up in Waterford and Simon and Theresa bought it in the factory shop in the town while we were there.

Purchased in an arts and crafts centre in Carvoeiro in Portugal is a rather nice **'Blue, White & Yellow Ashtray'** that still looks OK to my eye in the less bright sunny climbs of this country. I have generally found that what looks good and appropriate in other countries doesn't always fit suitably when brought home to this country. Caution needs to be exercised but the odd exception may be permitted so long as it is not too gross. The **'Small Square Blue and White Mosaic Olive-Stone Tray'** I nicked while dining out with my nephew and his wife in an open air restaurant in Ibiza where my sister Sue and brother in law Ken have had a two week part ownership in a bay side apartment in Calle Llonga for many years The tray caught my eye and though virtually worthless in money terms is unique to the Balearic Islands and I fell in love with it and it reminds me of two enjoyable holidays spent there with Sue and Ken. Tactfully, I thought it sensible not to mention to Ken, a retired Met Police Officer, that I had pocketed it at the end of a long, warm, increasingly stimulating and intoxicating evening unable to find the waiter to offer payment. I am pleased with my first ever attempt to decorate pottery. At a do it yourself pottery in Twyford, I painted a sea scene of a sailing/steam ship onto a blank butter dish and had it fired on site. I think of it as my **'J W M Turner Butter Dish'** and proudly bring it out for dinner parties and family gatherings.

Although not pottery the two presumably **'Brass Condiment Pots'** are no doubt of foreign origin; I would guess Indian. We only use them for ornament and remind me of the days of the British Empire on which the sun never set. I like to think they were given to me when Ros and I got married by my old school friend Tim Biddiscombe, alas no longer with us, or by his parents, his father having served in India as a Regimental Sergeant Major in the British Army during the Raj. His wife who was a very witty woman and from whom Tim inherited his sense of humour, used to joke that every morning he would march up and down the garden attached to their little bungalow in Hythe and call the flowers to attention "Tulips - stand up straight there!" Whether they came into our possession in this way or not and Ros assures me they didn't, I cling to my memories of the Biddiscombes that these two pleasantly wrought, items bring to mind. At the Grand Canyon I spotted a **'Navaho Native American Decorated Pot'** which in its simplicity was much more attractive than any of the modern day American style souvenirs available for purchase.

**TANKARDS, CUPS, GLASSES & DECANTER**

The rather **'Battered Pewter Tankard'** was given to me by my friends for my 21st Birthday. I have two more pewter tankards, this time in pristine condition given to me when I retired from HM Customs & Excise in 2000. The **'Flat Handled Pewter Tankard'** was presented to me by the Collector (Senior Regional Manager) and fellow members of the Thames Valley Collectorate (Divisional Managers). The **'Curly Handled Pewter Tankard'** which I value even more was given to me by The Debt Management Team, consisting of an initially largely suspicious and negative group of team leaders who I succeeded in forging into a very effective and influential operational force. I value this gift because it was unexpected and given as a spontaneous gesture of respect and gratitude and not simply because it was 'the done thing'. The **'Three German Stone Tankards'** were kindly given to Ros and me by Albert Muscat, Export Manager of Grenzebach in Bavaria who Ros worked with at Riverlock and whose daughter we had looked after a couple of times when she came over to the UK to improve her English. I have two pottery tankards. The **'Tutankhamen Tankard'** was purchased in the hotel shop in Taba Heights at the top end of the Red Sea on a holiday during which we visited Cairo and the Pyramids, travelling there and back across the Sinai Desert and Suez Canal. In the Cairo

Museum I was blown away by the magnificence, richness and beauty of the objects retrieved from Tutankhamen's tomb, a very minor pharaoh who died young and whose memory succeeding pharaohs and religious leaders had sought to erase completely. What, by comparison, you may ask must thc plundered and vanished treasure of the great pharaoh Ramses II have looked like! The decoration on this tankard is taken from some of the objects found in Tutankhamen's tomb: I particularly like the depiction of the loving tenderness and unostentatious humanity in the full length seated portrait of the young pharaoh and his consort. I bought the **'Prague Tankard'** in a Czech pub opposite Prague Castle during a trip to Prague, Brno and Bratislava with Ros and her mother not long after the 'Velvet Revolution' put a final end to the country's least willing adherence along with Hungary to the Russian dominated Soviet Communist Bloc. Also in my collection are a '**Tudor Leathern Tankard'** I bought at the Tower of London and a handcrafted '**Brown Pottery Beer Jug'** purchased on a new year's stay in Boscastle, Cornwall. I bought the **'Green Stone Goblet'** in Charmouth on the Jurassic Coast, a charming spot as the name of the cosy secluded seaside hamlet suggests, which we used to regularly frequent for the day as a family when we were staying with my parents in their retirement bungalow in nearby Bradpole. As regards my beer glasses, the beautifully decorated half litre **'Tile Glass'** was bought during a visit to the Museu National do Azulejo (National Tile Museum) just outside Lisbon. The **'Corsendonk Glass Goblet'** was bought when Ros and I visited Bruges. Each brewer in Belgium, of which there are many, has their own specially shaped and decorated range of glasses and this is but one example. While on a night out in a lively restaurant in Rio de Janeiro, I purchased the house **'Dusky Dancer Glass'** which I enjoy drinking from on festive family occasions including barbeques. I also have a splendid **'London Pride Straight'** – although it has to be said that I normally prefer 'Jugs' (beer glasses with handles). The glass itself is great and reminds me that I have shares in this long established brewer of traditional English Ales based in Chiswick, West London. London Pride is one of my favourite ales. I keep these last two in the kitchen cupboard. Finally in the glassware category, I have a nice **'Cut Glass Decanter'** presented to me by the London Airports Collectorate when I transferred in 1992 to Thames Valley Collection to take over the Maidenhead based VAT and Excise Division. I missed the twenty-four-seven buzz of working at the airports but this loss was more than outweighed by the benefit of working, for once, close to home for the last eight years of my service. At Shakespeare's birthplace I bought a nicely shaped **'Shakespeare Stone Goblet'** and was given a lovely **Stratford China Cup** by my daughter in law Theresa depicting the properties in the town associated with the great man. My other daughter in law Nicola gave me a **China Cup from Eriskay** in the Outer Hebrides where her maternal ancestors come from. It stands together with a similar shaped **'Ironbridge China Cup'** I bought on a memorable and interesting day spent in the town in Shropshire where the first the seeds of the worldwide industrial revolution were sown.

## MEDALS, SHIELDS ETC

When my mother died, my sister and I found my father's **'World War II Medals and Citation'** in a dressing table drawer in their bedroom. We never knew these existed. Neither my father nor my mother had ever spoken of them while they were alive. Notwithstanding the fact that my mother had always deprecated my father's contribution to the successful outcome of the war – selling his standard issue rifle, she alleged, to a passing Arab and demonstrating lack of ambition in rejecting the opportunity to become an officer because he didn't want to leave his mates – and allowing for the fact that the medals he received were no doubt issued to all military personnel who took part in the North Africa and Italian campaigns and did not signify any particular act of bravery on his part – I am sure that he suffered physical and psychological privations in doing his bit for the cause and that these medals represent a suitable and deserved recognition for the part he played in the conflict. Sue and I agreed to have the medals and citation framed and given to Simon to pass down to future generations. I had them tastefully framed on a Royal Air Force blue background and they can be viewed on display in the hallway of his house. The citation gives a description of the medals on one side and on the reverse side the citation itself which reads *'The Under-Secretary of State for Air presents his compliments and by Command of the Air Council has the honour to transmit the enclosed Awards granted for service during the war of 1939-45.'*

The Medals displayed in the showcase from left to right and top to bottom are – The Italy Star
The 1939-45 Star
The Africa Star
The War Medal 1939-45

**The Defence Medal**
In the middle of the top row, there is also a medal which must have been presented to my mother for some reason

while she was at school. It bears her name 'M. ARBER' and the inscription **The Kings Medal-LCC 1919-20.** She would have been eight years old at the time and must have been awarded this impressive token in recognition of some sporting or academic achievement. 'LCC' stands for London County Council which was the local government body responsible for schools and other local organisations and institutions for the London Boroughs at the time.

Although the 'medals' I was given during my time in HM Customs & Excise are hardly in the same league as my father and mother's medals, they afford pleasant memories of some of the enjoyable and important representative work I did at the London Airports in concert with foreign Customs services in order to improve international collaboration. The first was a **'French Customs Lapel Badge'** given to me during a trip to Paris with the Heathrow Customs Rugby Team to play their French counterparts on the weekend of the Five Nations match between our respective countries. During the Glasnost period and before the fall of the Berlin Wall, I hosted visiting Russian Customs officials taking them out to eat in the evening in Henley on Thames and was given the two **'Soviet Union Customs Medals'** for my efforts. For similar involvement with visiting Customs officials from Singapore, I was given a **'Silver Singapore Mounted Plate'**, a **'Smetana Vinyl Long Playing Record'** given to me by a Czech official, kept with my other vinyl LPs and an **'Australian Customs Necktie'** given to me by a Customs colleague from that country.

On a European Union sponsored two week reciprocal exchange under the auspices of the Matthaeus Programme to the Northern France Customs Department based in Lille,

I was given by the Director at the French Customs Training School near Rouen a **'Limoges French Customs Plate'** bearing the initial ENBD standing for the Ecole Nationale de Bureau de Douanes and a picture of an armed French Customs Officer in 1846 costume. Later the same day I was taken on a flight in a French Customs helicopter over the English Channel clutching my newly acquired gift.

When I retired from HM Customs & Excise I took with me unused presentation souvenirs that we gave to visiting officials and that were no longer required for that purpose. The first was a **'Thames Valley Collection Shield'** a **'HM Customs & Excise Paperweight'** and a **'Large HMC&E Ashtray'** from my days at the Airport. I had at one time on display two **'Mini Rugby Shields'** dating from the period when I was Chairman of the Maidenhead Rugby Club Mini Section. We had many successes both on and off the field of play and won lots of cups and shields in competition with other rugby clubs. The two I now have are just random ones that I or the boys retained for some reason. Though not specifically interesting or memorable they represent a tangible souvenir of so many enjoyable hours spent coaching and administering the affairs of the club from mini to senior level over 25 years.

**PRINTS & CERTIFICATES**

Hanging on our Dining Room wall is a lovely **'Print of Billingsgate Fish Market'** which I came across in a shop in Maidenhead shortly after we moved to the area. I admired this print which I had suitably framed not only for its intrinsic quality but also because of the association it conjures up in my mind with Ros' father who spent his working life in the market as a bookkeeper for one of the traders. It also reminds me of the pungent smell of fish that wafted from this famous building through the neighbouring Custom House designed by Christopher Wren where I spent my initial classroom training with HM Customs & Excise. Around the same time that I bought the Billingsgate print, Ros and I purchased, possibly in the same shop, the **'Limited Edition Print of Venice'** which brings back memories of the few days when we visited the city seemingly floating on light and water.

Other framed prints and certificates which are important to me because they echo my career in HM Customs & Excise are on display. They are my cancelled **'Commission as an Officer of HM Customs & Excise'** presented to me on my retirement from the Service in 2000, the **'Commendation from the Cabinet Secretary & Head of the Home Civil Service'** I received on behalf of my Division in 1995, and the **'Invitation to the Queen's Garden Party'** Ros and I received in 1990. The **'Print of St Katherine's Dock'** was given to me by Ros' sister Jackie and her husband Peter as a Christmas present one year. It is a nice print and is special because I worked from time to time in my early days in Customs at this dock. Indeed I delivered the final withdrawal of Customs Approval to the St Katherine's Dock Warehouse Keeper/Wharfinger as containerisation began the rapid demise of the docks, wharves and warehouses along the river. Towards the end, few ships ventured this far up-river. I remember tinctures and tea as the only commodities being imported and warehoused under bond before being sold onto the home market. Funnily enough, when Ros mother died, we inherited from her, a print by the same artist, Keith Charles. This **'Print of St Mary's Church'** depicts the church where Ros' mother worshiped and where Ros and I and her two sisters were married. We also have a similar and equally professional looking **'Print of St James the Less Church'** our local church by our organist and amateur artist David Colthup whose son used to work for me in the Thames Valley Area VAT Office in Maidenhead. Most recently on a trip to the Sunderland area in 2017, I was able to visit the church where my Cottee forebears were baptised, married and laid to rest. The church is now closed for religious services but is listed as historically important serving as it did in its heyday, the residents, including my family members of the adjacent commercially important seaport at the mouth of the river Weir. In the neighbouring and delightful small tea shop run by the charity responsible for its upkeep, I purchased the **'Canvas Print of Holy Trinity Church'**. When in Moscow for Ros' 50th birthday shortly after the fall of Communism, I purchased for a few kopeks a **'Hand Drawn Portrait of St Basil's Cathedral in Red Square'**; onion domes and all.

On a day trip to Salisbury Cathedral some years ago I was able to view one of the few remaining original versions of the Magna Carta sent to the cathedral in 1215 for information and safe-keeping and kept there ever since. It is a remarkable document representing the first steps to be taken in formalising the rule of law, affirming the application of impartial justice to all and accepting that government would henceforth become accountable to those who were being governed. In the cathedral shop, I purchased a copy in English translation of the original Latin version of **'The Magna Carta'** which I have had made into a desk pad for the Study. I believe that in the history of the world, this is one of the most important documents ever written, despite the fact that King John, the nominal author, repudiated it within weeks of giving it his approval. Likewise on a visit to the Library of Congress in Washington DC, I purchased a copy of the **'Declaration of Independence'** signed in 1776 by representatives of the first thirteen states of America. This, too, is to me an important document arguing as it does for fair and representative government for all men, despite the fact that it ignored the rights of slaves to enjoy the freedoms espoused. On the same US trip I also bought a **'Print of the Battle of Chancellorsville'** during a visit to the Civil War battlefield. Back home I had this nicely balanced and lively battle scene tastefully framed. As a souvenir of this tour with our friends Robbie and Margaret of the Southern States of America, I bought my friend Robbie Stevenson a lovely print of Commanding General Robert E Lee and Stonewall Jackson of the Confederate forces mounted on their horses Traveller and Little Sorrell which he has had framed. He bought me a framed **'Print of Harpers Ferry'** a place I particularly liked at the confluence of the Potomac and Shenandoah Rivers where we stayed for three days. I can't find this now and can't recall what I might have done with it. On this trip I discovered that my friend and I would have finished on different sides both in the American War of Independence which they call the Revolutionary War and also in the American Civil War. I guess there must have been many times in the past, including the English Civil War when friends and family members were faced with making agonising life changing choices between two different courses of action in support of differing sets of principles both of which embraced some degree of validity. For us, thankfully, these differences are only academic and do not involve the sacrifice of real flesh and blood and the loss of precious friendship.

In the delightful Egyptian town of Aswan on the Upper Nile, Ros bought me a **'Coronation Papyrus'** depicting the New Kingdom enthronement of Nefertari, the wife of Egypt's most powerful Pharaoh, Rameses II. It serves as a reminder of the unplanned extra week's holiday we enjoyed in April 2010 resulting from a weeklong suspension of flights to and from airports in Britain and in much of Europe caused by the sudden eruption of an Icelandic volcano throwing dust and ice into the atmosphere. In Athens I bought a beautiful **'Print of Ancient Athens and Its Surrounding Area'** by cartographer and engraver Ambroise Tardieu (1788-1841). I had it beautifully framed by Ann Carroll who was recommended to me by the art shop in Maidenhead. Prompted by a friend interested in art and a fine amateur artist in her own right, I recently framed some of **'My Doodles'** that I had drawn on official blank note paper in idle moments when undergoing my initial training as an Officer of Customs & Excise in Wren's notable Custom House in Lower Thames Street, London in 1960. I still have the semi abstract chalk picture titled **'Footprints in the Snow'** created by my sister in law Jacqui in the 1960s when she was at school, which I have had framed and greatly prize: it is worthy in my opinion of display in The Tate Gallery.

**HM CUSTOMS & EXCISE STUFF**

In an A4 box file in my Study can be found the four **'HM Customs & Excise Training Notebooks'** which I compiled during the course of my six months theory and practical induction training as a newly commissioned Officer of Customs & Excise in 1960. They provide interesting reading, for me anyway, after all these years. Also in the box is my **'Green Hard Back Travel Expenses Notebook'** relating to the time when I was 'Unattached' that is to say I occupied no fixed station other than the local region (Collection). With the passage of time, these documents written in my own fair hand bear some passing historical interest.

Also in the box and of some general historical interest are the 1959 booklet ' **Her Majesty's Customs & Excise'** which describes the work and responsibilities of the Department as it was when I joined, including an organisational chart, and a rather flashier more expensively produced booklet ' **The Call to Duty (1683-1983)'** commemorating the Tercentenary of the English Excise. Also, recently, I purchased a copy of '**Something to Declare – 1000 Years of Customs & Excise'** by Graham Smith the former Departmental Librarian and Archivist who I knew by site from my time in Headquarters. This gives a comprehensive review of the origins and history of the Department up to the 1980s, by which time I was in mid-career.

I still use my '**Parker Fountain Pen, Biro and Propelling Pencil'** given to me by my boss at the time, John Barnard, the Collector Thames Valley to commemorate 40 years service in the Department.

**MISCELLANEOUS**

The oldest item in this category is a miniature replica of an **'HMS Victory Cannon'**. I bought this before I was married when Ros and I visited the famous ship - Nelson's flagship at the Battle of Trafalgar - in Portsmouth Dockyard. I chose it firstly because I liked it and because it represented a suitable memento of a pleasant and interesting day out but secondly because, as I half jokingly suggested to her at the time, it was my first small contribution, literally and figuratively, to our 'bottom drawer' – indeed, the first article that I actually purchased for the furnishing of our future home together. Much later I purchased a metal miniature of an **'American Civil War Artillery Piece'** at the visitor centre in the Sharpsburg/Antietam Battlefield in Maryland USA during a tour in 2009 of the Southern States with our friends Robbie and Margaret.

I have kept the **'Peruvian Mat'** I bought in the Colca Canyon, famed for the gorge which is deeper than the Grand Canyon in Colorado and for the condors that inhabit the area. Unfortunately they weren't flying the day we were there. The overland journey from Arequipa into the Andes to reach Colca Canyon took us at one point to an altitude of 16666 feet above sea level. I suffered a slight headache that evening in the hotel in which we stayed but apart from that and the extra effort required to walk around and indulge in normal physical activities, I can't say that I suffered much from altitude sickness. This was fortunate because we moved on from there to Lake Titicaca lying at some 13000 feet for the next couple of days. I must say that Lake Titicaca is possibly the most magical place I have ever visited on this earth. I also bought an **'Andean Woollen Hat'** in the hotel on the edge of the lake where we stayed. I use this hat as a golf club cover.

A trip to Malta, an island of kaleidoscopic colour produced the magnetic **'Malta Bus'** and the **'Malta Boat'** which serves as a soap dish. The buses are brilliant. They are all beautifully preserved and lovingly customised British makes such as AEC, Austin, Bedford etc dating from the 1950s and 1960s. I loved them! The hot dry sunny climate on the island has kept the dreaded rust at bay and it is wonderful to watch and travel in these reincarnations of my boyhood era.

From my days of pipe smoking – I gave up in 2000 when I retired from full time working – I have kept the **'Austrian Curly Pipe'** complete with wind cap. I acquired this pipe during a very enjoyable family summer holiday in the Austrian Alps, when the boys were young, staying at the village of Westendorf not far from Kitzbuel and the famous Hannenkarm down-hill ski run which we visited. Most precious of all I keep my **'Meerschaum Pipe'** that Ros bought me some years ago now for my Birthday. I have been known to smoke it for old time's sake on Christmas Day but even that is now problematic with the grandchildren around and prevailing health considerations.

Before I got married, my old school friend Terry French gave me, for some reason, a **'Sword cum Bayonet and Scabbard'** that had reputedly, according to Terry, been the property of a French aristocrat around the time of the Franco Prussian War. The date on the haft reads 'Juillet (July) 1871'; just after the war ended in May of that year. It is also inscribed with an abbreviated name which West Street Antiques of Dorking believe to be Charlesville where it was probably manufactured. Around the hilt are the letters S F and on the scabbard the numbers G3708 and 085921. West Street Antiques valued it at £50 (August 2013). French infantry in the First World War carried such bayonets and often traded them with the British troops for bully beef and cigarettes in short supply in the French Army. Many of these bayonets thus acquired were brought back to

England as souvenirs. The sword has no connection with my ancestors, except in the general sense that my great, great grandmother lived during that period in Tubingen, in Southern Germany on the edge of the Black Forest not far from where some of the battles were fought. Moreover, she was apparently deeply averse to Prussian militarism and being a great Anglophile sent all her surviving sons including my great grandfather to England to avoid entanglement in the Prussian cause which amongst other things was to result in the unification under the Prussian monarchy of all German states including Schwabia where she and her ancestors had lived peacefully for many years. With that background in mind I shall try to find out more about the provenance of this weapon during the course of my researches into my family history.

I keep two walking sticks. The first is my **'Highland Walking Stick'** made form birch wood and deer antlers that I bought in Fort William at the foot of Ben Nevis hoping to climb this mountain, the highest in Great Britain, during a one week stay in the area in 1980. Alas the weather was mainly wet and cloudy throughout the week and I never did get round to the planned ascent. The second walking stick, my much admired **'Monks Ridge Walking Stick'** purchased in South Africa after a successful ascent and descent of one of the peaks in the Drakensburg range of mountains to see examples of early stone age rock paintings.

For my 2010 Christmas Tree present, Ros kindly bought me a miniature replica of my father's **Morris Traveller Company Car**. I learnt to drive and passed my test in this car and drove around in it until I acquired a car of my own. The Traveller was a great car to drive with a perky engine and olive green paintwork and golden varnished wood trim which was pleasing on the eye compared to some of the monstrosities around at that time. A photograph of me sitting at the wheel of this car is in my photo library.

Finally, in terms of treasured possessions, I must mention the splendid **'Barometer'** which also contains a thermometer and hangs in the Hall. This instrument was my mother's pride and joy and was probably given to her as a wedding present in 1936. I remember her religiously tapping it every morning from which scientific operation she carefully divined and forthrightly pronounced her prediction of the ensuing weather for each day. "Barometer's rising – it's going to be a good day" – "Barometer's falling – don't forget to take your Mac if you go out".

Also, my maternal Aunt Dorothy's husband Graham Hankinson, when he died aged 93 in January 2013, left me as a former revenue officer, by way of a placatory trust, a **'Back-Spring Flintlock Muzzle-Loading Carbine Bore Pistol'** willed to him by his great grandfather Jasper Read of Gillingham, Kent (also a former revenue officer). West Street Antiques of Dorking valued it at £200 (August 2013) and consider that it was manufactured in Birmingham between 1845 and 1850 and that it was probably purchased from the manufacturer by the Henry Robinson gun shop in Ipswich and sold privately by retail between 1845 and 1868 as a plain, basic serviceable pistol, unlikely to have been official government issue. I would like my grandson Austin to have it when I am no longer around together with the **Muzzle Loading Flintlock Stone Ammunition Balls** given to me by a tradesman fairly recently, noticing my interest in historic firearms displayed in my dining room cabinet. I would like my grandson Austin to have it when I am no longer around together with the three **Muzzle Loading Flintlock Stone Ammunition Balls** given to me by a tradesman fairly recently, noticing my interest in historic firearms displayed in my dining room cabinet. The two larger balls are standard bore and fit the pistol.

Finally in imagining the goods trinkets and mementoes I might wish to take with me on my inevitable journey into infinity, I must give mention to the grave goods 'as it were' that I have inherited from my Aunt Dorothy, the last of my maternal Arber ancestors, who in her lifetime had custody of her mother's and my Grandmother's **'Kornthal Sampler'.** This was made by my grandmother in 1899 while attending school in Korntal, Southern Germany and living during her teenage years with her German born father's relatives in Tübingen. I have had this remarkable heirloom cleaned and reframed and hope to pass it on in due course to my granddaughter Neve for care and safekeeping in posterity.

# POSTSCRIPT

I don't want to carry this rather self-indulgent conceit of Grave Goods too far but for the sake of verisimilitude I think it would not be entirely inappropriate to bring the contents of this Appendix to a close by making reference to my collection of audio-visual items.

I have recordings of Phillip and Nicola's and Simon and Theresa's wedding ceremonies and their receptions at each of which I gave a speech. I also appear briefly on a video recording of the April 2007 investiture by the Bishop of Reading of Keith Nichols the new vicar appointed to our local Parish of Burchetts Green. I also have recordings of some but by no means all and for my money not the best and most challenging radio interviews and phone-ins I gave to local radio stations, including BBC Radio Berkshire in my capacity as the Area Manager for Berkshire as part of 2001 National Census.

Also I have recordings taken from BBC Radio of a couple of memorable classical music concerts Ros and I attended. Our cheers and clapping can be heard as part of the rapturous applause both performances received. The first was given by Leonard Bernstein conducting the famous Vienna Symphony Orchestra during the Promenade season at the Royal Albert Hall in September 1987. The works they played included two of my special favourites; the Mozart Clarinet Concerto and Mahler's 5$^{th}$ Symphony. The second concert is recorded on DVD It was given by the

Philharmonia Orchestra at the Royal Festival Hall on 4 February 2010 and included $20^{th}$ Century pieces for which, in recent months, I have been developing an increasing taste: these by Benjamin, Stravinsky and Bartok.

In the 2010 Proms season, on our wedding anniversary, Ros and I attended a talk in the Royal College of Music given by novelist Philip Kerr, the subject of which was literature inspired by Berlin. The talk was recorded on BBC Radio 3 and broadcast later that evening during the interval of the Proms concert given by the Berlin Philharmonic conducted by Sir Simon Rattle which we also attended before travelling by rail the following day for a city break in the city of Berlin. The talk and concert including the audience response to which we contributed are recorded on DVD.

I have a fairly extensive music collection recorded on iTunes computer app, compact disc and vinyl. Most of the recordings are of classical music but there are some popular works as well.

I have DVD recordings of a few films that I particularly admire. They include, in no special order – Deliverance, Zulu, Carry On Up the Khyber, Monty Python's Life of Brian, Viva Maria, La Grande Illusion, The American Civil War, Hamlet, Don Giovanni (Opera), Henry V, Rusalka (Opera), King Lear, The Importance of Being Ernest, Paris Texas, The Last Valley

The following reflect many of the experiences I shared during my childhood.

This Happy Breed, Hope & Glory, Hop Skip and Jump.

My photograph collection dating from 1889 to the present day includes early photos that Rosalind and I inherited from our respective families but for the most part consists of photographs we have taken ourselves as we grew up and developed our family and circle of friends.

I have always been interested in photography and one of my first major purchases after I left school was a 35mm Minolta camera which I bought from a little photographic shop in Hartfield Road, Wimbledon on a ten month interest free loan. It had a magnificent lens, albeit I had to buy a separate exposure meter that had to be clipped to the top. Yet this was pretty advanced technology for its day. Eventually, while Phillip was at University, I replaced it with a more modern Canon reflex camera with built-in aperture and shutter speed functions, exchanging that in 2003, with a forthcoming trip to the Far East and Australia in mind, with a less cumbersome, easier to use recently introduced digital camera – a Pentax. The use of colour film around the time I acquired my Minolta was quite revolutionary. Before that, film was black and white only. Now of course film itself is no longer necessary. No more fiddly mucking about in the camera innards to retrieve old film from the spools without tearing or exposing it to the light, winding new rolls of film onto the spools and winding it forward and back after each successive picture has been taken.

When taking photos I have always tried to choose a subject, camera angle, magnification and exposure that would produce an artistic and interesting picture. Some have turned out better than others but on the whole I have been pleased with the results. Some of my favourite photos I have framed and hung on the walls of our house. I have also designed and had commercially printed album style portfolios of my artistically most satisfying and/or most significant photographs in terms of my personal family history.

Lightning Source UK Ltd.
Milton Keynes UK
UKHW050208030822
406766UK00007B/68

9 781803 811345